A BRIDGE TO JUSTICE

A Bridge to Justice

THE LIFE OF FRANKLIN H. WILLIAMS

Enid Gort and John M. Caher

FORDHAM UNIVERSITY PRESS   NEW YORK 2022

Fordham University Press has no responsibility for the persistence or
accuracy of URLs for external or third-party Internet websites referred
to in this publication and does not guarantee that any content on such
websites is, or will remain, accurate or appropriate.

Fordham University Press also publishes its books in a variety of electronic
formats. Some content that appears in print may not be available in
electronic books.

Visit us online at www.fordhampress.com.

Library of Congress Cataloging-in-Publication Data available online
at https://catalog.loc.gov.

Printed in the United States of America
24 23 22   5 4 3 2 1

First edition

To Kyle and Olivia, so they may understand the past,
the present, and their grandmother's lifelong
commitment to civil rights.
Enid Gort

To Erkeno, and my friends at the Franklin H. Williams
Judicial Commission, as together we strive
for justice by example and persistence.
John M. Caher

Contents

PREFACE   ix

NOTE FROM THE AUTHORS   xiii

Introduction   1

1 Roots   7

2 Coming of Age   17

3 An "Ole Lady" at Lincoln   31

4 The Real World   39

5 The American Veterans Committee   52

6 Civil Rights Lawyer   63

7 In the Courts   74

8 Legal Lynching   91

9 Passion and Power Plays   110

10 California Deliverance   122

11 The Washington Years   145

12 After Washington   165

Epilogue   183

ACKNOWLEDGMENTS   191

NOTES   193

INDEX   219

Preface

The morning after a dinner party welcoming me home from a three-year anthropological exploration in Swaziland, I was awakened by a telephone call from a complete stranger, a man I had never met. "Good morning," the unfamiliar and self-important voice said. "My name is Ambassador Franklin Hall Donald Lowry Williams, and I would like you to come over right now for an interview at the Phelps Stokes Fund!" When the caller realized (with exaggerated exasperation) that I had been sleeping at seven in the morning and was wasting my day away, he showed even less patience. I knew nothing of Franklin Williams and next to nothing about the Phelps Stokes Fund and would learn only later that it was nonprofit foundation that had been established in 1911 to increase educational opportunities for African Americans, Africans, Native Americans, and needy whites and to create housing for poor people in New York City.

My first impulse was to hang up and go back to sleep, but something about this strange call and strange man piqued my curiosity, and I agreed to the proposed meeting. I hurried over to 10 East Eighty-Seventh Street, where I found a marble-faced brownstone that had once been the home of Philip Buttenger, a noted scholar and bibliophile of Austrian Jewish descent, and rang the buzzer. A trim, neatly dressed young man offered a stiff, formal greeting and escorted me inside, gesturing toward a tiny elevator. We rode to the third floor, and the instant the doors opened I was face-to-face with the aforementioned Ambassador Williams.

The Ambassador, who had been playfully toying with me since interrupting my sleep, shot me a twinkle-eyed smile and ushered me into his small yet majestic office, embellished by African art and statuary, photographs, and memorabilia. He told me he'd received a call from Gil Jonas, a former chief fundraiser for the NAACP and a mutual friend with whom I had been at the dinner party the evening before. It seems Gil, without bothering to mention it to me, thought the Phelps Stokes Fund would be a good landing place as I continued to pursue my doctorate in anthropology and African studies at Columbia University. The Ambassador seemed intrigued that I had spent three years in Swaziland doing fieldwork, and he was quite interested in the exploratory studies I had conducted in Senegal, Togo, and especially Ghana, a country near to his heart. After asking only a handful of questions, he basically told me I was hired for a job for which I had not applied and wasn't at all sure I wanted. And what exactly would that job be? We'd figure it out later, along with the salary. I protested that I needed to begin writing my dissertation, a project that would consume all my time and energy. He shook off my concern with a dismissive wave of his hand and said not to worry about it, I could come and go as I liked.

The offer was bizarre, to say the least, and I told him I needed time to think about it, even though I'd already decided I wasn't interested. I walked home, where my husband was getting ready for work. I told Sy of my strange encounter and the odd job offer I intended to decline. He thought for a moment and urged me to reconsider, noting that the job location was unbelievably convenient, the foundation's work focused on my field of interest, and I'd have time to pursue my scholarly passion. What was there to lose? I had to agree, and I called Ambassador Williams and accepted the job.

The very next day I began work at Phelps Stokes, starting what would become an exhilarating, exciting, educational, and fruitful experience. For six years, I worked closely with Franklin Williams on a wide variety of projects. (This biography was never a part of my job, or even a thought.) Franklin was the most dramatic, kind, gentle, charismatic, and eloquent—not to mention infuriating and supercilious—man I had ever encountered. He could be incredibly thoughtful and maddeningly thoughtless. But he was always engaging and insightful and highly principled in most ways, and those of us who were privileged to know him forgave his excesses because, at least on some level, we knew we were in the presence of someone very special. At Phelps Stokes, I came to work at 6:00 a.m. so that I could complete my daily tasks in peace and quiet and spend the later afternoon in school. But inevitably, when I arrived, the office was already buzzing with activity and people who could not wait to come to work.

When Franklin arrived, everyone in the building gathered in the dining area for an early morning coffee klatch. Thelma Taylor, the housekeeper, made the coffee and Abu Sillah, the assistant comptroller, provided the muffins. During these informal meetings, the conversations ranged from current events and politics to the problems people were having with their work. Like a doting father, Franklin took an interest in all of us. He initiated ideas, created programs and identified the best people to run them. He inspired us with experiences, but more important, he listened to and learned from us. Sometimes, he brought guests such as Ellen Sirleaf Johnson, later the first woman president of Liberia, and Donna Shalala, then president of Hunter College, who would become the US Secretary of Health and Human Services, president of the University of Miami, and a member of the US House of Representatives. He showed an interest in everyone and everything, approached discussion with an open mind, and rarely passed up an opportunity to learn. Franklin thought there was much to discover from everyone, no matter how high or low their station in life, no matter what their academic pedigrees or lack thereof.

On one occasion, a Black secretary from South Africa arrived at the office visibly upset and told me that while browsing at a nearby shop during her lunch hour, she was stalked by an overbearing security guard just waiting for her to slip something into her pocket. This was a woman who came to the country where all are supposedly created equal to escape the racial caste system of her homeland, and the experience with the security guard was deeply upsetting. I was appalled and immediately relayed the story to Franklin, who, in a flash, grabbed his hat and coat and hurried over to the store, where he confronted the owner. It was a fascinating exchange to witness. Franklin did not yell or scream or berate or threaten to sue or picket the store or demand the security guard's job or throw a brick through the window. He merely explained in a calm, reasoned manner how the security guard's behavior opened barely healed wounds and how terribly hurtful it was to a woman who had come to this country in search of freedom and equality. It was a classic Franklin Williams teaching moment, the first of many I would witness and learn from in the coming years. He preferred converts to enemies and believed, sometimes naively, that he could reason with even the unreasonable.

Over the years, Sy and I became part of Franklin's and his wife Shirley's wide and diverse circle of friends. Shirley was a woman blessed with all of Franklin's good qualities, none of his bad ones, and an intellect that transcended almost everyone I've ever known. She spoke impeccable English and fluent French. She read the classics in both languages, adored the arts, abhorred gossip, and with quiet, understated strength possessed all the skills that would someday be demanded of a diplomat's wife. Shirley gently and gracefully brought balance to a relationship and family that, without her presence, would have become lost in Franklin's sizeable shadow and ego.

In researching this work, I came to appreciate the impact this man had, and the key, albeit somewhat behind the scenes, role he played in the civil rights movement. He granted me dozens of no-restriction interviews about his life and times and the experience of Black Americans in the twentieth century. Franklin Williams truly was a giant among men and a historic figure. This book endeavors to tell his story.

Note from the Authors

There is a concerted effort to purge from the language and cleanse from our culture a racial epithet beginning with the letter "n." We acknowledge that this word is jarring and offensive but choose to use it rather than revert to the preferred "n-word" style in quotations because we believe the historical record should reflect precisely what was said without sanitization. We agree with legal scholars Randall Kennedy and Eugene Volokh that "vocalizing any word for a legitimate pedagogical purpose—and in particular to accurately report facts—should not be made taboo."[1]

Except where specified, all interviews in this book were conducted by Enid Gort.

A BRIDGE TO JUSTICE

Introduction

Courageous and charismatic civil rights leaders such as Martin Luther King and Thurgood Marshall challenged the United States and, through the force of their personalities and the power of their intellect, transformed this country and made equal rights and equal opportunity not only the letter but also the spirit of the law. Those pioneers changed the course of history, and their accomplishments and contributions are beyond dispute. They were revered in their day, and they are revered now.

But somewhat behind the scenes were the "bridge figures," those a step or two outside the limelight who were perhaps less threatening and better able to navigate both Black and white circles and to span the more turbulent racial waters below. The bridge figures were a conduit between cultures, interpreters in a sense, who were able to persuade people who looked at the world in one way to view it in another. Late in his life, James Farmer, the main founder of the Congress of Racial Equality who helped shape the civil rights struggle in the 1950s and 1960s, described the role of a bridger: "I lived in two worlds. One was the volatile and explosive one of the new Black Jacobins and the other was the sophisticated and genteel one of the white and Black liberal establishment. As a bridge, I was called on by each side for help in the contacting the other."[1] Franklin Williams occupied a similar position.

Whites *and* Blacks could perhaps more easily relate to these "bridge figures," whereas they may have shunned the militant, revolutionary and incendiary rhetoric and tactics of a Bobby Seale, a Huey Newton, or a Malcolm X (at least until his break with the Nation of Islam). Although many of the bridge figures contributed mightily to the battle for equal rights, most have been sadly relegated to the footnotes of history, largely lost in the overwhelming shadows of

King and Marshall, to name just two of the titans of the civil rights movement. One could write a book on the entire group of bridge figures, but this one focuses on the contributions of a particular member of that clique: Franklin Hall Williams. Franklin Williams was more than merely a "bridge." He was an historic figure in his own right, and his influence on the civil rights movement and civil rights jurisprudence must be recognized and should be celebrated by those to whom he handed the baton of freedom and equality rather than the weapons of revenge.

Civil rights leader, lawyer, diplomat, organizer of the Peace Corps, United Nations representative, foundation president, associate of Thurgood Marshall on some of the seminal civil liberty cases of the past hundred years, Franklin Hall Williams was a visionary and trailblazer who devoted his life to the pursuit of civil rights—not through acrimony and violence and hatred, but through reason and example.

> I am not a Black militant. I am not a communist. I am not "crazy." I am a former American Ambassador, well-educated, sober and responsible. I believe my country is the second most racist nation in the world [after South Africa, which from 1948 until the early 1990s, had an institutionalized policy of racial segregation, or "apartheid"]. I believe this is a cancer in the body of our society which we have ignored for so many decades, so many generations that we are almost incapable of recognizing it for what it is and when we see it.[2]

Franklin loved his country, all the while hating the way it treated him, his family and his community. He abhorred violence and was ardently anticommunist, believing that the communists wanted to undermine the country and shred its Constitution. He believed to the core of his soul that the Constitution provided all the rights and protections necessary for Black America to gain equal footing. He did not think it was properly enforced—nor was it—but he thought all the necessary tools were in that constitutional toolbox. He believed in and trusted the rule of law and marshaled the power of the law and courts to defend innocent men, challenge prejudice and segregation and bring shame on businesses and businessmen who practiced discrimination. Even after enduring the segregated army, suffering cruel discrimination and barely escaping a murderous lynch mob eager to make him pay for zealously representing three innocent Black men falsely accused of rape, Franklin was not a hater. He believed that Americans in general were good people who were open to reason and, in their hearts, sympathetic to fairness and justice. He did not think the Ku Klux Klan was representative of the white majority any more than he thought the Nation of Islam represented mainstream Black attitudes and mores. And unlike both the white supremacists and the Black separatists, he was not a segregationist.

Williams would define "racism" intellectually as the unconscionable and mindless tendency to ascribe intellectual, moral or social significance based on something as incidental as one's genetic lineage. He believed in *individual* rights, the inalienable rights with which every person is born by virtue of being a human being. At the same time, Franklin accepted the importance of the group dynamic, understanding all too well that the discrimination he suffered was not directed to him as an individual but as a member of a particular group. So, while the philosophical construct of individual as opposed to group rights was persuasive and appealing to his mind and moral compass, Franklin's pragmatic side recognized the need to mobilize his group and appeal to other groups.

Franklin Hall Williams was born in Flushing, Queens, New York, on October 22, 1917. He was a veritable one-man melting pot: Williams's forebears include Native Americans, Black freedmen, runaway slaves, and slave owners, as well as Dutch and English immigrants. His mother died from a botched abortion when he was only two, and his father, a traveling musician, was absent for much of his life. Williams was reared by a stern, self-righteous maternal grandfather who looked down his nose equally on "white trash" and the Black equivalent.

As a young man, Franklin Williams grew up in a culture in which he was not allowed to use the public swimming pool or sit in the orchestra seats at the theater. He was denied membership to the YMCA because of his race, and he suffered the indignities and insults imposed as a matter of course on Black Americans during the first half of the twentieth century. Yet this abject discrimination did not make him bitter; it made him better. It made him thoughtful, and that thoughtfulness was nurtured during his years at Lincoln University, the first degree-granting historically Black university in the United States. In time, Williams would emerge as a reasoned voice on civil rights.

At Lincoln University (also the alma mater of Thurgood Marshall), "Frankie" Williams majored in philosophy and was a member and manager of the male chorus, the philosophy club, and Phi Kappa Sigma fraternity. He was involved in intramural track and basketball. His senior yearbook described him as "dominant," "capable," "definite asset," self-sufficient," and "altruistic." Other words associated with his name were "we the people" and "democracy."[3] He was salutatorian of his class. Vitally, he learned self-awareness and accepted the fact that a Black man who wants to succeed must first come to terms with and defeat his own demons.

Franklin was admitted to Fordham Law School, but before he completed his studies, World War II beckoned. Service in the segregated US Army scarred

Williams far more than the discrimination he had experienced as a child and young man.

After his military service, much of which was spent in an army hospital for reasons that to this day are unclear, Williams returned to the Fordham University School of Law, graduating in 1945. For the next fourteen years, he worked with the National Association for the Advancement of Colored People (NAACP), first as a special counsel to Thurgood Marshall and later as West Coast regional director.

Williams successfully argued key civil rights cases before the US Supreme Court and laid the foundation for the Court, in *Batson v. Kentucky*,[4] to declare once and for all that Blacks could not be systematically excluded from juries. He represented Isaac Woodard, a just-discharged Black soldier who was blinded by a police officer who thought the Negro on the bus didn't show proper deference to the white bus driver. The case forever closed Woodard's eyes, but, with the help of Franklin Williams, it opened America's eyes to racial injustice (and inspired folk music icon Woody Guthrie to write "The Blinding of Isaac Woodard"). He literally put his life on the line for three Black youths wrongly accused of raping a white woman, the subject of Gilbert King's brilliant Pulitzer Prize–winning book *Devil in the Grove*; battled to integrate the armed forces; and embarked on vitally important NAACP fundraising tours with Woodard, Jackie Robinson, and Joe Louis. Quickly, Franklin proved an eloquent intellectual companion—and, occasionally, competitor—of Thurgood Marshall.

Marshall and Williams clashed often, partially owing to competing egos but mainly because of principled, albeit spirited, disagreement. Marshall was leery of taking a case to the Supreme Court unless he was quite sure he would prevail because he knew that a defeat could establish a devastating precedent and set the movement back a generation or more. Williams, on the other hand, would take that risk and confront the justices in Washington with the blunt reality of what was happening in America.

Further, Marshall was reluctant to represent through the NAACP Legal Defense Fund individuals who were clearly guilty of gruesome crimes, fearing few would contribute to the fund if it was viewed as a vehicle for helping murderers and rapists (especially *Black* murderers and rapists) beat the rap on a "technicality." Williams, again, would take that risk to make the point that if the US Constitution doesn't protect the rights of the most wretched defendant imaginable, it doesn't protect anyone. In Williams's view, confessions beaten out of the guilty were no less repulsive than confessions beaten out of the innocent. Marshall shared that view, of course, but he wasn't willing to risk his organization's credibility standing up for vicious criminals, at least in the early days. Williams, again, would have rolled the dice.

Williams was also unabashedly ambitious, more than a little arrogant, and not the least hesitant to lecture Marshall and tell one of the greatest civil rights lawyers in history that he, the barely thirty-year-old neophyte with meager legal experience, knew better. Early in his career, Williams was privileged to watch Marshall argue before the Supreme Court a case in which a Black woman had been arrested and fined for refusing to move to the back of a Greyhound bus. Marshall's bravura performance mesmerized everyone—with the exception of Williams, who thought he would have done a better job and said so.

The tension became so great that Williams was transferred to the West Coast in 1950, about as far away from Marshall as possible. But once out of Marshall's shadow, Williams shone and largely built the NAACP in a region that includes the states of Alaska, Arizona, California, Hawaii, Idaho, Nevada, Oregon, Utah, and Washington. In California, Williams challenged housing and employment discrimination, won the first school desegregation case and, later, as an assistant attorney general, created the first Constitutional Rights Section within the state's Department of Justice.

His growing prominence and reasoned approach brought him to the attention of the Kennedy administration and in 1961 Sargent Shriver—President John F. Kennedy's brother-in-law—invited Williams to join the newly established Peace Corps. Shriver wanted the Peace Corps to set an example as the very first fully integrated government agency, and he began that quest by recruiting Williams. Shriver and Williams, seemingly an odd pair, traveled the world together, consulting with the heads of state in nine countries before deploying Peace Corps volunteers. Williams fulfilled several roles in his short but vital stint with the Peace Corps and completed his tenure as regional director for Africa. Shortly after President Kennedy's assassination, President Lyndon Baines Johnson appointed Williams to serve as the US representative to the Economic and Social Council of the United Nations.

In 1965, Johnson named Williams ambassador to Ghana, a tenure that remains controversial because some believed he was complicit in the coup that overthrew President Kwame Nkrumah, his Lincoln University classmate. To the day he died, Williams swore he had nothing to do with the coup, and nothing has emerged in the decades since to prove otherwise. Ultimately, even Nkrumah reversed himself and agreed that Williams had not been involved. But those more interested in narratives than facts continue to insist that Williams sold out. After three years abroad, Williams returned home to New York.

In New York, Williams assumed the directorship of the Urban Center at Columbia University, a position he held for only two years. For the following twenty years, he served as president of the Phelps Stokes Fund, an educational foundation dedicated to advancing opportunities for Africans, African

Americans, and Native Americans. He sat on the boards of Consolidated Edison, Borden Inc., Chemical Bank, the American Stock Exchange, Lincoln University, the Boys' Choir of Harlem, and the Barnes Foundation, among others. And he continued to speak and write on civil rights.

In 1988, Williams received a cold call from a man he had never met, Sol Wachtler, New York State's chief judge. Judge Wachtler was deeply concerned with the lack of minorities in the court system and the way minorities interacting with the court system were treated. He wanted to set up an aggressive commission and needed an aggressive chair, but he didn't know who to call. He asked Thurgood Marshall for advice, and Marshall told Wachtler that there was only one person he should consider: Franklin Williams. After getting Wachtler's assurance that the commission would be totally independent of the courts and that the courts would cooperate fully, Williams was appointed chairman of the newly created New York State Judicial Commission on Minorities, the first body of its kind in the nation. Under Williams's leadership, the Commission undertook a comprehensive and groundbreaking study on minority participation in the courts and legal profession, issuing a blistering report. The report led to extensive and enduring reform, and today the commission is named in his honor: the Franklin H. Williams Judicial Commission. It was Williams's final project before lung cancer caught him off guard and claimed his life on May 20, 1990.

Even with the optics of time and hindsight, it is difficult to pigeonhole Franklin Williams. He was not an intellectual in the manner of W. E. B. Du Bois or a legal scholar, mainly because he was impatient and result-oriented rather than theoretical or academic. He did not come out of the Black church, like Martin Luther King; in fact, he was at best indifferent to religion, and occasionally hostile. He was not a "populist" figure such as Jesse Jackson. Historically, he belongs in the company of the likes of James Farmer, Loren Miller, Whitney Young, Vernon Jordan, Dorothy Height, and Andrew Young. Williams was a practical, pragmatic bridge builder, a brilliant yet complex individual whose life story reflects the opportunities and constraints of an intellectually elite Black man in the twentieth century.

1

Roots

Franklin Williams grew up in something of a protective family cocoon, but his autocratic grandfather and supportive phalanx of relatives could not entirely shield him from the childhood slights and bigotry that would scar him for life.

As a young adult, Franklin endured the indignity of the segregated US Army, witnessed the tangible impact of systemic racism through the blinding of Isaac Woodard, and then barely escaped a lynch mob eager to put the uppity Black attorney in his "place"—and in their minds, his "place" was dangling from a tree with a noose around his neck. As he gradually came to terms with his own identity and as racism hit closer to home, Franklin slowly came to realize his calling in life, his character, his destiny. Yet he never broke completely free from the yoke of racial defensiveness. In 1988, at the age of seventy-one, he confessed:

> I am still handicapped by a consciousness of my race. . . . I always
> think there are people sitting there saying, "What is he doing here?"
> I have never gotten over that. It's so bad that I have few shoes that fit
> me because when I go into a shoe store and I try on a pair of shoes,
> after the third or fourth pair I become so goddamn self-conscious that
> I'm thinking this guy is thinking, "This poor nigger doesn't have any
> business in here in the first place and he obviously can't afford these
> shoes. That's why he's not buying them." I have never walked out of a
> shoe store without buying shoes. I tell you, it's a horrible thing. I hate
> it. I can't do it. I can't get up and walk of that store. . . . Isn't it terrible
> to be my age and never to have been able to rid yourself of those fears?[1]

Those were fears developed throughout his life, even though he was brought up to view himself and his family as superior rather than inferior. Racial "inferiority" was something he would learn when he ventured outside the family shell.

Franklin Hall Donald Lowry Williams was the youngest of three sons to Alinda and Arthur Williams, as well as the youngest of five related children living together in Flushing, New York, all of them raised by a stern and self-righteous grandfather. The family stubbornly refused to view itself as second-class, even if much of society, and the law, did. Indeed, the family was rather haughty, a trait that certainly rubbed off on Franklin. The five children, each a year apart, lived within a large extended family household in a middle-class, neighborhood.[2] All were adored, even pampered as young heirs of the family tradition. But it was ebullient, inquisitive and charming "Frankie" who most often commandeered the center of attention. Assertive and smart, self-confident and assured, Franklin embodied from the very start many qualities that would eventually help him rise to prominence and hone his natural leadership skills.

Like many Black Long Islanders, Williams could trace his ancestry back through three or four generations of Black freepersons, runaway slaves, Native Americans, and colonial Europeans. His maternal great-grandmother, Annise Elizabeth Tobias Davis (known as Lizzie), was a full-blooded Matinecock, descended from people who had once lived in birchbark longhouses and hunted in areas that are now part of metropolitan New York City and Long Island.[3] Lizzie was a huge presence, literally and figuratively, a three-hundred-pound woman with braided hair "so long she could sit on it," Williams recalled. She dressed in Indian attire, wore moccasins instead of conventional footwear, and seemed tightly connected with the Native American community. She was also blind.

In 1863, with the Union soldiers losing ground to the Confederacy, poor whites were incensed to learn that their government intended to conscript them into military service. A congressional act, allowing those with the money to buy their way out for $300, pushed them over the edge. New Yorkers who could not afford the $300 and bitterly resented those who could waged the so-called Draft Riots attack on their wealthier neighbors. When the police broke up the riots and shielded the wealthy whites, the frustrated rioters turned their wrath on the Black community, shooting and killing people of color for "causing" the Civil War.[4] Lizzie, caught up in the hysteria, was trampled by a policeman's horse, resulting in injuries that damaged her optic nerve and slowly led to blindness.[5]

Williams remembered Lizzie associating with "big fat women who looked like her [and] would come to church on Sunday afternoons to complain about the 'government people' who were threatening to widen the roads 'down the Island' and disturb their families' graves." Increasingly, as New Yorkers sought respite from the hot summers and as Long Island towns grew, roads were built to accommodate the traffic, with little or no concern for the indigenous residents. Indian burial grounds were often desecrated in the process. In the 1930s, sacred grounds were dug up to clear the way for Marathon Parkway in Douglaston and Northern Boulevard in Little Neck, a highway that reportedly trampled the historic trail linking Matinecock settlements.[6]

For Franklin, it was an early primer in social justice, minority concerns and government power. Lizzie's colorful stories, rich in historical and social detail, fascinated the young boy and planted questions that troubled him into adulthood: Who was he? Where did he fit in? The sessions with his great-grandmother, the undisputed matriarch of the household, were the beginning of his lifelong engagement with matters of identity and race.

Sometime in the late 1860s, Lizzie and her sister, Mary Tobias, were hired by the uptown Willets family to serve as live-in servant-companions to their daughters. In that era, it was common for well-to-do white families to employ Black servants, and doing so was a sign of social status. During the decades following emancipation, nearly a third of African Americans in New York City worked as domestics for whites.[7] The Tobias girls were educated along with their upper-class Willets "sisters" and brought along as servants on exotic family vacations to Paris and Rome. In 1870, when Lizzie was about seventeen, she became pregnant. Some of her descendants claim that the father was a Willets. Others say it was a soldier.[8] Whoever fathered her child, a noticeably pregnant Lizzie married John Davis, a dark-skinned Black porter, and soon thereafter gave birth to a fair-skinned, red-headed daughter named Caroline, nicknamed Cab. Later, the three Tobias sisters and their families (the married names were Davis, Spencer, and Craig) decided to form a combined household, creating a family unit that remained intact for the next forty-one years.[9]

At first the family lived in a succession of three-story frame buildings located in the East Eighties off Third Avenue in Manhattan. Their racially mixed, working-class neighborhood, only steps away from the busy East River waterfront, abutted an industrial area of breweries, lumberyards, and slaughterhouses. It was a neighborhood in flux, and the family was eager to move out and move up. By 1891, they had saved enough money to move to Flushing, a quiet, residential Long Island town of twelve thousand.

As a center of the agricultural nursery industry, Flushing was a community of tree-lined streets, well-kept gardens, and townspeople proud that their town had been a station on the Underground Railroad. Activist Blacks and abolitionist Quakers had helped runaway slaves move northward, sheltering them at residences like the Bowne House (still standing on Bowne Street) and the Aspinwall House (Northern Boulevard), or hiding them beneath the basement of the Macedonia African Methodist Episcopal (AME) Church.[10] But Flushing was not a model of perfection, nor did it entirely deserve its reputation as a haven of tolerance. Certain congregations, such as the Methodist and Baptist ones, were repressed, as generally were Blacks and Native Americans.[11] Although manumission in Flushing began in 1799, it was not until 1825 that all slaves were finally freed. Not until 1902, and "after much resistance," were public schools in Flushing finally integrated.[12]

Despite its sketchy history, Flushing in the early 1800s attracted freed slaves and other people of color who were convinced that the Quakers were more serious than others about creating an equal and just society. Many Quakers were abolitionists, and some extended themselves to help dark-skinned new-comers. However, all too many others did not. Thus, Flushing was polarized from the beginning—first by religious differences and ultimately by race.

Lizzie Davis, along with her sisters (Alinda and Mary) and their families, entered this world when they arrived in Flushing in 1891. Initially, the family rented a twenty-one-room house at 65 State Street that commanded the south-west corner atop State Street hill. In 1905, Lizzie somehow came up with $5,450, a staggering sum in those days, to buy the property.[13] The origins of the windfall are unclear, although the family speculates that it came from the Willets, which, if true, could lend support to the theory that someone in that family fathered Cab. Years later, Franklin Williams could recall every feature of it in detail—"the great veranda, the coal-fired stove in the kitchen, the rabbit hutch in the backyard and the containers of lard and sugar on the pantry shelves."[14]

The house lent itself to entertaining, which the sisters, who for years had observed the social rituals of wealthy families, did stylishly even with limited financial resources. A social column from 1905 described a party held to celebrate the purchase and attended by the Black elite.[15] One of the attendees was Thaddeus Lowry, Franklin Williams's grandfather. Thaddeus, a slim and handsome man, had met and married Cab around the time of the move to Flushing.

In 1881, at the age of thirteen, Thadd left Newville, Virginia, a peanut, corn, and hog-raising town thirty-five miles south of Petersburg in rural Sussex County, and came north to take his chances in New York, bringing with him a highly developed racial consciousness and value system. Thadd made his way to the "Tenderloin," an area on the west side of Manhattan that was a haven for new arrivals and a center of intellectual and entrepreneurial activity.[16] Writers, actors, and other artistic types congregated on the lively streets, as did members of the Black and white underworld who ran gambling parlors and

Franklin Williams's grandparents Caroline ("Cab") and Thaddeus Lowry. Franklin and his brothers were raised largely by their grandparents. (Enid Gort collection)

brothels. Thadd supported himself by playing cards and shooting pool until he found a job as chauffeur to Edward Holbrook, president of the Gorham Sterling Silver Company.

Although generally good-humored, Thadd was known to have "attitudes"— biases explicit and implicit and derived, in the main, from his own relatively privileged antecedents, people like those W. E. B. Du Bois had in mind when he wrote somewhat reverentially of "the industrious and property accumulating class of the Negro citizens [who] best represent . . . the general tendencies of the group."[17] Thadd Lowry's mores mirrored those of Blacks—often, lighter-skinned

Blacks—who viewed themselves a cut above much of white and Black society. They mimicked the mannerisms of upscale whites, embraced social and literary associations, wanted their sons and daughters to marry higher-class Blacks to ensure "good breeding" and viewed travel, especially travel abroad, as an important status symbol.[18] Neither Thadd nor his new employer, Holbrook, cared to mix with people who did not wear jackets, shirts, and ties to work. Both held immigrants and Catholics in contempt and aligned with the Republican Party.[19] Franklin recalled: "During the Smith-Hoover campaign of 1928, a little girl down the street wrote on the sidewalk 'Smith for president.' I erased it and wrote 'Hoover for President,' because I'd heard my grandfather say, "You can't have a Catholic president. The pope will come over here, and people will have to kneel down and kiss his ring.'"[20]

Thadd was a quintessential joiner, a characteristic of the "Black bourgeoisie" that he passed on to his youngest grandson.[21] He was particularly proud of his affiliation with the Prince Hall chapter of the Thirty-third Degree Masons, a unit of the international fraternal organization composed of middle-class Black men considered preeminent in their communities.[22] Although cynical about religion and rarely a churchgoer, Thadd was deeply involved in the social affairs of the African Methodist Episcopal Church, the first major denomination in the Western world that was established for racial rather than theological reasons.[23] He was the unquestioned patriarch of a lively and vibrant household. Thadd encouraged his children, Alinda (Franklin's mother), Frederick Lawson ("Freddie"), and John Edward ("Eddie"), to associate with boys and girls with "good" hair and fair skin, who took education seriously and had plans for professional careers.

For adult company, Thadd associated with the "Smart Set," a loosely organized social circle whose members were drawn from the networks of middle-class Black families who had established themselves in Harlem, Brooklyn, and to a lesser extent in the Queens communities of Corona, Jamaica, and Flushing. Almost every Sunday, members of the Smart Set met at the Lowry home, a gathering place for the Black bourgeoisie.[24] Among the regulars on State Street was Alinda Lowry's best friend, May Chinn, an extraordinary woman who had come to New York from Great Barrington, Massachusetts, to study music at Columbia University, but decided she wanted to become a doctor—an almost absurd aspiration for a Black woman in the 1920s. Still, in 1926, Chinn became the first Black woman graduate of Bellevue Hospital Medical College; she was also the first Black woman to intern at Harlem Hospital, where she served as a physician until retiring in 1977 at the age of eighty-one.[25] Others included Eslanda "Essie" Goode, the future wife of Paul Robeson, the acclaimed singer, actor, and social activist, and an anthropologist in her later life; and Earl Johnson,

Thadd Lowry, Franklin's autocratic grandfather, holds court over the "Smart Set," a group of educated and socially prominent Blacks whom Lowry convened. Thaddeus is seated at the bottom left, smoking his pipe. Franklin's mother, Alinda, is at the far right of the back row, and next to her is Franklin's godmother, May Edward Chinn. (Enid Gort collection)

who with his wife Anna established the first Black husband-and-wife dental practice in Harlem.

Thadd directed and participated in most of the Smart Set activities, holding court over the group, impressing the guests with his storytelling ability and expansive vocabulary (including grand-sounding words and phrases he invented from whole cloth, such as "asterperious" and "risorial"), and organizing fiercely competitive poker games. Thadd loved the strategy of poker, distracting his competitors with his endless commentary and warning his family of the danger of overthinking the hands: "Think long, think wrong," he would admonish.

Thadd Lowry delighted in his children, the product of his patriarchy and the hope of his race. He was concerned about their appearance as much as their abilities and knew all too well that dark-skinned Blacks who spoke in the vernacular of the race were at a particular disadvantage. One son, Freddie, could easily have passed for white. Alinda and her brother Eddie had high cheekbones and were copper-colored, resembling their American Indian forebears. Both boys were excellent basketball players. Eddie, a four-letter man, was salutatorian of his class and a legend in the annals of academic achievement at Flushing High School. He became a physician, a rare accomplishment for a "colored boy" in the early twentieth century; John Edward Lowry was the first Black elected to the presidency of the Queens County Medical Society.

Alinda Lowry Williams (*left*), circa 1915. (Enid Gort collection)

Alinda, however, was her father's favorite, a gentle, sweet-faced girl who attracted eligible young suitors from her own area as well as more distant neighborhoods in New York City and Brooklyn.

It was probably on one of those Sunday afternoons in 1912 when Earl Johnson, the dentist, brought a young pianist named Arthur Lee Williams to State Street to play for the weekly gathering of the Smart Set. Tall, imposing, and stylishly dressed, Arthur Lee enchanted Alinda Lowry with his dark, seductive eyes and an engaging charm that he would pass along to at least one of his sons. After a brief courtship, Arthur and Alinda married and added three little boys to the State Street homestead: Arthur Robert (1913), John Frederick (1915) and Franklin Hall (1917).[26] But the marriage was troubled from the start.

When Arthur arrived, New York City was on the brink of becoming the world's premier entertainment center, and the Harlem musical revolution created unprecedented opportunities for Black musicians.[27] Even Broadway was hiring

Franklin's mother, Alinda Lowry, died of a botched abortion attempt when he was fifteen months old. His father, Arthur Williams, was an itinerant musician who was banished from the
household by his father-in-law and had little involvement in the
lives of his sons. The child in the photograph is Alinda's first-
born, Arthur Williams Jr. (Enid Gort collection)

Black musicians for musical comedies, albeit casting them as dim-witted,
shiftless, happy-go-lucky "Negroes" to the amusement of white audiences.
Arthur, however, couldn't break in. He spent long periods away from home
and did little to support his family, conduct utterly unacceptable to Thaddeus
Lowry. He had largely outworn his welcome when, on January 29, 1919, Arthur
lost his wife and his boys lost their mother. The brothers always believed their
mother died from a virulent attack of influenza. The death certificate tells a
different story: Alinda died of septicemia, blood poisoning that apparently
followed a self-induced abortion.[28]

Thaddeus discouraged visits by Arthur and dissuaded any connection between the boys and their paternal relatives. Even if Arthur tried to be a good father—and perhaps he did—it is entirely possible he was shut out by and demeaned by his father-in-law. In Franklin's mind, coming of age without a biological father in the picture had little impact since Thadd filled that role admirably. But growing up without a mother is something he never got over.

Even as an adult, Williams seemed at times preoccupied with thoughts of a mother he never knew, for he was only fifteen months old when his mother died.[29] He displayed characteristics that psychologists and sociologists say are not uncommon in boys who grow up without a mother.[30] He was tough and resilient, but at times could be cold and insensitive. He disliked being alone and transformed his anger over maternal "desertion" into an indictment of social injustice.

2

Coming of Age

With his background, heritage, and sheltered upbringing, Franklin Williams was blissfully ignorant of racism as a child. But when it hit, it hit hard, and he carried the albatross of discrimination and race-based self-doubt with him for most of his life. As an adult in 1964, Williams reflected: "I am a Negro-American who learned from personal experience that, given equality of opportunity, human dignity resides in a man's being equal to himself. . . . The process of self-discovery, however, is not an easy one for any man. It is especially difficult for a Negro in America, whose 'cultural heritage'—if one may call it that—is a deeply ingrained sense of his own inferiority."[1]

Those were sentiments that would develop over a lifetime.[2] Despite the presence of grandparents who adored him, devoted uncles, as well as brothers and cousins his own age, he seems to have felt an unappeased longing for someone or something missing from his life.

It may have been the lack of a consistent maternal presence that led him to spend much of his time cultivating the attention and affection of women in the household. Foremost there was his great-grandmother Lizzie. Ella Spencer, who did the family cooking and painted watercolors, exercised a marked influence on Williams's creative ability: one day he would paint well enough to sell his work and, for a while anyhow, at least one of his paintings was on display in the White House.[3] Edith ("Daisy") Craig Butler was a confidante even in later years. Molly, a young woman from a nearby orphanage, helped care for the children. Franklin especially loved his grandmother. Unfortunately, she had little time to give him, overburdened as she was caring for Lizzie, now bedridden and totally blind, her husband, her son Freddie (Eddie was away at school), and three active grandchildren.[4] Somewhat guiltily, Williams would recall how his grandmother labored on behalf of her family. "She did everything for us," he recalled. "She washed our clothes and ironed them and fed us and took care of her mother's bedpan and emptied our piss pot. She just worked and never complained, until finally she just gave up." Yet the boys were not without compassion. On several occasions they felt so sorry for her that instead of sleeping in their separate beds, they would pile into one in order to make her cleanup work easier.

While Franklin delighted in the company of his older brothers, he spent most of his time with Daisy Butler's son, Charles Jr. Everyone called them "Frankie-n-Charlie," as if they were one, because they were usually together and getting underfoot. Less than a year apart, the boys shared their belongings and their earliest, most memorable experiences: first haircuts, first automobile rides, first encounters with racism.

One hot afternoon in the summer of 1922, before Frankie entered elementary school, he and Charlie decided to examine Flushing's first automobile dealership, with its giant plates of glass providing an unobstructed view of the shiny new Fords inside. As the two young children stood with noses pressed against the glass and staring wide-eyed at the marvelous vehicles inside, three white men sauntered outside. "How about it, boys?" one asked. "If you tap dance for us, we'll give you money to buy ice cream cones." Neither Frankie nor Charlie knew a thing about tap dancing, but the bribe was enough for them to jump around and shuffle their feet to the raucous amusement of the white men who tossed coins at their feet. Franklin had a nagging sense something was wrong, but the ice cream quickly quelled his brief feelings of embarrassment and shame. Still, his first rather minor brush with racism was something he would recall clearly decades later. In elementary school that fall, Franklin was the sole Black child at PS 20 at Union and Sandford Avenues in Flushing. While he could not recall any incidents of racial hostility on the part of teachers or students, he remembered agonizing over questions of self-definition: Who am I and where do I belong?

> All of the kids in my . . . class were "something." They were Poles, Germans and Russians—all immigrants. One day the teacher asked everybody to tell what they were and where they were from. I was so scared I wanted to cry because I didn't know what I was or where I was from. . . . Since my name is Williams, I went last. As the other students took their turn, I became more and more anxious. I couldn't say I was colored, because if you're colored, then what are you and where are you from? So, when my turn finally came, I said, "I'm an Indian from Indianapolis." And that was it. The teacher never batted an eye. But I went home and cried.[5]

The Williams boys and their cousin Charlie, Franklin's best childhood friend, outside the Flushing home they shared. (*Front row*), Charlie Butler and Franklin Williams; (*back row*), Johnny and Arthur Williams. (Enid Gort collection)

Although his schoolmates admired Frankie as "a fast runner and one of the smartest boys in class,"[6] he made few friends and suffered from a confused identity. Unfortunately, his concerns about race and origin were off-limits in Thadd's household:

> I couldn't talk to anybody about it because in my family we didn't talk about race. It was a non-issue. My grandfather had only one thing to say on the topic of race: "Stay in your own back yard. You're better than those dirty kikes or those dirty Irishmen or those dirty wops." My grandfather was a valet, so he always wore a collar and a tie. That made us "better" than those other folks.[7]

Thadd wanted his grandsons to play with Black children like Eugene and Adele Jones, the son and daughter of Eugene Kinkle Jones, head of the Urban League, or with Gerald and Winifred Norman, whose grandfather, Lewis H. Latimer, invented the carbon filament for Edison's incandescent light bulbs.[8] But these young people were contemporaries of his brothers, Arthur and Johnnie, and they lived on the other side of town.[9] Franklin could not find nearby friends that met with his grandfather's approval, so he was often lonely. He became tense and defensive around strangers, a trait he carried throughout his life: at first, Franklin would appear remote and arrogant when introduced to someone he didn't know. Only after sizing the person up would Franklin open the door a crack and begin to relax. Psychologically, in some ways, he never escaped the State Street cocoon.

Within that protective bubble, Arthur, Johnnie, and Frankie Williams and Charlie Butler constituted a closely knit, exclusively male cadre. Mary (Mamie) Butler, Charlie's sister, recalls that they frequently made her life miserable: "As the only girl I was always being chased. Some adult would have to stop them from chasing me around the yard and through the house and up and down the stairs."[10] Of the boys, Arthur Jr. was the most conscientious and responsible. Nicknamed "Sakes" because "sakes!" was the strongest curse he could muster, he tried, with limited success, to keep the younger, more mischievous ones in line. Everyone's favorite was skinny, sickly Johnnie, so winsome and imaginative that no one could resist him; one family member would later describe him as "the sweetest man the Lord ever put on earth."[11] Cousin Charlie was a round, ebullient elf of a child, a willing sidekick to his energetic younger cousin Frankie, who was intense, determined, controlling, and often oblivious to the feelings of those around him. When easygoing Charlie needed to escape the pressure, he would seek a forgotten room or closet to hide in until Frankie tired of pursuing him. Since childhood, Franklin had a presence or aura that was overwhelming at times and impossible to ignore. Charlie, at times, would find

Franklin, in the middle, was the youngest of the Williams boys. Here he is flanked by his brothers Arthur (*right*) and Johnnie (*left*). At that point, roughly 1920, their mother was dead and their father was absent. The woman on the right was a girl from a local orphanage who helped care for the children of the Lowry household. (Enid Gort collection)

respite in a closet when he needed a break from his cousin's unbridled exuberance. This self-absorbed little whirlwind was often too much to bear for some of his relatives. "We all knew he had a quick mind, but Frankie didn't have an ounce of sweetness in him," one relative recalled.[12]

In the family, Franklin developed a natural and strong bond with his grandfather, who was immensely pleased with the child. "Frankie has the vapors," Thadd Lowry would declare proudly. Thadd and Franklin shared a love of sports and games, and a capacity to turn simple activities into grand adventures. It was from his grandfather that he learned to fish, catch and clean crabs, ice skate, and play cards.

By the mid-1920s, the household that already contained parts of four families—the Spencers, Craigs, Butlers, and Lowrys—expanded. After graduating from Howard Medical School, Eddie Lowry moved back home, along with his new wife, Ethel Skinker, a delicate, fine-featured young woman from the elite Le Droit Park section of Washington, DC. Ethel's father, Buckley Merriman Skinker, was a wealthy white planter who had been driven from Carolina County, Virginia, when he insisted on living openly with a Black woman, with whom he fathered eight children, including Ethel. Ethel's presence, which some in the family resented, forced the household to acknowledge what it should have come to terms with earlier: they simply couldn't afford the big house. For years, they had attempted to get by just paying the taxes and interest, never making a dent in the mortgage. The house was finally sold in 1925.[13] Mamie Butler would later blame Ethel for loosening the extended family ties: "Ethel Skinker had delusions of grandeur because she married a doctor."[14] Franklin, on the other hand, adored Ethel and wistfully imagined that she was his mother.

The Craigs and Butlers relocated to a smaller home on Roosevelt Avenue in Flushing and then to one at a less prestigious address on MacDonough Street in the Bedford-Stuyvesant section of Brooklyn. The Lowrys—Lizzie, Thadd and Cab, Freddie, Eddie, and Aunt Ethel and the three boys—moved less than a mile away, to a three-story, nine-room Victorian house at 180 Barclay Street. Eddie had an office and waiting room on the first floor, furnished with the ancient maroon sofa and chairs they had taken from the State Street parlor. Before long, Freddie married and his wife, Gussie Hernandez, moved in.

The five and one-half years Franklin spent on Barclay Street were marked by loss of companionship, family income, and family solidarity. Nothing could make Franklin feel lonelier than the absence of attentive women, a dilemma he faced on Barclay Street. A massive heart attack killed Lizzie in 1928, two years after the move. Aunt Gussie was out of the house all day working at the post office. His beloved Aunt Ethel, unable to find a teaching position locally, taught school in Washington DC, and was home only on weekends. Beside his taciturn grandmother, there was no one else at home to talk to.

In 1926, the Gorham Sterling Silver Company relocated to Providence, Rhode Island, and Thadd was fired.[15] After thirty years with the company as the loyal chauffeur to the president, Thadd naively expected a pension, but Gorham sent him packing without a dime. Thadd was both furious and deeply hurt, and the family's financial straits forced him to accept a demeaning position as a messenger. The loss of stature hurt more than the loss of income; Thadd's self-image as the pillar of a Black middle-class family was badly bruised. Consumed by his own troubles, Thadd was no longer the rock of stability that Frankie had so adored and respected. Frankie turned to his brothers to help him get his bearings in a household that seemed to be disintegrating, only to find them less accessible as they matured and developed their own interests. The mood in the household, once playful and fun, was tense and often bitter. For the first time, Franklin witnessed ongoing and harsh arguments among people he loved, and sought to build bridges between them. He was eager to assume that bridge-building role, and was a natural at it, and it stands to reason that the skills honed early in life became manifest decades later when he brought diverse people together, whether it was for purely social purposes or to further the greater goal of civil rights.

In those tense years, there was an ongoing power struggle between Thadd, who would always consider himself the head of the household, and Freddie's wife, Gussie, who would not cede to the authority of her father-in-law. Rather than eat communally, Gussie insisted on cooking meals for herself and her husband and demanded the right to a refrigerator of her own. Thadd, struggling to maintain his self-respect and his position of prominence and respect in the family, resented her attempt to establish a household within a household. Many evenings Franklin would hear their angry voices penetrate the door of his third-floor bedroom: "I would pray that the person toward whom a statement was made would not answer back, because I could actually feel the arguments escalating. It was very painful, listening to people whom I loved arguing."

Arthur, a high school freshman, had become a serious student, but he had to study hard to maintain good grades. Johnnie, a substandard and often truant student, was "discharged"—a euphemism for "expelled"—from Flushing High School. He enrolled in Textile High in Manhattan, and then dropped out of school altogether.[16] An easygoing person averse to rules and restrictions, Johnnie would stay out beyond curfew, infuriating Thadd and Cab and adding to the growing tension in the household.

During those lonely years on Barclay Street, Franklin amused himself with solitary hobbies such as stamp collecting. He bought small packets of foreign stamps from the neighborhood candy store, placed each new stamp in the window allotted in his album, and wrote a description of the stamp and the country from which it came. Collecting, an avocation throughout his life, proved to be more than an intellectually satisfying exercise. It was a way of retreating from potentially hurtful relationships to find solace in objects over which he had complete control.

Franklin also began keeping scrapbooks, chronicling his life much as his mother may have had she lived—filling the oversized pages with Boy Scout badges, invitations, and ticket stubs, identifying each item with captions or commentary. An article from a local newspaper, mounted on one page, describes how Franklin, who could barely swim, rescued an infant and its mother from the waters of Long Island Sound after their boat exploded.[17] The incident, in which two people drowned, was reported by a journalist who, consistent with journalistic practices of the day, described the boys in racial terms despite the fact that race was not germane to the story:

> Two Flushing colored boys played a prominent part in the rescue work. Frank Williams of Barclay Avenue, Flushing, plunged overboard and took one baby from its mother and . . . Daniel Broadnax, also colored of Grove street [sic], Flushing, fearing that Williams would become panicky leaped into the water and took the child from him and brought it to the shore.[18]

Franklin yearned for companionship and in 1930, approaching adolescence, he began to venture beyond the confines of his household. He joined the local Boy Scouts—an integrated troop sponsored by St. George's Episcopal Church—and Christian Endeavor, a church-run youth group. On Saturday afternoons with friends, Black and white, male and female, he enjoyed movies in a neighborhood theater, the Janus. After school, he joined the young people who congregated in Kissena Park or who ice skated when their local pond froze over. Racial restrictions did not yet hamper him, but like other Black children he was aware that his participation was complicated in ways not experienced by his white companions.

Some local institutions were segregated, and some were not. Making sense of the situation was difficult for Franklin and for other Black children, not just because they faced restrictions but because the restrictions were vague and arbitrary. For instance, the local YMCA, which for years had solicited funds from the community at large to build its facility, refused to offer memberships to Black families when its building was completed in 1926. The Y did allow Flushing High School's basketball team to use its courts and pool.

Consequently, Arthur, because he was an athlete, could use the facilities while his brothers were barred solely because of their skin color.[19]

Frankie did not understand why he could not join the Y, take classes there, or play on its teams. It simply baffled him. Similarly, Franklin's Boy Scout troop was integrated, but the camp was not. While discrimination was never Boy Scout policy, troop leaders and others in authority often took positions that reflected the attitudes of the times.[20] So, Franklin and Johnnie were sent to camp in Manhattan where they bunked with five other Black "rejects" from other troops. Relationships with white neighbors could be equally confusing. Some neighbors were bigots, some were kind and gracious, and others behaved so inconsistently that it was difficult to gauge their feelings or predict their responses. It wasn't always obvious who would be a friend and who would be an enemy. As a child, Franklin thought it all very puzzling and found psychological refuge in the belief, instilled by Thadd, that his family was a cut above:

> I couldn't play on the private soccer team or join the Y because I was colored, and that hurt because I was denied the opportunity to participate. But deep down I knew that I was better than they were because my family was better educated, more socially conscious, and so much more cultured than the average white person that I dealt with on a day-to-day basis.

During the summer of 1930, Franklin learned agonizing and lasting lessons in racial relations and was forced to accept the painful fact that skin color transcended friendship. He and blonde, blue-eyed Carolyn Robertson had been classmates and buddies since kindergarten and part of the crowd that frequented the Janus Theater and Kissena Park. Both were good students, well-liked and attractive. Increasingly, they spent time together, usually in the company of their best friends, Bill Meier and Lillian Myers. On one occasion, the four decided to take the bus downtown to see their first evening movie.

Fortified with Milky Ways and Baby Ruths, they laughed and ate their way through the newsreels and the feature. After the movie, they emerged from the darkened theater to the brightly lit and crowded lobby where they were confronted by Carolyn's angry parents. Her father grabbed Franklin by the shirt and threatened him: "Williams, you're old enough to be going out with girls of your own race. If I ever see you with my daughter again, I'm going to have you arrested." As his wife screamed racial epithets, Mr. Robertson ushered both girls from the theater, leaving Franklin humiliated, terrified, and dumbfounded.

Later that summer, Franklin's Boy Scout troop decided to visit the new public swimming pool recently opened on Northern Boulevard. His white friends were readily admitted, but Franklin was stopped at the gate and told Negroes and other undesirables were unwelcome at the public pool. "See that bum?" the ticket taker said contemptuously. "If we let you in, we'll have to let him in, and all the other bums as well." What hurt Franklin most was not the ignorant rantings of a racist buffoon, but that boys he thought were his friends abandoned him; not even one stood up for their Black friend. They simply left him behind to run home and cry alone in his bedroom. It was a slight that he never forgot or forgave.

That fall, Franklin entered Flushing High School. While he did not encounter racial hostility in the school, he had learned that it raged outside and sought to shield himself from the psychic pain and hurt he knew awaited beyond the school doors. He restricted himself to school-sponsored activities, cautiously limited his friendships, and became almost frenetically involved in activities that would keep him in school. He joined the basketball, cross-country, football, and track teams, the biology and stamp clubs, and the chorus and served on the traffic squad and the parents' entertainment and lost-and-found committees. He worked on the school newspaper and as a library guard and gym squad leader, and he was even an "agent" for the DeMasi-Smith Fund, a group that raised scholarship money in the name of two Flushing high school graduates who had died in a fire at Dartmouth College.[21]

Franklin's classmates elected him to the Service League and the Government Organization Council, the premier associations of student government. He earned and nurtured a lofty reputation; one faculty member called him one of "the best and most deserving students in the school" and "an example for the rest of the student body to follow."[22] Despite the respect he earned from faculty and students, he was reluctant to again expose himself to the risk of rejection because of race. When school and school activities ended, he went home and stayed home.

Home was now at 3305 Murray Street, a three-story, red brick colonial that Eddie and Ethel bought to house their growing family (their son John Edward Lowry Jr., or "Chunk," had been born in April 1931) as well as his parents and nephews. Arthur proudly went off to Lincoln University, thanks to Eddie's generosity, in a limousine Thadd borrowed from the local undertaker.[23] But after two years, Eddie could no longer afford the expense alone. The family turned to Freddie, who had a steady if low-paying job in the post office, but he refused to help: "I never went to college. Let Arthur go out and work."[24] Arthur was forced to drop out. He may have forgiven his uncle, but Franklin never did. Meanwhile, Franklin started coming out of his social cocoon.

In the late spring of 1933, Franklin met Adelaide DeFrance, a tall, slender sixteen-year-old with a captivating air of sophistication who would become his first girlfriend. "I had never met colored girls my age that were particularly attractive," Williams recalled, "and it was pretty clear that Adelaide liked me." The following Sunday, he took the Number 7 train from Flushing and the A train up to Harlem. It was a trip the eager teenager would take with unbridled delight almost every weekend for the next four years.

Adelaide was at the center of a social circle that linked the children of Harlem's elite to their counterparts in Brooklyn and the Bronx,[25] and she introduced Franklin to that world. Through Adelaide he met a number of the junior members of New York City's "talented tenth," the term coined by Du Bois to characterize elite Black Americans.[26] Among them were Jane White, the daughter of Walter White, executive secretary of the NAACP; Robert (Bobby) Braddicks, the son of the vice president of the Dunbar National Bank; the Bishop sisters, Beth and Eloise, daughters of the Rev. Shelton Hale Bishop of St. Philip's Episcopal Church; Barbara Watson, whose father, James S. Watson, was a judge; and Jimmie Williams, the son of Wesley Williams, New York City's first Black fire chief and the grandson of James H. Wilson, director of redcaps at Grand Central Terminal. Franklin's association with Adelaide and her clique was pivotal. He learned to hold intelligent conversation on the issues of the day, and although he certainly did not know it at the time, Franklin was honing skills that would one day make him a talented debater and then litigator. He would purposely take a contrarian position just to see if he could successfully defend his argument.[27] Williams created and initiated parlor games and learned valuable lessons about group dynamics and diplomacy.[28]

In the 1930s, Harlem was replete with organizations created to promote social relationships; by 1932, there were an estimated two thousand such clubs, and the Lowry household was part of that scene.[29] In their later teens, Franklin, his brothers, and his cousins attended debuts, spring frolics, and tea dances, invariably sponsored by adult members of social clubs made up of parents who wished to create an environment where their children could meet others like themselves, those who were "light, bright and damned near white."[30] They learned social graces, heard scintillating conversation, and began to establish themselves among the upper echelon. Franklin began appearing in the gossip columns of ad hoc publications with titles such as *The Smut, Spadeville,* and *Fence Talk.*[31] He was clearly quite popular, but not with everyone.

In the 1933 issue of *Fence Talk,* an anonymous contributor lambasted Williams for his "extreme" ego, complaining that while he "derived of a well family" he was hypersensitive to his own feelings and often indifferent to the feelings of others. The assessment of Franklin was not entirely off the mark. While never intentionally cruel or mean-spirited, he could be direct, opinionated, and self-centered and too often took offense, typically racial offense, when none was intended. For example, toward the end of his life, Williams was riding a bicycle in front of a beach club in the resort town of Bridgehampton, New York. Feeling suddenly tired and slightly unwell, he stretched out on a grassy patch of lawn to regain his strength. A young white woman entering the club stopped to inquire if he was ill. It was simply a kind gesture of genuine concern, with no tone of condescension whatsoever. Frankly became surly, cynically remarking after the woman moved on, "I guess they don't like niggers sprawled out on their lawns!" When his bicycling companion suggested that if the woman had ignored him, he would have also taken offense, Williams thought for a moment and then quietly acknowledged that was true.[32] Throughout his life, Franklin would wrestle with that defensiveness, which he attributed to a sense of inferiority burned into the psyche of every American Negro.

In January 1935, Franklin was graduated from Flushing High School, ninety-sixth in a class of 238, six months later than his classmates because he lacked the requisite credits.[33] Throughout his high school years, Franklin had occasionally made the honor roll, but his approach to academic work in general had been haphazard—his grades, reflecting his moods, ranged from A to F. But during his final two semesters, he buckled down and ultimately graduated with high honors—an achievement he celebrated alone. His relatives, preoccupied and distracted by their own troubles, did not attend the ceremony.

Franklin was disappointed, of course, but understood that the Lowrys were emotionally and financially drained. Arthur, working as a messenger/receptionist at National Distillers, was supporting the household, much to the resentment of his wife, Roberta Braddicks. The quick-tempered daughter of a Harlem banker, Roberta controlled the $35 a week that Arthur brought home and clashed repeatedly with Thadd over finances and purchases. She recalled:

> Now I want to remind you that they [the Lowrys] were poor as poor can be. I came home one day and there was no food in the house. I said, "Grandpa, I gave you the food money. Where is it?" He said, "The boys needed pants." Then I blew my stack. He said, "If you talk to me like that I'm going to hit you over the head with this dishpan." Then I said, "Old man, if you touch me, I'm going to kill you."[34]

Thadd and his spirited daughter-in-law fought relentlessly until they noticed the toll their arguments were taking on Cab, who would sit off to the side, quietly weeping. One evening, after a fight so fierce it sent Arthur fleeing from the house, Roberta stormed up to her room. About an hour later, Thadd came knocking on her door: "Gal, we should not fight like that. Let's have a drink." Roberta was surprised and touched by Thadd's desire to reconcile with a toast, particularly since he didn't drink.[35] Downstairs, Thadd had arranged the miniature liquor bottles Arthur brought home from National Distillers like soldiers marching two by two down the center of the dining room table. "By the time Arthur returned, Thadd and I were sailing, and we'd become the best of friends," Roberta said. The two vowed not to fight again, and they never did, but their truce had come too late. Years of caretaking, financial insecurity, and dissension were to take a serious toll on Cab, who became increasingly depressed. She died of heart failure in 1936, and with her death the family split apart.[36] The constant bickering left lasting scars on Franklin as well. The chaos and dissension that marked that period of Franklin's life were traumatizing, and he vowed he would one day create a secure and happy home for himself and his future family.

Thadd went to live with Eddie Lowry's family. Frankie and Johnnie moved in with their older brother and his wife. But Roberta, at twenty-one, had neither the interest nor inclination to act in loco parentis to her two teenage brothers-in-law—especially Frankie, who didn't like her any more than she liked him. With considerable prodding, and begging, Roberta allowed the boys to move into their one-bedroom apartment on St. Nicholas Avenue in Harlem.[37] The brothers slept together on Roberta's battered living room couch.[38]

Franklin saw college as his only way out and started working multiple jobs to earn enough money for tuition. He drove a truck for the Palace Chow Mein Company, carting vats of steaming food through the streets of Brooklyn, stopping often to sample the deliveries. At Kramer Brothers Freight Line, he learned to drive a tractor-trailer. He washed dishes at Kress's Five and Ten and bused tables at Connie's Inn. Franklin and his friends adopted the living patterns of musicians, entertainers, and waiters who worked all night and slept all day. In the late afternoons, they lounged around the public pool on 146th Street between Lenox and Seventh Avenues. After hours, they frequented smoke-filled hideaways like the Red Rooster and Mimo's, or hung out at the Moulin Rouge, the Cavalcade, or the more disreputable bars along Lenox Avenue where both booze and sex were available.[39] During that same period Williams was slowly gaining racial consciousness and slowly growing up. After landing a relatively cushy job sweeping tents and shining shoes as an "assistant servant" for a National Guard regiment, Franklin was fired when he learned that the Black domestics were expected to perform racially charged skits for the entertainment of the soldiers and refused to participate. He recalled the incident from childhood when he had naively humiliated himself by performing a tap dance in exchange for ice cream money and wasn't about to lower himself to that level again.

But he was foundering. Franklin had planned to attend the tuition-free City College of New York, but with his mediocre high school grades he failed to make the cut. It was a rude awakening: Franklin Williams was not used to rejection. He enrolled in night school. But working odd jobs all day and going to school at night proved too much for the teenager, and he dropped out.

Despondent and deflated, Franklin was walking aimlessly past the corner of Seventh Avenue and 142nd Street in Harlem when he happened to notice a sign that read "Dr. May Chinn" in the window of a ground floor office. It was a name he had heard in his household all is life. Chinn had been his mother's friend and a central figure in the Smart Set, the group of young Black achievers who liked to relax on Sunday afternoons at the Lowry's house on State Street. But Franklin had never met her. On a lark, he rang the doorbell, which Chinn answered. Her eyes filled with tears when Franklin introduced himself as the youngest son of Alinda Williams.

Chinn invited Franklin in and spoke with him at length through lunch and then dinner. She captivated Franklin with cherished memories of the mother he never knew. Chinn demanded to know his plans and listened intently as Franklin dejectedly told her that college seemed farfetched. He admitted that City College had rejected him, and that he had no interest in venturing south into the "land of segregation and racial hatred." Franklin spoke wistfully of Lincoln University, the historically Black college his oldest brother had attended until the money ran out, but said the fees seemed out of reach. May Chinn cut him off: "Apply to Lincoln," she instructed. "Work during the summers and take campus jobs. If you still have financial difficulties, I will stand behind you." Her advice and promise of support would change his life forever.

3

An "Ole Lady" at Lincoln

"This is the happiest day of my life," Franklin Williams scribbled in the margin of his letter of acceptance from Lincoln University before preserving it in his scrapbook.[1]

Over the next four years, the small rural school in southeastern Pennsylvania would be more like home than any place he had lived since his family lost their house on State Street. Franklin loved Lincoln from the moment the bus from Philadelphia left him standing beneath the golden arch that marked the path leading to the campus on September 16, 1937. Situated on 275 acres surrounded by farmlands and wooded hills, the nineteenth-century campus consisted of a Gothic chapel, several two- and three-story red brick dormitories and lecture halls, and professors' residences—frame houses with wide porches. "Never in my life had I pictured anything . . . quite as beautiful, [nor] had I thought about living in such surroundings."[2]

Lincoln, an all-male school at the time, offered more than scenic beauty to the young man who, since childhood, had been unsure of who he was and where he belonged. It offered a safe, sequestered world where bright, ambitious Black men like himself, most with plans to enter the professions, could strive and were expected to thrive. Lincoln preached intellectual discipline and re-minded impatient students that progress in race relations was a battle that started long before they arrived and would continue long after they were gone. But they were also reminded that attending such a college was a privilege, and in exchange for that gift, Lincoln students and graduates were expected to excel as scholars and citizens.

The first degree-granting historically Black university in America, Lincoln was originally called Ashmun Institute.[3] It was founded in 1854—the eve of the

Civil War—by John Miller Dickey, a white Presbyterian minister, and his Quaker wife, Sarah Cresson Dickey. Both came from families of abolitionists, and the seminary/liberal arts college they started offered a classical education to Black men who intended to become teachers or missionaries. Over time, it would attract high achievers—men like the poet Langston Hughes; future Supreme Court Justice Thurgood Marshall; Nnamdi Azikiwe, the first African governor general of Nigeria; and Kwame Nkrumah, the first president of an independent Ghana.

When Franklin arrived at Lincoln, he was assigned to Cresson Hall and quickly arranged to room with Robert "Bobby" Freeman, a handsome New Yorker who agreed to be Franklin's "ole lady" (roommate). The two had met at a party in Harlem barely weeks before the term began and found that they liked each other and had mutual interests, including Lincoln University and attractive women. Yet they were the odd couple that complemented and brought out the best in each other: Bobby was gentle, soft-spoken, and conciliating. Franklin was considered brash and aggressive and overly ambitious, particularly by southerners who preferred Bobby's understated personality.[4] Franklin was "exceptionally smart, competitive, driven, and not apologizing for it,"[5] while Bobby was humbler, easier to take, but perhaps a bit too naturally reticent. "Frankie would pull me up and push me ahead," Freeman recalled, "and I'd hold him back, and pick up the pieces that were broken when he did the wrong thing."[6]

The "campus twins" roomed together for all four years in 10 Cresson Hall, and the friends they made became close friends, men of distinction: Roy Nichols would become the first Black bishop of the United Methodist Church; Theodore Bolden would be a dean at the Meharry Medical College; Jesse Gloster would hold a chair in political science at Texas Southern University; and Henry Mitchell would become a Baptist minister, educator, and author. Their small group, interested in serious music and serious conversation,[7] would, according to Freeman, "get together in the evening after classes and after dinner . . . and go to each other's rooms . . . sit down and pick a subject, and everybody would expound on that subject to the extent of their knowledge, and we learned from each other and respected each other."[8] They were poor but resourceful, and conscious of their attire. These young men sifted through barrels of clothes donated by Presbyterians, occasionally added new items as budgets allowed, making sure each combination of sport coat, pants, shirt, and tie matched,[9] and then shared the wardrobe communally. By year's end, they earned reputations as being among the best-dressed men on campus.

Two years older than most freshmen who entered Lincoln right out of high school, Williams was comparatively worldly. He had lived on his own, survived

Robert "Bobby" Freeman (*left*) and Franklin roomed together at Lincoln University for four years and remained the closest of friends their entire lives. This photo would have been taken around 1940. (Enid Gort collection)

the tough streets of Harlem, and enjoyed an unusual amount of success with women. His breadth of experience made him attractive to students who were not threatened by his brusque facade. But since he was a little older and perhaps a bit more self-assured, Franklin had little patience with some of the customs and traditions that freshmen were expected to accept. At Lincoln, the most juvenile and unpleasant of these was a form of hazing called "rabbling." Sophomores, and to a lesser extent seniors, inflicted cruel treatment on freshmen, who were called "dogs." The "dogs" were beaten with two-foot-long wooden paddles shaped like oars and made to do foolish and sometimes dangerous things, such as climb the school's water tower.[10] Incoming freshmen had to wear beanies, attend chapel every day, refrain from eating in the refectory, and avoid areas where other students congregated. Sophomores could stop them at any time and demand to hear the alma mater song or a litany of the school's history. If the recitation was poorly done—and more often than not it was—the hapless freshman had to "assume the position" and prepare for a paddling.

Williams wouldn't subjugate himself to anyone, certainly not someone who supposed superiority simply because he happened to be a "sophomore." He openly opposed rabbling and defiantly refused to do what was demanded of him by upperclassmen, resulting in a stern reprimand from the Dean, warning Williams that if he didn't allow himself to be humiliated, why, he wouldn't be allowed to humiliate others when he became an upperclassman. The absurdity of the threat made Franklin laugh. Lincoln had always been a conservative, tradition-bound institution, but it struck Franklin as illogical that a Black university would be tethered to class distinction. Franklin understood that Blacks had survived by banding together under certain traditions and customs, but doing something for no better reason than that's how it was done in the past struck him as nonsensical. Williams, and a handful of others, rebelled against the status quo, much to the chagrin of The Lincolnian, Lincoln's school newspaper: "Has the entire student body lost its ideas of class distinction? It seems in each edition of the paper we must ask the same questions: Juniors sitting in Seniors seats in Chapel. . . . Freshman and Sophomores walking on the library steps. . . . What is Lincoln coming to?"[11]

It was customary on graduation eve for the seniors to march en masse to the rooms of freshmen, ripping off their clothes and paddling them. In the spring of 1938, when the seniors launched their attack upon Cresson Hall, Frankie, Bobby, and their friends decided that having suffered throughout the year, they had had enough. When they heard the approaching shouts and threats, the quick-thinking underclassmen armed themselves with small rocks and stones, climbed up to an attic space called "Gut Bucket," and pulled the ladder up behind them. As the seniors closed in, the freshman pelted them with stones, a rebellion that caused a campus riot and forced the administration to take notice. The school's president, Walter Livingston Wright, convened a meeting of the student council, and posed a question: "Is it necessary to haze freshmen brutally in order to make them true Lincoln men?"[12] Masterminded by Franklin, the siege of Gut Bucket became the legendary act that defined the class of 1941. When its members graduated, the Cresson men were praised as "the Gutbucketteers who . . . took a position against destructive tradition and began to make [a] contribution toward a better Lincoln."[13]

But when it came to Greek life, Franklin acquiesced to tradition and swallowed his pride. Fraternities wielded enormous power at Lincoln. They controlled the part-time jobs by which students earned tuition money and provided admission to professional and social networks after graduation. None was more prestigious or powerful than Alpha Phi Alpha, so naturally that is the one Franklin wanted to pledge. He was also under some pressure to do so; when he left for school, his Uncle Eddie warned, "Don't come home from Lincoln if you're not an Alpha man." Uncle Eddie was serious; at Lincoln and beyond, APA membership unlocked doors.

Founded in 1906 by seven Black Cornell University students who were denied the opportunity to participate in social life, Alpha Phi Alpha was the first intercollegiate Greek letter fraternity established for Black Americans. To this day, it carries tremendous prestige, and a legacy that includes Martin Luther King Jr., W. E. B. Du Bois, Duke Ellington, Paul Robeson, Thurgood Marshall, Frederick D. Patterson, and John Hope Franklin. Hubert H. Humphrey, who served as vice president to Lyndon B. Johnson, was inducted as an honorary member after the fraternity started accepting whites in 1945. From its inception, Alpha Phi Alpha had a distinctly academic focus and attracted only those interested in serious academic achievement. Williams did not make Alpha in his freshman year. His acceptance came the following year, but not until he had proven his mettle by enduring a hazing, a tradition he immediately challenged once he was accepted into APA with a powerful letter to the national office. His letter prompted the fraternity to abolish "Hell Week."[14]

Williams had come to Lincoln intending to become a dentist. But when lab periods scheduled in the late afternoon conflicted with his need to work to pay tuition, he was hardly disappointed. He switched to liberal arts and majored in philosophy, with minors in French and sociology. He was inspired by three professors: Joseph Newton Hill, a Black English professor and a stickler for proper usage and pronunciation; John Davis, a young Black political scientist interested in raising awareness about social and political issues affecting Blacks; and Josef Herbert Furth, a Jewish refugee from Austria who taught economics. Like many other intellectuals who had fled from Nazi Germany,

Furth, one of the few PhDs on campus, wound up teaching at a historically Black college.[15]

Franklin found that with relatively meager effort he could maintain an A–average, which left plenty of time for extracurriculars. Only two months into his freshmen year, he was chosen for the Delta Rho Forensic Society, Hill's renowned debate team. The Lincoln team debated both Black universities and white schools in the Pennsylvania conference, such as Swarthmore, the University of Pennsylvania, Lehigh, Franklin and Marshall, and Bucknell. Franklin looked forward to debates at white schools and particularly enjoyed beating their teams. The Lincoln team was first-rate, as one professor from Bucknell acknowledged, writing, "I want to commend your student representatives for their knowledge of the question and skill in meeting arguments and the unfailing courtesy in conducting an animated discussion. . . . We found them to compare very well with the best debaters we meet from various schools."[16]

The note was both flattering and condescending; it is doubtful whether this professor would have employed that language to congratulate competent debaters from a white institution. Franklin was simultaneously pleased with the compliment and piqued at the patronizing racism inherent in its tone; it was as if the professor were surprised that Black students could excel at debating.

In addition to debating, Franklin was interested in singing. He joined the chorus, partially because it came with a $60 stipend and included seemingly exotic trips to cities up and down the East Coast and throughout the Midwest.[17] The problem was, chorus members had to read music, a skill Franklin lacked. He faked it, learning his parts by rote. The charade fell apart when he was selected for a quartet and the glee club and it became clear that, when it came to reading music, Franklin was illiterate. Characteristically resourceful, Franklin ran for and was elected business manager and made himself indispensable. The chorus became a source of managerial experience, and the outings became a source of girlfriends.

Because of John Edward Lowry's ties to old friends, fellow graduates of the University of Pennsylvania, his nephew was invited to the homes of successful professional men in and around the Philadelphia area whose families were considered among the elite of Black America.[18] However, it was Franklin's own good looks and engaging personality that attracted the attention of their daughters. He courted or made friends with Doris and Marie Christmas, the daughters of Lawrence Christmas, a prominent physician, and Cordelia and Mary Hinkson, known respectively as Betty and Bunny, the daughters of Major DeHaven Hinkson, the first Black to head a US Army hospital (at Tuskegee). The *Ladies Home Journal* featured the Hinksons in a glossy pictorial review. It was a rare and possibly unique instance where a magazine with a national readership depicted the daily life of an upper-class Black family.[19] Franklin also developed a friendship with Georgine Upshur, whose father, William A. Upshur Jr., was a state legislator and proprietor of the funeral home that buried Bessie Smith, the famed blues singer.[20] Franklin's relationship with the Upshur family became so close that, at their urging, he used their address to establish his eligibility for a scholarship from the state of Pennsylvania.[21]

Family connections and skin tone alone determined admittance into this rarified world, and Franklin considered himself lucky to be accepted. However, he became disenchanted when he found that Roy Nichols and his darker-skinned Lincoln friends were not warmly welcomed in these homes. Increasingly, he rejected the assumption that light skin color and "good" hair—or any skin tone, or any hair—were measures of a person's worth. At Lincoln, Williams began thinking deeply about race and racial relations as he drifted further and further from the State Street cocoon of his younger years.

Like most of the other northern students, Franklin had never experienced blatant racial segregation; at worst, he had been made to feel uncomfortable. However, the grisly stories told by southern students about the way they were treated in their home states disturbed him. He was appalled and disgusted by what he saw and experienced once he left the safe seclusion of the Lincoln campus. Once, during a choir trip to the South, a restaurant manager refused service to the entire choir solely because of their skin color.[22] Closer to home, Lincoln students, all of whom were Black, were barred from the movie theater in nearby Oxford.

The discrimination and segregation, however, tended to unite the Lincoln students, but that unity did not generally extend to students from Africa. The African students tended to be older and more serious than the African American students and had neither the time nor patience for sophomoric activity and silly traditions like hazing and rabbling. Some were nobility in their home nations and were used to a certain deference from commoners. But the Africans were a minority, and like any minority, they were outsiders. Even Kwame Nkrumah, an upperclassman and recognized intellectual who would become the first president of Ghana, was harassed for the simple and simplistic reason that he was different. Few American Blacks, including Franklin, made much attempt to get to know or understand the Africans, and probably vice versa.

Yet Williams did have a natural affinity for the underdog, and actively intervened when his classmates called a second-generation West Indies immigrant a "monkey chaser" and tried to force him to climb the water tower. Williams took the student, Bruce Wright, under his wing, got him onto the debate team, and supported a protest the African students staged against discrimination by the track team."[23] Williams's mentoring interests also extended to the small community of Blacks who lived in the surrounding area. In his sophomore year, he became director of the YMCA-sponsored Lincoln University Boys Club, a group formed to promote the welfare of local boys attending an impoverished and segregated Black school in what had formerly been a barn.[24] His actions earned him trust, respect, and, crucially, loyalty. He would employ a "helping others helps yourself" approach for the remainder of his life.

On June 3, 1941, Franklin was graduated from Lincoln University as salutatorian, second in his class of sixty-eight, earning mention in *Who's Who in American Colleges and Universities* and election into Phi Kappa Epsilon, the national scholarship and research fraternity. His fellow seniors described him as "dominant," "capable," "self-sufficient" and "altruistic" and used the phrase "we the people" and the word "democracy."[25] They also described him as "most superficial," and cited him in the yearbook for his "suave smugness." He was all of those things, as both a young man and an adult. He also had a natural knack for public speaking, and his classmates chose him as commencement speaker. Franklin spoke intelligently and articulately about the dilemma of going into a world where "megalomaniacs like Hitler and Mussolini" were drawing America into war. May Chinn, Eddie and Ethel Lowry, Franklin's brothers, and Roberta Williams were all in attendance for what could be viewed as Franklin's true public speaking debut. His speech inspired a thoughtful note from a total stranger who happened to be in the audience: "While I orally congratulated you upon the address which you made at the Commencement exercises, I wish also to send you this note to say that it was for me a true and impressive statement on the way in which a man should look upon the present problems of the world. . . . You will make for yourself real opportunities for accomplishment."[26]

Williams would return to the Lincoln stage twenty-five years later when, as ambassador to Ghana, he was invited to deliver the 1966 commencement address. He told the students that the most important things he learned at Lincoln were respect for human dignity, concern for human understanding, and a commitment to excellence, creativity, and integrity.[27] It was at Lincoln that Williams developed his passion for justice and discovered his own leadership and oratorical skills.

4
The Real World

In 1941, with his degree from Lincoln in one pocket and an acceptance letter from Fordham University School of Law in the other, Franklin Williams was more than optimistic, even euphoric.[1] His future could not have seemed brighter, and he and Bobby Freeman looked forward to a summer working as bellhops in the plush resorts of Saratoga Springs.

Nestled in the foothills of the Adirondacks, Saratoga Springs is a quaint little city of wide boulevards, handsome Victorian mansions, and grand hotels. Established in the years after the Civil War as a quiet resort for people seeking rejuvenation from the waters of its mineral-rich underground springs, the town's introduction of horse racing and casinos made it a rakish place, even though its seamy side was hard to detect behind the facade of elegance and refinement.[2] By the 1940s, visitors to Saratoga Springs came less to take the waters than to lose their inhibitions. Saratoga Springs would teach Franklin and Bobby, as sophisticated as they thought they were, more about life than they bargained for.

When the young men arrived at the Worden Hotel at the northeast corner of Broadway and Division Street, they were assigned one bed in a room hardly bigger than a closet, living off tips and picking up extra money catering at illegal poker dens and escorting willing women to the rooms of male guests. "We didn't realize it at the time—we were just going along with the way of life and trying to stay out of trouble—but now, as I look back on it, we were pimping,"[3] Freeman recalled. Along the way they had their share of adventures and misadventures—the homosexual priest who tried to lock Bobby in his room; the white dowager who tried to confine Franklin in hers; and the half-dressed revelers at a private party who cornered Franklin when he delivered their champagne and threatened him when he declined an invitation to join them. Franklin and Bobby each cleared $150 that summer, the most money either of them had ever earned.

When the summer ended, Franklin returned to New York City and entered Fordham Law, a Jesuit school housed on the twenty-eighth floor of the Woolworth Building at 233 Broadway. Fordham's stated mission included providing educational opportunities to disadvantaged minorities and the success of the earlier pioneers—such as Ruth Whitehead Whaley and Oliver D. Williams, the first two Black graduates of the law school in 1924—helped pave the way for Franklin.[4] Whaley, a cum laude graduate of Fordham, became the first African American woman to practice law in New York State, and Oliver Williams was one of the first elected to the New York State Supreme Court.[5] For Franklin, the Jesuit school checked off multiple boxes: full-time students could attend classes either in the morning or the afternoon, leaving time for part-time jobs; he could live rent-free with Arthur and Roberta Williams, who by then had a two-bedroom apartment on the top floor of a brownstone at 511 Macon Street in Brooklyn; Lincoln graduates, because their alma mater was highly regarded academically, were exempt from Fordham's qualifying examinations; and for several years, Fordham had at least one Lincoln man on campus. Lincoln men at Fordham felt part of a tradition, a legacy Franklin yearned to join.

Still, during his first days, Franklin's self-confidence was atypically low as he worried whether he could keep up with white classmates with undergraduate degrees from the likes of Georgetown and Swarthmore. He was intimidated when his professor, a renowned legal scholar named I. Maurice Wormser, gave him his first assignment:

> We had to read these old cases, and some of them had Latin in them. I was sitting in my little bedroom trying to brief them, as they told us we had to do. About quarter to 11, I was so mentally exhausted, that I almost began to cry. I felt I just couldn't hack it. . . . The next day Wormser started to call on people. I realized that they were stumbling all over the place and [that] I [could] do better. . . . He finally called on me and I stood up and explained the case. He scratched a little sore on his head and said, "Now, there's a man who understands the law."

With his confidence restored, Williams got on with the business of making friends. There was only one other Black student in his class of approximately sixty students, a shy, studious, young woman named Joyce Philips. "Who could forget Franklin Williams?" she asked. "His mind was like a machine—click, click, click, you could look into his eyes and think you could see it working."[6] Franklin quickly established himself as leader in a circle which was ethnic if not racially diverse and included "an Italian girl named Helen Paladino, a couple of WASP guys, and a Jewish girl, who was the brightest girl in our class." He was amazed to discover that prejudice at Fordham was directed more toward Jews than Blacks, most of whom the students assumed were Catholics: "I can remember one day an Irish girl coming over to Helen Paladino, who was standing with me and said, 'Helen, you better stop hanging out with that Jewish girl, otherwise the boys are not going to date you.' What a relief it was that nobody came over and said to Helen, 'You better stop hanging out with that Negro, otherwise guys won't date you.'"

Hampered as usual by a lack of money, Franklin secured a clerkship in the law office of Ruth Whitehead Whaley, an attorney who in 1924 was the first Black woman to graduate from Fordham University School of Law and only the third Black woman admitted to practice in New York. Whaley had a general private practice at 277 Broadway, just steps from Fordham, and kept a rein on expenses by refusing to hire secretaries. Thus, it was Williams's task, besides doing legal research, to take dictation, type, and file court papers. The early exposure to the nuts and bolts of legal work and office administration helped him develop a lifelong appreciation for back-office staff. He did not take for granted secretaries, bookkeepers, and others who perform critical yet often unappreciated office chores.

Just three months into Williams's law school education, the Japanese attacked Pearl Harbor and America was at war, bringing to the fore a discussion and debate that had been in the abstract. While still at Lincoln, Franklin and his fellow students had closely followed Germany's occupation of its European neighbors and debated whether or not Americans should be involved overseas. Some were pacifists who opposed the war. Others recited the experiences of Black soldiers who had fought in World War I: Blacks were first discouraged from enlisting and then drafted without the possibility of deferment; Jim Crow restrictions on servicemen, including the few Black officers, were rigorously enforced, and French army officials, to whom Black units were assigned, were warned against treating Black soldiers with dignity, lest they get the impression they were worthy of equal treatment.[7] Still, most students could not help but notice that Hitler's doctrine of racial hierarchy was directed as much against them as against Jews, and they believed that democracy itself was being threatened and registered with the draft board, as required. Recruits were racially categorized based on the skin shade of the person ahead of them in line and behind; they had no other way to determine who was a Negro other than to compare his skin tone to that of another man.[8]

With just a month remaining in the spring semester at law school, Franklin was drafted in April 1942. He requested a one-month deferment to take his final exams and complete the semester but was flatly rejected by the all-white draft board. He left law school and departed for Fort Dix, New Jersey, for processing.[9]

The night Franklin arrived was cold and rainy, and the recruits were immediately divided according to race. White soldiers were promptly marched to brightly lit wooden barracks, while the Blacks were forced to stand at attention in the rain and mud while watching their Caucasian counterparts settle into relatively nice quarters. Soon, lively music blared from their radios. After they were sufficiently soaked, filthy, and humiliated, the Black soldiers were marched miles away and put up in tents. The next morning, he stood in a segregated line for breakfast. Franklin seethed and knew at that instant that he would hate the army and the army would hate him. He had not expected such blatant discrimination north of the Mason-Dixon line, and he wouldn't stand for it. But the abandonment by his white friends hurt the most and brought back childhood memories of the incident at the pool when he was turned away because of his race and none of his friends stood by him.

> I was drafted with white friends, but I and other colored men were segregated from the moment we entered the Fort Dix reception center. From that point on, although previously these white friends had never felt any superiority, I began to recognize in them an almost unconscious acceptance of the principle that we couldn't live or fight together, and I rebelled against it, and I couldn't throw myself into the business of being a good soldier.[10]

After days of physical examinations and intelligence and competency tests, Williams found himself on a train filled with Black soldiers ordered to Fort Huachuca, Arizona, under the supervision of a few white officers. The train traveled only at night, with the window shades drawn for fear of German bombers and the anticipation of a mainland attack that never came.

At 11:00 a.m. on May 23, 1942, five and a half days after his journey had begun, Williams stepped from the train. He blinked to shield his eyes from the sun, the hottest and strongest he had ever encountered, and surveyed the landscape: rows and rows of two-story wooden barracks, some still under construction, amid miles of fine brown sand. Purple blue mountains with canyons like velvet folds rose in the background. A Black sergeant announced, "Welcome to Fort Huachuca."

Since 1892, the army had stationed its Black soldiers at this remote installation at the edge of the Chihuahua Desert. Initially, they had been battle-hardened Civil War veterans, happy for full-time work and willing to help tame the western frontier.[11] Tough and wily soldiers, they had fought hostile Indians,

In the segregated US Army, Williams, well-educated and a student at Fordham Law, rebelled against discrimination. (Enid Gort collection)

patrolled the Mexican borders, and assisted civil authorities to keep cattle rustlers, land-grabbers, and other renegades in check.[12] But by 1931 Huachuca was a forgotten outpost, not only because the region had become relatively peaceful but also because the army wanted to reduce the number of Black men serving in the military. White racists in government knew that Blacks in a military uniform threatened to destroy the stereotype of the inferior, subservient Black man. Despite documented accounts of the intelligence and courage displayed by Black men in battle, southern congressmen in 1916 sponsored a bill to eliminate Black soldiers and sailors from the armed forces by preventing their enlistment or reenlistment.[13] The army achieved its goal. By 1939, two years before the United States entered World War II, there were only 3,640 Black men in uniform and only three Black combat officers, far fewer than in 1900.[14]

Williams arrived at Fort Huachuca at a time when mounting pressure from the Black community and the urgent need for manpower had forced President Franklin D. Roosevelt to make good on his election year promise "that Black military manpower [would] be maintained at a ratio approximating the proportion of Blacks in the national population—that is, from 9 to 10 percent."[15] This order sent the military brass scrambling to find "suitable" bases for training Black troops. "Suitable" was defined as far enough from civilian populations that would be offended by the presence of Black men in their midst.[16] In the remote desert and surrounded by mountains, Fort Huachuca was ideal from the army's point of view, though the men relegated to the Fort "Wegotcha" outpost thought otherwise.

After processing, Williams was assigned to the Ninety-Third Infantry Division, Adjutant General's Department.[17] Franklin was thrilled, assuming he'd get a chance to put some of his legal training to good use. But he was woefully ignorant of the fact that the last thing the army wanted was an educated Negro who just might think for himself and, horror of horrors, prove to be smarter or more capable than a white officer.[18] Williams, a well-educated man with legal training, was relegated to the typing pool.

After three weeks, Williams received his first $21 paycheck, the equivalent of roughly $340 today.[19] He immediately headed off to the "Hook," a recreation site just outside the southern gate, where he was startled to see hundreds of Black soldiers lined up to have sex with prostitutes, one after the other, in squatters' huts.[20] He was appalled that the activity was essentially sanctioned by the army, with military police there to escort the Black soldiers to the prostitutes. It was not only a den of iniquity, but a pocket of disease with syphilis spreading like wildfire.

Williams complained that while nothing was being done to safeguard soldiers' health at the Hook, the one place Blacks could socialize, authorities were taking every precaution elsewhere. A Black warrant officer listened impassively and then threw Williams out of his office. Angry and frustrated, Williams fired off letters to Adam Clayton Powell, the Black congressman from New York, and to Walter White, executive director of the National Association for the Advancement of Colored People (NAACP), in which he described how the army was contributing to the spread of venereal disease among Black servicemen. He and other Black soldiers also complained about the lack of Black officers, the disrespect shown to those few who were Black, and the racism and incompetence of white officers, 95 percent of whom were southerners.[21] In late November of 1942, the NAACP responded to the barrage of letters by sending assistant secretary Roy Wilkins to investigate conditions at Fort Huachuca.[22] Several months later, the Hook was declared off-limits and the prostitutes were dispersed or arrested.[23]

Not long after, Williams caught what he believed was a bad chest cold, one that made him uncomfortable enough to seek treatment at the segregated base hospital where he remained for several weeks, serving as the doctors' unofficial assistant. But he was not improving and the facility lacked the capacity to deal with more than routine ailments, so Williams was transferred to Beaumont General Hospital, a desegregated facility at Fort Bliss, Texas, for observation. He underwent a battery of tests for shortness of breath, fever, and a slight cough. Test after test proved inconclusive, and the days stretched on.

About three weeks into his hospital stay, Williams received an invitation to be the best man at Bobby Freeman's wedding. Bobby had been ineligible for the draft because of a chronic ulcer and was working for the War Production Board in Washington, DC, where he met and fell in love with Mary Jones, an animated young woman with the face of a child and the gravelly voice of stage and screen legend Tallulah Bankhead. Williams applied for and was granted a thirty-day pass and bought a ticket on a segregated train. The trouble began immediately. Barred from entering the colored coach by a conductor who seemed to think he was Mexican, Williams was steered to the white coach, where the conductor accused of him of trying to pass for a white and ordered him back to the colored section.[24]

The Jim Crow coach, located just behind the engine, was perpetually contaminated with filthy black smoke and soot, not to mention the overflowing toilet that would go unrepaired for the duration. The stench was overwhelming, and the Black passengers had no choice but to keep the windows open. Williams didn't even have a seat—all the seats were taken while he was shuffled between the Black and white sections—and spent Thursday night and Friday on the floor, with his duffel bag as a pillow, and watching the growing circle of toilet sewage creeping closer. To add insult to injury, since Williams had never been on a segregated train before, he didn't know enough to bring food and just assumed he'd purchase meals along the way. But the white passengers got first crack at whatever food was on board, and by the time the porter got to the Jim Crow car there was nothing left but peanuts, soda, and a few pieces of fruit. Williams was at the breaking point—sitting on the floor (and soon in sewage), exhausted and starving, and fearing he was on the verge of a nervous breakdown. A well-dressed, well-spoken Black man quickly noted Williams's distress. "Son, you're in trouble," said the dignified, middle-aged man, dressed in a crisp, three-piece suit, and wearing thick rimless glasses. Williams had spotted the man earlier and marveled at his calm demeanor and capacity to tolerate the intolerable conditions. "I'm Dr. J. J. Rhoads, president of Bishop College, and I want you to get off in Marshall, Texas, with me."[25] Williams wasn't sure if it was an offer or an order, but he quickly agreed, and the two men got off just before the Louisiana state line, where they found an old sedan and chauffeur waiting. The chauffeur drove them down a tree-lined boulevard past stately buildings with wide verandas and screened-in porches, stopping at

Rhoads's much more modest home, where they were greeted by a huge Black woman. "Mother, I'm bringing you a 'Son,'" Rhoads said.

The president's wife, sensing that Williams was a young man in turmoil, scooped him up in her mammoth arms and held him tight. "I just wept," Williams later recalled, "because I finally felt safe." After a bath to calm his nerves, he joined Rhoads in a dining room, where they chatted comfortably. Rhoads showed him around campus the next day, while that evening some students came to the president's home to hear the views of their northern visitor from Lincoln University and Fordham School of Law. The following morning, feeling refreshed and rejuvenated and ready to resume his journey—and equipped with a bag full of homemade snacks from Mrs. Rhoads's kitchen—Williams boarded the next train. Once again, he was dispatched to the Jim Crow car, but this time he made it all the way to Washington.

In retrospect, if it were possible to name the moment that Williams's outrage over racial inequality crossed the line from the abstract to the personal, it was as a result of this ride on the Jim Crow train. Suddenly, it hit home that the majority of white America viewed him as lower on society's totem pole than any ignorant, unaccomplished white. From that day on, he viewed discrimination as a personal insult.

Once Williams arrived in Washington, he tried to put the incident behind him and enjoy Bobby's wedding, but he showed up in sergeant's stripes he had not earned and had no business wearing.[26] Shallowly fearing that some guests (in particular, Mary Freeman's beautiful sisters) might wonder why he had not made more progress after eight months in the army, he had purchased the stripes and sewn them on his jacket for the ceremony and reception thereafter.

Like many apparently self-assured people, Williams hid a deep and festering insecurity, a holdover from his earlier years, when he could not be sure of the judgments people outside his extended family were making about him. In the moments between not knowing he could dominate a group of people and learning that he could, he might betray his discomfort by behaving in ways that were, at best, disingenuous, and in this instance almost unimaginably foolish. If caught, he likely would have been court-martialed, which would have ended his legal career before it started. It was a foolish and largely unprecedented risk by an insecure, immature young man.

By New Year's Day, Williams was back at Fort Huachuca's typing pool, and within a few weeks he was back in the base hospital and then transferred back to the William Beaumont General Hospital. His symptoms were perhaps stress-induced, but without a diagnosis and conclusion, the doctors would not clear him for duty. So, he spent months in a ward with twenty-five white soldiers, organizing poker games, reciting poems, and sharing commentary and insight with the other patients, one of whom recalled, "Franklin let us know that stereotypes worked both ways. He told me that some people thought all Italians were banana salesmen who 'spoka da lousy in-ga-lish,' and he called our other buddy, who was German, 'Sauerkraut.' He really got us thinking about things."[27]

Williams had plenty of time on his hands during his hospitalization since he wasn't really very ill. He spent some of it writing letters to the press over whatever issue of the moment got under his skin. When he read that the mother of Dorie Miller, the first Black American to receive the Navy Cross for heroics during the attack on Pearl Harbor, had been invited to attend a military ceremony in honor of her son, he pointed out the irony of her traveling in a Jim Crow coach to get there. In a letter to the *El Paso Times*, he argued that the poll tax was a mechanism to disenfranchise Black voters.

> You condemn those members of Congress who insist on the passage of an Anti-Poll Tax Bill now—and in the same breath you say that the South, "Is coming out of its swaddling clothes." If this be true, if the South is truly "growing up" at last, then let them demonstrate this by granting freedom of the polls—at least in federal elections—to the citizens of their respective states regardless of their ability or inability to pay a tax . . .
>
> We all know the *raison d'etre* of poll tax laws. We all know—though some won't admit—that they were originally established for the express purpose of disenfranchising a large portion of the Southern people because of their race or economic status. Is this just? Is this a democratic act? Is this one of the principles for which millions of us are fighting and thousands dying? Is this one of the practices we are holding out to the peoples of the various conquered nations? I say, "It is not!"—It is, rather, one of the things we are frankly ashamed of.[28]

Three months later, he condemned the editors of the El Paso *Herald-Post* for their support of columnist Westbrook Pegler, who had denounced the Black press.[29]

> Some weeks ago, your paper editorially supported Westbrook Pegler in his condemnation of the Negro press. Having read some of those papers at various times, I disagree with your allegations concerning them. I have, since your statements, familiarized myself with the history, personnel and general policies of the Negro press from the time of its first publication in 1827 to the present.

My general impressions have been as follows: Negro newspapers stress mistreatment of colored people because mistreatment is a fact and the white press ignores it or plays it down. They bend over backward in giving credit to white people even when they make only a gesture of being fair. Observe the play given by them to Mrs. Roosevelt, Pearl Buck, and Wendell Wilkie. But when Negroes are beaten and killed, exploited and robbed, insulted and humiliated because they were fortunate or unfortunate enough to be born Negroes, their press would be worthless if it remained silent.

Newspapers are supposed to report the news, addressing that which is of the greatest importance to the greatest number. This rule compels Negro newspapers to prominently report cases of discrimination, segregation and humiliation because of color and they'd have no *raison d'etre* if they didn't.[30]

Williams knew that the major in charge of the ward was reading his letters but didn't particularly care until learning that special investigators had him under surveillance and were documenting his public missives.

On November 19, 1943, after spending a year and a half in the military service—285 days of which were spent in government hospitals—Williams received a Certificate of Disability and was discharged from the army. He had been found unfit for military service based on a diagnosis of pulmonary fibrosis, or scarring of the lungs, a potentially serious and permanent condition, as well as valvular heart disease.[31] Years later, tests established that he'd never had pulmonary fibrosis and had no issue with his heart valve.[32] It is possible he was simply misdiagnosed by incompetent doctors; it is also possible he was intentionally misdiagnosed so the army could rid itself of a potential troublemaker. It is also possible that he was malingering, which was considered a major problem by military authorities at Fort Huachuca, where, by the end of 1942, a third of the patients on the medical wards were thought to be exhibiting symptoms associated with psychosomatic illnesses.[33] The truth will probably never be known, since most of Franklin Williams's military records were destroyed in a fire in the National Archives Records Administration in 1973.[34]

Williams returned to New York and reapplied to Fordham Law, where he was accepted on the condition that he repeat the term he had nearly completed before the draft. His older brother, Arthur, was still in the service, and his sister-in-law, Roberta, allowed him to move into her Brooklyn apartment. She felt a sense of obligation to her youngest brother-in-law even though she still considered him "the biggest pain that ever came down the pike."[35] While waiting for the spring term to begin, Williams took a clerical job in the Empire

State Building and spent his evenings catching up with old friends and making new ones. According to Roberta: "I had trouble with my landlord because of Frankie. One day he called me down and said, 'Now I want you to know that when you're at work, Frankie brings women in here.' I replied, 'Mr. Neusome, where else would he bring them? This is his home.' But he certainly did bring in a lot of women."[36]

At a Christmas party dance at the Comus Club, Williams was introduced to a slender young woman whose off-the-shoulder gown of ice-blue brocade accentuated her serious dark brown eyes and warm olive complexion. Williams took the girl's hand and led her to the dance floor, and before the set was over he decided that Shirley Marie-Louise Broyard was the woman he would marry. Five years his junior, Shirley was the youngest of Edna and Anatole Broyard's children, and a woman with an exotic mix of African, French, and Iberian ancestry.

As a young child, Shirley lived with her family in a tiny three-room house in the French Quarter of New Orleans. Financial difficulties forced the family to move north, to Brooklyn, and when the Depression hit the children were expected to earn wages and not squander their time in school.[37] Regardless,

Shirley Broyard Williams. (Photo courtesy of Franklin H. Williams Judicial Commission)

Shirley and her brother, Anatole Jr. (or "Buddy"), had an intellectual streak
that could not be suppressed.

Buddy openly defied his parents and enrolled in tuition-free Brooklyn College, dropping out one course shy of graduation. In time, Buddy became a part
of the New York intellectual elite and enjoyed a long career as a book critic,
columnist, and editor for *The New York Times*. As an adult, Anatole estranged
himself and his family from their relatives. A light-skinned man who did not
publicly, or even privately, acknowledge his African American heritage, his
children never met their uncle, Franklin Williams. Black pride did not take
root until perhaps the 1970s, and many lighter-skinned Black people who could
"pass" for white chose to do so.[38]

Buddy interested his younger sister in literature, introducing her to Kafka,
Wallace Stevens, D. H. Lawrence, Ferdinand Céline, and others.[39] Shirley read
widely as well and gravitated toward the theater. Even as a teenager, she preferred to venture alone to the Fifth Avenue Playhouse for a matinee performance
of *Les enfants du paradise* or Jean Cocteau's *La belle et la bête* than socialize
with friends.

In 1939, Shirley's parents reluctantly allowed her to enroll in Hunter College,
a tuition-free, all-girls' school in New York City, but under the condition that
she obtain a marketable degree, namely teaching. Although Shirley had no
interest in teaching, she acceded to her parents' demands by majoring in education, minoring in French, which she adored, in understated rebellion. She
was an outstanding student, elected to Phi Beta Kappa in her junior year and
awarded a graduate scholarship to Smith College after graduation. But her
parents insisted she turn down the scholarship and get to work. Although Shirley was the first Broyard ever to graduate from college, her family was indifferent
to her achievement, a slight that left a lasting scar, similar to the disappointment
Franklin felt when his family declined to attend his high school graduation.[40]
Even with her degree, credentials, and a teaching license, Shirley could find
only temporary substitute teaching assignments.

On New Year's Eve, Franklin and Shirley ran into each other at another
party, both of them accompanied by dates. Regardless, they spent most of the
evening together, and a serious courtship ensued. With the beginning of the
spring semester, Franklin returned to Fordham, located one block north of the
Municipal Building, where Shirley was working. Each morning, the two met
and took the subway from Brooklyn to downtown Manhattan; each lunch hour
they shared a sandwich; each evening they met to make the return trip together.
One day on the crowded subway, amid the early morning rush, Franklin inquired: "Did you ever think of marrying a lawyer?" Apparently, she had or
would; they were married May 27, 1944, just six months after they met. After

a honeymoon weekend at the home of Eddie and Ethel Lowry, the couple moved into a third-floor apartment in the same brownstone where Shirley's parents lived, getting by on a combined income of $53.

In June 1944, Congress passed the G.I. Bill, which provided tuition payments and stipends to returning veterans. This enabled Franklin to take classes over the summer. He earned high marks, made the law review, and passed the New York State Bar examination five months before he was graduated in October 1945.[41] Williams was unsure where his law degree would take him, and in 1945 he applied for a position with the FBI. In his application, Williams noted that his parents were deceased, and in response to a question on where his father was born, responded "New York?" with a question mark, as if he wasn't sure.[42] In response to the question: "To what extent are you financially indebted to others and to whom?" Williams wrote, "None at all."[43] He was not offered a position with the FBI but was not particularly bothered since he really wanted to be a trial lawyer.

Williams viewed constitutional law as the surest, quickest, and most legitimate manner of securing basic civil rights for himself, his family, and his community. He believed to his core in the power of reason and was convinced that most Americans were reasonable people. He believed that the Constitution, if properly applied, provided the rights and protections that had historically been denied to African Americans. And he hoped to be among the top attorneys chosen by the prestigious NAACP who would be allowed strategically and expertly to take the cause of civil liberty—a lost cause in the legislative and executive branches of dozens of states—to the judiciary. But that was the future, and Franklin knew he would need experience before he could realize his dream of arguing civil rights cases in the nation's courts.

During his last year at Fordham, Williams clerked at the law office of Thomas B. Dyett and Harold Stevens.[44] The two Black men were active in the Democratic Party, and their practice was essentially political. Williams hoped that Dyett and Stevens would have a job for him after he graduated, but they did not and instead referred him to Carson DeWitt Baker and Harry G. Bragg, attorneys with connections to the man who held the post of special counsel to the NAACP: Thurgood Marshall.[45]

5

The American Veterans Committee

Much like his grandfather, Thaddeus Lowry, Franklin Williams was a joiner and natural leader. He liked to be part of fraternal and other organizations, and he liked to be in charge.

In August 1945, at twenty-eight years old, a year and a half after his discharge from the army and a few months before he would begin his stint as an NAACP civil rights lawyer, Franklin was eager to align himself with a veterans' organization. But he wanted nothing to do with the American Legion or Veterans of Foreign Wars, both of which were conservative-leaning associations that relegated Black members to segregated chapters.[1] In an uncharacteristically sloppy letter to I. F. Stone, the progressive editor of *PM*, a left-wing New York City newspaper, Williams sought help in finding a veterans' organization with which he could identify.

Dear Sir,

I am a daily reader and confirmed follower of *PM* and have been since its first appearance on the newsstands of New York. I read it during my 19 months in the Army and have always felt that the various fights you have fought have been worthwhile, necessary and fruitful. . . . Since my discharge . . . I have been most desirous of associating myself with some veteren's [sic] organization which stood for the principles to which I have always subscribed and *PM* has always propounded and defended. Being just another veteran . . . it has not been easy to find such an organization. . . . I am now appealing to your paper's investigatory ability and staff to put me and the thousands of other GIs in a similar quandry [sic] straight.[2]

It is unclear whether Stone ever responded, but shortly thereafter Williams learned about the American Veterans Committee (AVC), and what he learned, he liked.

The AVC was the brainchild of Army Air Force Sergeant Gilbert Harrison, a UCLA psychology graduate who had been active with the Interfaith University Religious Conference (IURC) in Los Angeles. Harrison was thinking of forming a new veterans' organization, a liberal alternative to the mainstream groups and one that agreed with the principles underlying Franklin Roosevelt's New Deal. In late 1942, he reached out to a group of like-minded friends to gauge their interest in establishing an association "based not on what [they] could get as veterans, but what [they] would contribute to the postwar world."[3] He urged his friends to think about how they "might achieve the kind of world they wanted to live in after the war."[4]

The response was enthusiastic. Harrison and four UCLA buddies who were part of the IURC—Clifford Dancer, Wadsworth Lightly, Edward Ladd, and Samuel Spencer Jr.—hammered out a general letter of intent for what the new organization would be and the principles it would espouse.[5] A year later, in February 1944, Harrison traveled to Washington to bring his idea of a progressive veterans' organization to Eleanor Roosevelt, a friend of his before the war who led him to Charles Bolte, a writer for the Office of War Information who was disenchanted with the narrow focus and jingoistic approach of veterans' organizations and despondent in general.[6]

Refusing to stand by idly while nation after nation fell to Germany's National Socialist Party and the United States demurred, Bolte volunteered to fight with the British before America was finally lured into the war. He served more than admirably, sacrificing a leg at the battle of El Alamein in North Africa, but returned despondent and brooding over whether, in the "razzle-dazzle" of victory, Americans had lost sight of the democratic principles for which he had given his leg. He feared the country had stuck its collective head in the sand and "lacked a positive national policy."[7]

Harrison came along at precisely the right time, offering Bolte both a mission and a part-time job. Bolte jumped at the opportunity, and his part-time job quickly became a full-time obsession. He quit his government job to devote all his energy to the cause. In the summer of 1944, Bolte recruited a handful of veterans to join a planning committee to create the type of progressive organization he had in mind, one that focused on "Citizens First, Veterans Second"—the line that became their slogan.

As the membership grew, the program broadened and the fledgling organization morphed into a political action committee, essentially, that embraced a domestic agenda that included increasing the amount of low-cost housing,

maintaining price controls, supporting health insurance bills, raising the minimum wage, and ensuring both full and fair employment. On the international
front, the group aimed to foster worldwide cooperation in keeping the peace.
Only secondarily did they expect to press for rewards due veterans as a special
interest group; in fact, they opposed cash bonuses and other short-range ben-
efits. Again, "Citizens first, Veterans second."

By January 1945, the AVC had chapters in Washington, Los Angeles, Cleveland, and New York, with a combined membership of under a thousand; by
May 1946, the organization had 47,000 members in 470 chapters across the
country and overseas.[8] Its members included well-known figures such as actors
Ronald Reagan—then a liberal—and George Reeves ("Superman" in the 1950s
hit program); war hero Audie Murphy; the Pulitzer Prize–winning cartoonist
Bill Mauldin; newspaper publisher and congressman Will Rogers Jr., the son
of the famous humorist; civil rights activist Medgar Evers; and oral historian
Studs Terkel, all of whom were interested in addressing global issues in the
wake of the Second World War.[9] From the beginning, though, the group was
balkanized between two factions, progressives and communists. John F. Kennedy, uneasy with both the liberal and communist wings, shied away.[10] Unlike
Kennedy, Williams did not see the writing on the wall, and his naivete led to
both his rise and fall within the organization, and inflicted painful yet forma-
tive lessons on racial politics and leadership.

Williams, who at the time was living at 249 Decatur Street in Brooklyn,
joined Brooklyn Chapter One in mid-1945. The liberal, predominantly Jewish
membership, delighted to have such a well-spoken Black man in their midst
and perhaps eager to display their enlightened attitude toward African Americans, immediately elected him as their legal counsel. A few months later,
Williams, Chapter One Chairman Harry Heller and several other chapter
leaders from the New York City area organized the Metropolitan Area Council,
bringing the ninety-five New York City chapters of the AVC under one umbrella.[11] At the recommendation of a few chapter heads, they hired as day-to-day
administrator Lawrence Knobel, a former infantry captain who was awarded
two Purple Hearts and a Bronze Star for his heroism during the D-Day invasion
of Normandy. Knobel proved to be hardworking, creative, and programmati-
cally innovative.[12]

The Metropolitan Area Council made news regularly throughout the spring
and summer of 1946 and clearly distinguished the AVC as a political organization in comparison to the VFW and the American Legion, which were more
akin to social clubs. The New York Times printed photographs of members
picketing Macy's and other stores in protest over the weakening of price controls.[13] Articles reported that members invaded the offices of the New York Real

Estate Board to call attention to the lack of affordable housing, lined up to donate blood when shortages were reported and protested against racial and religious quotas at institutions of higher learning.[14] Congress passed a bill to provide specially equipped vehicles to paraplegic veterans, a proposal conceived and advanced by the Metropolitan Council. Williams learned of and became at least tangentially active in social causes to which he had given little thought before joining the AVC.

Williams was uncomfortable from the start with the open warfare and the backroom back-biting between AVC members holding liberal/ progressive views and those who hewed more closely to the communist line. Yet, he failed to appreciate the depth of the animosity, the lengths the warring factions would go to in advancing their agenda and tamping down the other side's, or the ways in which he was being exploited because of his race. His ignorance of ideological issues and the longstanding feuds between the left-wing factions left him vulnerable and he found himself misunderstood and vilified by both sides.

Although the AVC attracted members across class and racial lines, two groups tended to dominate its leadership, particularly in urban areas—upper-class "WASPS" and the children of Jewish working-class parents. These were the same groups, and in many instances the very same people, who had been at the forefront of the liberal, socialist, and communist student movements in the 1930s.[15]

With Europe unraveling between 1935 and 1938—the Nazis' intervention in support of Spanish fascists and Germany's annexation of Austria and invasions of Poland and Czechoslovakia, along with its pogroms—students on the political left, regardless of orientation, saw the need to unite against fascism and formed an organization, the American Student Union (ASU), a merger of socialist and communist factions. The merger was doomed from the start with each faction fighting for supremacy within the organization. The communists, fearing a Nazi invasion of the Soviet Union, urged American intervention. The socialists and independent radicals opposed intervention on the grounds that waging war furthered capitalist and imperialist aspirations. All sides resorted to dissembling and dirty tricks to undermine the efforts of their opponents. The communists often misrepresented themselves by lying about their party affiliations and denying against credulity that they were puppets of the Communist Party.

Still, until the signing of the Nazi-Soviet Pact in 1939, the warring ASU factions struggled to at least present an appearance of unification against the common enemy: Fascism. Joseph Lash, the executive secretary of the ASU, who later became an AVC member, struggled mightily to keep the group together and was successful until 1939 when Soviet dictator Joseph Stalin invaded neighboring Finland, an unprovoked attack against a small, neutral nation that enraged most Americans. At that critical moment, to the shock of the organization's majority, communists openly cheered the Soviet invasion and called for American neutrality, claiming that they spoke for the majority of ASU students. In fact, they did not, but they had swiftly and stealthily usurped leadership. The machinations of the communist students destroyed the ASU and eventually the student movement that had arisen in the 1930s. The independent radicals, socialists, and liberals would never again trust the communists. Justin Feldman, the director of veterans' affairs for the AVC, explained the mindset of those who defined themselves as "liberals" after the war:

> We had gone through depression, we had gone through a war, we had seen the Spanish Civil War, we had seen the Soviet-Nazi pact. Those of us who had been political—and I was born political—had a sense of the dynamics of all the personalities. We had seen the fights within the trade unions develop, the takeovers of the trade unions, the takeover of the IUE by the Communist Party, and the ousting of Jim Carey in the International Union of Electrical Workers, the fights with Philip Murray and the steel workers. This was a very virulent fight. . . . We were not going to let [the Communists] take over the veterans' movement. . . . We saw what was coming and decided to gird for it.[16]

If Williams knew anything at all about the ASU and its history, he would not have been as blindsided as he was by ideological maneuvering and manipulation of the AVC and may have seen the writing on the wall. As it was, Williams wasn't even aware of the existence of warring AVC factions until several months after joining. He was under the naïve illusion that the AVC was what it claimed to be—a liberal/ progressive alternative to the VFW and American Legion that was committed to, among other things, racial fairness. In May 1946, when the Metropolitan Area Council convened at the Manhattan Center to adopt a platform and elect officers,[17] the divisions and their implications began to sink in.

As legal counsel, Williams was selected to chair the opening session.[18] But at the following night's executive committee meeting, half the members and the chairman, Harry Heller, representing the liberal wing, were absent. Puzzled, Williams inquired, only to learn that the missing were holding a separate meeting at the Thirty-Fourth Street home of a garment center executive. He rushed over to Thirty-Fourth Street, where he found several representatives of the national board, including Franklin Roosevelt Jr., Merle Miller, and Michael Straight, prominent white liberals from distinguished families. An unfamiliar thirty-seven-year-old man, Joseph Lash, who had previously served as executive secretary of the American Student Union and was intimately familiar with the communists' ploys, was chairing the meeting. Williams entered just in time to hear Lash's dire prediction: "We're gathered here tonight because at the next session there will be an organized effort by the Communist Party to take over the Metropolitan Area Council!" Lash warned.[19] Williams was astonished and confused: "My heart went down in my stomach. . . . I had joined [AVC] because of its commitment to nondiscrimination and a totally integrated veterans' association. Here I was in a meeting with prominent people whose names I knew, and they feared the motives and machinations of the Communist Party."[20]

Lash suggested that to ward off the onslaught they put together a slate of nominees for the upcoming election of officers. Two candidates were considered for chairman of the Independent Progressive Caucus, the liberal faction: Harry Heller and Franklin Williams. Williams, although he didn't realize it at the time, was being used. In the past, the communists had promoted Blacks because they knew that nothing brought liberals to their knees quicker than any insinuation of racism and figured they could get a puppet figure entrenched because the progressives wouldn't dare challenge a Black man. In this instance, the liberals attempted to play exactly the same game—promoting Franklin Williams because they thought he was "educable" about the evils of communism and suspecting that the communists would be just as loath as the liberals to openly oppose a Black man.[21] While the Independent Progressive Caucus may have figured Williams as a pawn for their clique, Franklin immediately asserted his independence from either faction: "Look, if I'm elected chairman, I'm going to fight to see that nobody takes over the Metropolitan Area Council, no political group, as Communist, no Republicans, no Democrats," Williams told the group.

Williams was elected chairman of the Metropolitan Area Council by acclimation and endorsed as a candidate for the National Planning Council. But members of the Unity Caucus—the communist wing—won every other office after nominating another Black man, Arnold Johnson, for third vice chair. It was beginning to sink in. Williams began to realize that "almost any Black guy could have won anything in that atmosphere [because everyone] was leaning over backwards to prove their liberalism." The predominance of Unity Caucus (Communist) candidates prompted an outburst by the president of the Greenwich Village chapter, who claimed the convention was rigged and urged his faction to abandon the event.

As the Greenwich Village delegates began their exodus, Williams ran to the stage and, exhibiting the leadership qualities that would fully develop over time, stated: "You all elected me unanimously as chairman. If you stay in this convention, I assure you as long as I am chair, nobody will take over the

Metropolitan Council, no caucus of any kind will take it over." Apparently he was convincing, because the delegates returned to their seats. In the coming months, as Williams worked closely with the officers elected by the Unity Caucus, he began to question whether some of them were truly ideological communists or merely opportunistic. He was particularly friendly with one of the Unity Caucus members, a Black attorney and Lincoln University graduate named Howie Paine, and knew Paine "was no more communist than I." That gave him hope that he could mediate the differences and restore unity. But it wasn't to be.

In mid-June 1946, Williams flew to Des Moines, Iowa, for the AVC's first annual conference, and while he was busy networking the Independent Progressives and the Unity Caucus factions continued to maneuver, manipulate, and battle for control, a conflict that manifested itself openly in the race for the vice chairmanship. The chairman, Charles Bolte, whose sympathies lay with the liberal wing, was quite popular and running unopposed. Consequently, the vice chairmanship was crucial: The liberal wing figured that if they could take that position, they could rid the organization of communists, at least on the national level; the communists knew that to remain relevant in the leadership structure, they had to take that position. Williams, who found the political games tiresome, attempted to remain above the fray and neutral, which of course only angered both camps. He found the manipulations childish and unimportant, particularly when he was distracted by an issue far more important than petty politics.

On the Saturday night of the conference, when two Black AVC members were refused service at the Rose Bowl Café in downtown Des Moines, Williams, New York attorney Oren Root (the great-nephew of Elihu Root, President Theodore Roosevelt's secretary of state, and a prominent Republican), and Charles Howard, the local NAACP attorney, immediately went to court, accusing the café's manager of violating the civil rights provision in the Iowa Code. Additionally, Williams organized a picket line, with fifty of the delegates on the street in front of the café chanting, "Jim Crow must go!"[22]

When Williams returned to his room, Larry Knobel—the communist faction delegate with whom he happened to be rooming—told him that the Unity Caucus was withdrawing its support because "we couldn't count on you when the chips were down."[23] Williams shrugged it off: "That's fine with me. I'm on the Independent Progressive slate." A few hours later, the other shoe dropped when he was summoned to the Independent Progressive Caucus suite by Franklin Roosevelt Jr. and told, "You're off our slate because you wouldn't do as you were told. We needed your support for Gil Harrison and we didn't get it."[24]

Williams retreated to the lobby, his head spinning, wondering how in the span of twelve hours he had gone from being everybody's candidate to nobody's candidate, apparently because he refused to play favorites. When Oren Root found Williams, he interceded, and the Independent Progressives put him back on the slate. Justin Feldman recalled, "We put him back only when we found that [the Unity Caucus] had dropped him. We couldn't afford to be seen as anti-Black [and] we knew he would appeal to some of the neutrals and to the Black voters. There were not many of them, but we were struggling to pick up votes wherever we could."[25]

Comically, when the communist faction learned that the liberals abandoned Williams, they put him back on their ticket.[26] The two factions were outdueling each other to prove they weren't racists, when both sides were exploiting the race card. Williams was not only elected to the committee but won a landslide victory, garnering nearly 24,000 votes, 1,300 more than his nearest competitor. He received more votes than such prominent figures as Roosevelt, Root, Robert Nathan (President Franklin Roosevelt's economic advisor), and Michael Straight, editor of the *New Republic*.[27]

For the remainder of his time with the organization, Williams found himself in favor, out of favor, supported by both groups, and opposed by both groups. In later years, Williams conceded that he was probably "naive" in believing that he could avoid making enemies by remaining neutral. Indeed, he made enemies in both camps and lost the trust of each: "We never knew where Williams stood ideologically," recalled Justin Feldman of the progressive wing.[28] Gil Harrison later complained: "What was important to Franklin Williams was being Mr. Franklin Williams, who played both sides. He had no ideology at all; he stood wherever it benefited him."[29]

Both those statements are inaccurate and unfair. Williams joined the AVC solely because of its apparent commitment to nondiscrimination, and race matters were clearly his priority. He made his position clear in an interview he gave to Norma J. Gould, a *New York Post* reporter who was so apparently smitten with Williams that she described him as a "self-assured 28-year-old with a tall forehead, straight well-defined eyebrows above luminous eyes—large eyes that look at you and yet far beyond you . . . [as he] pours out his words evenly, unemotionally, without too much rhetoric."[30] Williams told the reporter in September 1946 that he'd like to see the AVC adopt an uncompromising position opposing Jim Crow laws and all forms of discrimination, whether by business, government, or labor unions. He made a similar statement a month later when *Mademoiselle*, the popular women's magazine, featured him as one of the nation's future leaders. He told the magazine: "I believe that the youth of

America which fought a war for peace and equality for all . . . are prepared to back a similar struggle in our own country."[31]

Meanwhile, although the Independent Progressive group was largely successful in beating back the Unity Caucus faction, the communists remained a powerful subset within the AVC and the infighting continued, growing ever more divisive and bitter as the year progressed. The first meeting of the newly elected National Committee provided yet another occasion for the two sides to display their sophomoric animosity, for Williams's behavior to be misunderstood, and for his efforts to heal those wounds to be distorted through insecurity and racial politics.

The meeting took place at Apple Green, a ninety-acre Westbury estate on Long Island owned by Michael Straight, with a fourteen-bedroom main house, several brick cottages, and elegant Chinese gardens.[32] Williams arrived in a foul mood, angry that the meeting was held in a location somewhat inconvenient for him and feeling slighted when assigned accommodations in the carriage house rather than the main house with the "rich liberals." The location, the setting, and the growing realization that he was being used as a racial pawn brought out the worst in Williams's insecurities, and the others were getting tired of walking on eggshells in his presence. The meeting was tense, with Williams hypersensitive to what he perceived as racial slights and with both the Unity Caucus and Independent Progressives demanding that he choose one faction over the other. Justin Feldman, among others, was growing impatient: "It was a pain in the ass . . . catering to his concern. I felt if I wanted to tell him, 'Franklin, you're a jerk, you're stupid and you don't know what you are doing,' I should be able to do so without being told, 'Oh, you think that way because I'm Black.'"[33]

Despite the hostility that Williams faced from the Independent Progressives and the distrust of the Unity Caucus, he still had broad support among his base, the rank-and-file members of the Metropolitan Area Council. At their raucous second annual convention in October of 1946—a meeting punctuated by "hissing, clapping, booing and stamping of feet"[34]—Williams was reelected chairman, defeating his opponent two-to-one. Despite what appeared to be a solid mandate, Williams could not diffuse the tension between the progressives and communists, and the AVC was so distracted over whether it was or wasn't a front for the Communist Party that its original mission was nearly forgotten.

The National Planning Committee met the weekend of November 9, 1946, at the Plaza Hotel in New York City, and the first order of business was a resolution proposed by New England Regional Vice Chairman Arnold Rivkin stating the organization's opposition to "the entrance into our ranks of members

of the Communist Party" and commitment to "prevent them . . . from attempting to use AVC as a sounding board for their own perverse philosophy." While
Rivkin's resolution concluded that while the political affiliations of AVC members are generally of no concern, "members of the AVC must subscribe to the
Preamble of the AVC Constitution, which obliges them to 'preserve the Constitution of the United States' [and protect] the rights of free speech, free press,
free worship, free assembly and free elections [while maintaining] full production and full employment in our country under a system of private enterprise
in which business, labor, agriculture and government cooperate."

Williams proposed a compromise that generally supported Rivkin's statement
but would not automatically exclude honorably discharged veterans who happened to be Communists. After his version was rejected by both camps, Williams reluctantly voted in favor of Rivkin's resolution, but it was a vote he
immediately regretted. Williams asked Thurgood Marshall, then a member
of the national board of the American Civil Liberties Union, for advice; Marshall told Williams he should not have supported the resolution, though some
years later Marshall passed information to the FBI about Communist efforts
to infiltrate the NAACP.[35] Williams returned to the meeting and changed his
vote. His single vote, however, did not change the outcome, and the AVC adopted Rivkin's anticommunist resolution. Williams saw that the constant infighting and bickering would ultimately doom the AVC and, along with Michael
Straight and Louis Frank, formed a third caucus: "Build AVC."[36]

Williams promised that Build AVC would be "independent, democratic,
unaffiliated and non-machine" and would "protect AVC against Communist
or other outside control . . . without imposing the Communist test upon every
person, program and policy."[37] In an article, "Democracy in Action" written
for the AVC Bulletin, Williams castigated Secretary of State George Marshall
for promoting American-style democracy to an audience of Russian officials
while ignoring the fact that Black Americans did not enjoy the very freedoms
he was urging the Russians to embrace. Contending that America's hypocrisy
on the race issue adversely affected its relationship with foreign governments,
Williams urged the AVC to "dedicate more of its time" to securing equal rights
for Blacks, "Our red-white-and-blue slip is showing and the dirt on it is not at
all attractive," he wrote in the AVC Bulletin of March 15, 1947.[38] The new faction rushed to draft a formal platform and prepare a slate of candidates prior
to the AVC's second annual conference.

On June 20, 1947, two thousand AVC delegates descended on Milwaukee
for the start of a three-day conference.[39] The delegates overwhelmingly agreed
with several proposals such as support for the United Nations and the Marshall
Plan and opposition to veterans' bonuses and universal military training, but

they struggled to get past the ideological issues, such as whether the United States should maintain its stock of atomic weapons until an effective international control system was established (as urged by the Independent Progressives) or disarm immediately (as the Unity Caucus insisted).[40]

Each of the three factions put up candidates for the top two positions, chairman and vice chairman. The new Build AVC group endorsed Charles Ebey, a college professor from Chico, California, and Williams; the Independent Progressives promoted Chat Paterson and Richard Walker Bolling, then an organizer with Americans for Democratic Action and later a seventeen-term Democratic congressman from Missouri; the Unity Caucus went with Ken Pettus and Don Rothenberg.

The night before the election, the Independent Progressives started a rumor that Williams had recently been fired from the NAACP because of communist affiliations,[41] a lie that spread quickly until the NAACP flatly denied it. Two decades later, when Williams underwent an exhaustive background check prior to his appointment as ambassador to Ghana, the FBI uncovered a Communist Party pledge card signed by "Franklin H. Williams." The FBI concluded that it was a forgery, but who forged it and why remains a matter of speculation. Ironically, while Williams's opponents were busy spinning a falsehood, they neglected to challenge him where he was vulnerable: on his war record. Franklin had misleadingly implied he had served in the Pacific during the war when in reality almost all of his service time was spent in a hospital in El Paso.[42] In any case, Franklin lost his seat on the National Planning Committee to Dick Bolling and, dejected, returned to New York to continue as chair of the Metropolitan Council. But his patience was wearing thin, and his days were numbered as the underhanded politics of the AVC continued to undermine both the organization and Franklin Williams. In the months that followed, Williams tried to press for new programs but grew frustrated when every discussion on every issue devolved into left-vs.-farther left and little was accomplished. At a meeting one evening, Williams reached his limit and summarily announced: "I resign."

He left the meeting, severed his ties with the AVC, and decided to reserve his energies for his paying job as an attorney with the National Association for the Advancement of Colored People. In that capacity, he would become even more familiar with and disdainful of communist infiltration.

6
Civil Rights Lawyer

Franklin Williams adamantly and stubbornly resisted the notion that the battle for civil rights was rooted in the activism of the 1960s. Rather, he argued that the fight began when the first slave fled to freedom and contended that the organized movement began to gain traction in 1935, when the National Association for the Advancement of Colored People (NAACP) hired Charles Hamilton Houston, the organization's first full-time, salaried special counsel, to direct its legal efforts to end racial discrimination.

It's not that Williams gave short shrift to the impact of marches and sit-ins and freedom rides, the brilliant eloquence of Martin Luther King. Not at all. Those efforts, he knew, galvanized public support, which was absolutely crucial. He recognized that the court of public opinion was paramount—but not paramount to the court of law. With his legally trained mind and reverence for the United States Constitution, Franklin believed the rule of law was the only way to effect structural and *permanent* reform, reform that was not contingent on the subjective whim of the era or the majority. It was a message he loved to share, particularly with the young.

"Can anyone tell me when the Civil Rights movement began?" Franklin asked a group of Queens College undergraduates in the spring of 1989. When a young man seated in the back of the crowded hall took the bait and offered the cliché response about bus strikes and lunch counter sit-ins and the like, Williams grasped his teaching moment. "Don't you know that if the NAACP's legal department hadn't laid the groundwork, none of those demonstrations could have taken place?" Williams asked in a fatherly tone. "The Civil Rights movement was born when the first slave ran away in search of freedom." He delved into his spiel, his adenoidal yet resonant New York City voice echoing through the auditorium, and spoke of the Black resistance to Jim Crow; the debt owed to W. E. B. Du Bois, one of the founding fathers of the NAACP; the energy and vision of Walter White; and the legal work of courageous and pioneering attorneys.

Williams understood that the political/democratic branches of government—the legislative and executive departments—were inherently and appropriately tools of the majority, designed to pander to the broader public; that's the definition of democracy, majority rule. But the judicial branch, with its counter-majoritarian mission, was the branch that protected the individual liberties delineated in the Constitution, the branch that shielded the minority from the tyranny of the majority. It was within the halls of justice, not the halls of Congress, where Williams saw enduring relief for his people, with the NAACP leading the way.

The NAACP was founded in 1909 by two diverse groups after white rioters forced two thousand Blacks to flee their homes in Springfield, Illinois, the city that had been home to Abraham Lincoln. The first group was led by W. E. B. Du Bois and consisted of Black intellectuals who had been part of the all-Black Niagara Movement, a civil rights organization founded by Du Bois and William Monroe Trotter on the Canadian side of Niagara Falls, since no hotel on the American side would allow them access.[1] Its name and location were symbolic, representing the mighty and irrepressible current that pushed the waters from four of the five Great Lakes over the precipice in perpetuity. Unfortunately, the Niagara Movement had little impact and less money, since it was an all-Black group. An alliance with a group of brave white visionaries such as social worker Jane Addams, novelist William Dean Howells, editor Oswald Garrison Villard (the grandson of William Lloyd Garrison, the Boston abolitionist), philosopher John Dewey, social reformer William Walling, literary critic (and NAACP president throughout the 1930s) Joel Elias Spingarn, and social workers Mary White Ovington and Henry Moskowitz, led to the formation of the NAACP. The NAACP's organizers hired Du Bois, the country's leading Black intellectual, as the organization's Director of Publicity and Research.

A Harvard University graduate, Du Bois was a scholar, writer, and social activist. One of his first tasks was to create a monthly magazine, *The Crisis*, that in addition to current events, political analysis, and literary work would feature "The Burden," a section that brought the news of white atrocities out of rural backwaters and onto the pages of a national publication. He wrote a scathing editorial each month, in which he and others described the poisonous effects of racism as it permeated every level of society, undermined the human spirit, and was antithetical to the basic tenets of democracy. *The Crisis* was geared toward educated Blacks, had a scholarly bent, and appealed to men and women of both principle and intellect—in other words, thoughtful future leaders such as Franklin Williams.

Du Bois brought a fundamentally different view from Booker T. Washington's, the old guard of the civil rights movement who preached a philosophy of accommodation and self-help, urging Blacks to tolerate discrimination for the time being and focus instead on elevating their economic status through hard work and education. Du Bois disagreed, believing that such détente would merely perpetuate white oppression. He advocated political activism and a pro-active civil rights agenda that resonated with Williams. Years later, in a speech to the Virginia State Conference of NAACP Branches, Williams spoke of the W. E. B. Du Bois vs. Booker T. Washington "battle for the minds of Negroes": "The failure of the grand design of Negro leadership was rooted in the fact that racial discrimination was deeply rooted in industry, in labor unions, in government service, in schools, in political parties, in service clubs, in churches, in professional groups, in trade associations, in sports, and in that vast array of voluntary organizations which play such a key role in our society."[2]

The NAACP was at a critical juncture in the mid-1940s. The end of World War II brought vast social change to America, and Blacks were no longer willing to accept second-class citizenship. Their sons had fought and died to prove that claims of racial superiority were a sham. It was time to bring the battle home. Now the goal was to utilize the right to vote, to obtain housing, education, employment, and to receive fair treatment in the courts, and the FDR-constructed Supreme Court seemed receptive. New Deal appointees such as Felix Frankfurter, William O. Douglas, Hugo Black, and Frank Murphy were leery of Jim Crow laws and believed, states' rights notwithstanding, that the Constitution set a higher standard. The NAACP prepared itself to move aggressively to end segregation and to ensure that the constitutional rights guaranteed all Americans were extended equally to Black citizens.

On November 15, 1945, shortly after completing his clerkship at Dyett and Stevens, Williams joined the staff of the Legal and Educational Fund and assumed responsibility for all legal matters dealing with the armed forces.[3] His first task was to review applications to reverse dishonorable discharges and retroactively challenge court-martials. Williams scoured the records, seeking to ascertain whether the defendant had been denied a fair trial because of his race, or if the sentence imposed was disproportionate to those white soldiers had received for similar offenses. If so, he would seek review by the Judge Advocate General. But there were so many meritorious cases that Williams had time only for the most egregious, and even with those cases success was rare.

As a young attorney with the NAACP, Franklin was actively involved in recruiting volunteers for the organization's various initiatives. Here he is with a volunteer helping to promote the Fair Employment Practices effort. (Photo courtesy of Franklin H. Williams Judicial Commission)

He was struck by the gross injustice of soldiers "who had been railroaded by these courts-martial proceedings . . . used by bigoted whites to take out their racist feelings on Black soldiers."[4]

One of his cases involved a soldier named Arthur C. Essex, who refused to cut wood unless provided with food. He was thrown into a ten-by-four-foot latrine pit which he shared with another wayward soldier, and then sentenced to ten years of hard labor. Williams fought to reduce the sentence in that case and many others, and he often went a step beyond and directly targeted the white officers who, by their brutal conduct, had violated army regulations. He lost every single case. In one case, a white lieutenant had ordered a Black private to stand naked in the snow and then dig a six-foot hole with a spoon. The all-white military juror found that the officer had done nothing wrong.[5]

The most difficult and highest-stake cases where those in which a Black soldier was accused of raping a white woman. Since the prevailing attitude was that no decent white woman would willfully sleep with a Black man, the Black soldier was presumed guilty. Evidence and facts mattered little. Sometimes, white officers who could not stomach the thought of sexual activity between Black men and white women persuaded indigent white prostitutes to solicit Blacks and then bring rape charges. The NAACP almost never prevailed, which demoralized and frustrated Williams. However, the experience enabled him to hone his skills as an attorney, and his oratorial skills were beginning to impress the NAACP leadership and, more and more, he was called upon to speak in public.

Williams's first-ever speech for the NAACP, entitled "The Battle Continues," was delivered to a small audience at a White Plains, New York, YMCA in late December 1945.[6] It was so well received that Williams was promptly asked to speak at the YMCA in Paterson, New Jersey, at Harlem Hospital in New York City, and at the All Souls Unitarian Church in Plainfield, New Jersey.[7] They were small events of little real consequence, but word was spreading both within the NAACP and outside it that Franklin Williams was a rare talent, an unusually effective and rousing speaker. Three months after he was hired, Ella Baker, the NAACP's field secretary and an outstanding orator herself, recommended that Williams speak in her place.[8] One colleague described Franklin as a "fabulous speaker, the best the NAACP ever had. He was dramatic, yet very direct, smooth, but never condescending."[9] Still another recalled, "Williams may have been the most gifted speaker I ever heard—his admirers use the term 'silver-tongued,' but even that didn't seem adequate to describe his oratorical skills."[10] By 1946, public speaking was an important part of Williams's duties, and his oratorical skills quickly surpassed those of Thurgood Marshall, who was seemingly threatened by this brash young upstart. Almost from the start, Marshall and Williams were at odds.

Gloster F. Current, National Director of Branches from 1946 to 1976, recollected that "there was always tension in the air when the two were together. Thurgood had no love for Franklin Williams and they were never on the greatest terms."[11] Famed civil rights attorney and legal scholar Jack Greenberg, who came to the NAACP in 1949 as assistant counsel, recalled in his memoir *Crusaders in the Courts* that "when Frank was in Thurgood's office behind a closed door, we sometimes heard . . . angry shouting."[12]

In hindsight, it is understandable why the two never meshed. Williams was assertive and ambitious, qualities that Marshall recognized in himself. Both were "outside men," who preferred generating ideas and speaking about issues, rather than "desk men," intellectual types who relished the solitude of research and brief writing. Both were highly competitive, told great stories, sought the limelight, and required the kind of loyalty from subordinates that bordered on subservience. Perhaps the only difference between the two was that Marshall had the common touch; he enjoyed being around plain folks, liked to speak in the dialect of uneducated southern Blacks, and could be loud and vulgar in mixed company; Williams preferred to associate with educated people, prided himself on his knowledge of grammar and syntax, and rarely used profanity. It was a case of two giant egos rubbing against each other in the same office, creating friction and heat. What began as a personality conflict took on a more serious tone in the years to come.

Marshall, in Williams's eyes, was too timid, too cautious, too reluctant to take important cases when the odds of winning were poor. From Marshall's perspective, Williams was strategically ignorant, lacking the sophistication to realize that an adverse decision by the Supreme Court would set the movement back generations; better to go with the sure winners. He thought Williams naively failed to appreciate that if NAACP took on the cases of heinous criminals whose rights were egregiously violated, garnering a reputation for getting murderers and rapists off on "technicalities," it would alienate patrons and cripple fundraising efforts; better to put its resources toward defending those who were truly innocent and not the guilty who confessed only after illegal beatings.

Williams was, without a doubt, presumptuous, impatient, ill-suited to be anyone's employee, and perhaps disinclined to afford Marshall, ten years his elder and with a wealth of experience, the deference his boss had earned. For example, Williams was at the NAACP less than a year when he submitted an audacious, five-page, single-spaced memo in which he laid out his suggestions for "running our office in a more businesslike manner" and suggesting that

Franklin Williams as a young
professional, roughly 1950.
(Photo courtesy of Franklin H.
Williams Judicial Commission)

Marshall was a poor administrator.[13] Basically, the new kid in the office was telling the boss how to sail the ship, and the boss didn't like it one bit. Unlike Marshall, Williams was willing to nurture the talent of those who served under him. Marshall at times seemed threatened by ambitious assistants.

But while Williams often lacked Marshall's support, he had a key ally in Walter White, whose daughter he had dated as a teenager. White viewed Williams as a son, admiring his precise use of language, his penchant for three-piece suits and the social confidence that mirrored his own.[14] He took a personal interest in the problems of returning veterans and advised Presidents Roosevelt, Truman, and Eisenhower on the issue, and he was looking for a particularly egregious case to make a point. The case was that of Isaac Woodard Jr., a decorated World War II veteran who served honorably in the Pacific Theater.

Woodard joined the US Army at Fort Jackson, South Carolina, in 1942, when he was twenty-three years old. He served in the labor battalion as a longshoreman and was promoted to sergeant. For his service, Woodard was awarded a Battle Star, a Good Conduct Medal, a Service Medal, and a World War II Victory Medal.

On the morning of February 12, 1946, Woodard was discharged after returning from a fifteen-month tour of duty in New Guinea and the Philippines. He was looking forward to a reunion with his wife at her parents' home in South Carolina and boarded a northbound Greyhound bus from Camp Gordon in Augusta, Georgia. Woodard and several other Black soldiers dutifully retreated to the back of the bus and settled in for a long ride. When the bus stopped, Woodard asked to get off to use the restroom. The driver refused and started to curse him. Woodard cursed back, adding, "Talk to me like I'm talking to you, I'm a man just like you."[15] The driver relented. Woodard got off, quickly returned, and the bus continued. Few passengers paid attention when, sometime later, the driver stopped in Batesburg to place a phone call.

Within minutes, three policemen arrived, including the chief of police, Lynwood Shull. The driver led them down the aisle, pointed to Woodard, and accused him of being drunk and disorderly. The policemen pulled Woodard from the bus and marched him down the street and into an alley behind a building. Once they rounded the corner and were out of sight of the bus and its witnesses, the powerfully built Shull asked Woodard whether he had been discharged from the army.[16] When Woodward replied "Yes" rather than "Yes, sir," the police beat him with nightclubs and dragged him to jail, where the poundings continued. Police repeatedly jabbed Woodard in the face with a nightstick, rupturing both eyeballs and beating him unconscious.[17] Woodard woke up in a jail cell, unable to see, his face grotesquely swollen and caked with blood. Police drove him to a Veteran's Hospital and left him at the door. In the hospital, Woodard learned that he would never see again.[18]

Three months later, on April 23, 1947, Woodard brought his story to the New York office of the NAACP but was unsure of two critical facts: precisely where the attack had taken place and the name of the officer who had blinded him. White was quick to recognize the emotional appeal of Woodard's story and its benefit to the organization. President Truman condemned the attack. A benefit at Lewisohn Stadium in New York City attended by heavyweight boxing champion Joe Louis and scores of other celebrities, raised $22,000. White provided Woodard's affidavit to actor and filmmaker Orson Welles, who was appalled. On Sunday, July 28, Welles read Woodard's tragic statement over his weekly radio show for ABC—the first of five consecutive broadcasts he devoted to Isaac Woodard—and sought to identify the officer who had blinded Woodard: "Wash your hands, Officer X. Wash them well, scrub and scour . . . and if you assume another name, I will find you. We have an appointment, you and I."[19] The August 1946 broadcasts were among Welles's last for ABC. The network terminated his show on October 6, and while the station maintained that the cancellation had nothing to do with the racial controversy he created, Welles never believed them.[20]

In any case, he did make a grievous error in his first broadcast, inadvertently stating that the event had taken place in Aitken, South Carolina. His blunder generated storms of protest from the mayor of the town and its indignant citizens, who demanded not only the removal of his show from the airwaves but also the banning of his films from movie theaters.[21] But the mistake proved fortuitous, for it shamed two passengers who had been afraid to come forward into providing accurate information. The two later testified against Lynwood Lanier Shull, chief of the three-man police force in Batesburg, South Carolina, who turned out to be the officer in question. That enabled the US Department of Justice, under pressure, to bring charges, which the state of South Carolina had refused to do.

Williams was assigned to represent Woodard at what became a sham trial scheduled for November 5, 1946. He knew that the Klan was threatening the NAACP, and he knew that the federal prosecutors were merely going through the motions and knew little about the facts of the case. "The trial was purely for show."[22] He spent the following day consulting with Fred Rogers, the special assistant prosecutor sent by the Justice Department to oversee the case, and Claude Sapp, the local US Attorney. Neither seemed to know or care much about the case.[23] The trial began the next morning on an unseasonably warm November day as Williams and Woodard entered the courthouse, walking through a phalanx of observers, Blacks on one side of the stairway, whites on the other.[24]

If Williams had any hope that the Justice Department would pursue the case competently and aggressively, since President Truman himself had made it an issue, he was bitterly disappointed. Sapp mispronounced Woodard's name, neglected to subpoena hospital records that would have documented the victim's injuries, refused to put the admitting physician on the stand, and declined to call two witnesses—one Black and one white—to testify that Woodard appeared sober and well-behaved; he did call them as rebuttal witnesses, however, after the bus driver testified that Isaac was drunk.[25] He also failed to object when the defense asserted that Woodard belonged to "an inferior race."[26] In his summation, Sapp never even asked the all-white jury for a guilty verdict. "Whatever verdict you gentlemen bring in, the government will be satisfied with," Sapp told the jury.[27]

The defense case relied largely on the word of Shull, who admitted striking Woodard but claimed he acted out of self-defense when the drunken and belligerent veteran attempted to wrestle the club from his hand. Shull said that it was purely by chance that his single blow had inadvertently ruptured both of Woodard's eyes, a ridiculous claim. In his summation, Shull's defense attorney noted that Woodard admitted he had cursed at the bus driver and argued, "That's not the talk of a sober niggra from the state of South Carolina."[28]

The jury began deliberations at 3:30 p.m. It took all of twenty-eight minutes for the all-white jury to find Shull not guilty. Shull's acquittal was front-page news in the leading Black newspapers, and even the mainstream press reported the unfortunate verdict.[29] As one editor contended, "Even the most cynical thought that the culprit would be convicted." Indeed, a large segment of the public seemed dismayed by the outcome.[30]

Williams, however, could not fault the jury. The prosecution's case was so slim and so full of holes that, based on the evidence in court, even he couldn't have found Shull guilty beyond a reasonable doubt, the high standard the government must meet to convict a citizen of a crime. Rather, Williams targeted his anger at the prosecutors who basically undermined their own case, and the judge, US District Judge Julius Waties Waring, who initially seemed complicit. However, as the case went on and Waring witnessed the feeble efforts of the prosecution, he was "shocked at the hypocrisy of my government . . . in submitting that disgraceful case before a jury. . . [and] I was also hurt that I was made a party to it."[31]

Judge Waring was at the beginning stages of a conversion that would make him a leader in upending the Jim Crow laws, and the Woodard case pushed him over the edge. A classic "Southern gentleman" raised in the tradition and culture of his community, Waring had grown increasingly concerned with the racial injustice he was witnessing regularly in his courtroom and began standing up to racism.[32]

He put an end to the practice of placing a "c" next to the name of Black jurors to indicate "colored." He ordered the bailiff to desegregate seating in the jury box and in the courtroom. He directed court personnel to address Black witnesses as "Mr." or "Mrs."[33] just as they would a white witness. Although the US Supreme Court wouldn't forbid the stacking of juries by race until 1986 in Batson v. Kentucky, Waring at least ensured Blacks were in the mix, even if they had little if any chance of actually being selected for a jury. Finally, he appointed John Fleming as bailiff, the first Black in the South to hold such a position.[34] Judge Waring's transformation seemingly came much quicker than that of the town, which is now Batesburg-Leesville; in 2019, seventy-three years after the incident, the town finally took ownership of the Woodard case, installing a permanent historic marker downtown as a reminder of the racial injustice that occurred.[35]

At first Judge Waring's colleagues and friends merely grumbled about his rulings and innovations, viewing him something of a maverick or harmless eccentric on the subject of race. But there was a limit to their endurance. After the judge ruled in *Rice v. Elmore*[36] (1947) that all-white primaries were illegal and wrote a dissent in *Briggs v. Elliot*[37] (1952) that "segregation is per se inequality," public opinion turned decidedly negative.[38] Waring and his wife, driven from their Charleston home, moved to New York, where they became ardent supporters of the NAACP and social friends with Franklin and Shirley Williams.[39] Judge Waring revealed why the Woodard jury took so "long"—less than half an hour—to exonerate Chief Shull. "[It was] because Mrs. Waring and I decided to take a walk, otherwise they would have been back in two minutes."[40] In other words, the only reason the jury didn't return a verdict much earlier is the judge wasn't there to accept it.

The NAACP complained to the US Department of Justice based on Williams's report of prosecutorial malfeasance. But Georgia peace officers, South Carolina's sheriffs, and other law enforcement officers counterattacked, accusing the Justice Department of "needlessly meddling in local law enforcement."[41] The Justice Department essentially ignored both the NAACP and the law enforcement organizations and dropped the matter.

After the trial, Williams undertook a major fundraising effort in the Midwest and the Eastern Seaboard and was exceptionally successful, according to Gloster Current, the NAACP branch director who arranged the tour.[42] However, he had no luck suing the Atlantic Greyhound Bus Company on the weak theory that their driver unlawfully ejected Woodard from the bus.

In his first eighteen months with the Legal Defense Fund, Williams had fought for the rights of soldiers stationed at home and overseas, raised funds, and made a name for himself as a public speaker. His future looked bright, and Williams finally felt secure enough to move his growing family into their first real home.

7

In the Courts

In the summer of 1947 the war was over, the economy was booming, the nation was eager to move forward. The Williams family—Franklin, Shirley, and Franklin Hall Williams Jr., born on Valentine's Day 1946—moved from their cramped Brooklyn apartment to Riverton, a newly built housing complex on Fifth Avenue between 135th and 138th Streets in Harlem. With Franklin bringing in a solidly middle-class salary of $3,000 a year (precisely the median income of American families in 1947, equating to about $35,000 today)[1] at the NAACP, they could afford bigger quarters, an electric vacuum cleaner, and Venetian blinds while dreaming of an even better life in the future.

Riverton, to the Williams family, was an idyllic island of suburbia nestled like a hidden jewel within the grimy reality of Harlem life. Each of its seven buildings rose thirteen stories, not very tall by New York City standards, but tall enough to seem stately. The towers were surrounded by green grass, trees, and playgrounds. At $12.50 per room/ per month, utilities included, the apartments were in great demand—22,000 families applied for 1,200 units—and Franklin and Shirley felt fortunate to win that lottery.[2] There was only one problem, which they chose to overlook: Riverton was built on a foundation of discrimination and segregation. It was a consolation prize when Blacks were turned away from Stuyvesant Town, a mammoth postwar housing complex on the East Side of Manhattan.

The Metropolitan Life Insurance Company took advantage of a New York City tax abatement program created to address the postwar housing shortage,[3] happily taking government money aimed at ensuring decent housing for veterans, regardless of color. But the chairman of Metropolitan Life explained: "Negroes and whites don't mix. Perhaps they will in one hundred years, but not now."[4] Harlem was the place for Blacks, and New York's power structure meant to keep them there. Thus, Riverton was built as the separate-but-equal cousin to Stuyvesant Town. "StuyTown" consisted of 110 buildings and 11,250 apartments, but it didn't have room for Black veterans and their families.

Riverton was controversial from the start, both with Blacks and whites who opposed the perpetuation of segregation and with prior residents of the area who had nowhere to go once their tenements were torn down to make room for the new apartments. In "Fifth Avenue, Uptown, A Letter From Harlem," James Baldwin expressed outrage: "Harlem watched Riverton go up in the most violent bitterness of spirit, and . . . began hating it about the time people began moving out of the condemned houses to make room for this additional proof of how thoroughly the white world despised them."[5] Although Baldwin did not blame the occupants of Riverton for "making the best of a dreadful bargain," he warned them never to forget that they undoubtedly had made one: "anyone who imagines that he has not struck this bargain or that what he takes to be his status . . . protects him against the common pain, demoralization and danger, is simply self-deluded."[6]

Williams despised segregation, and within a few years would become a leader in opposing housing discrimination. But the chance to obtain decent housing for his family at a reasonable rent took precedence over what he knew at the time would be a cut-off-your-nose-to-spite-your-face protest.[7] Despite the segregation, Williams loved Riverton and the all-Black culture that re-minded him somewhat of Lincoln University. Riverton was home base for the "Gaylords," a small society of upper echelon Blacks that Williams modeled after the "Smart Set" his grandfather had once convened in Queens. The Gaylords met weekly, planned social events, and sponsored an annual dinner dance at the Essex House, a grand hotel on Central Park South where the members would don tie and tails and their wives or dates would dress glam-orously. It was a not-so-subtle message to New York society that, like it or not, Blacks were arriving.

Riverton was full of talented young men with attractive young wives with attractive friends, sisters, and relatives who came to visit. It was a close-knit community, and one rife for indiscretions. Although he cherished Shirley, Williams was an inveterate philanderer, and often involved himself with women in his family's immediate social circle. His sister-in-law, Roberta Braddicks Williams, recalled:

One day Shirley called and asked me to come upstairs. When I did she gave me this letter. It was an unsigned letter—although I knew exactly who it was from—telling about Frank running around with this one and that one. Shirley was crying. Then, I said, "Shirley—you take this letter out to the incinerator and put it right in there. And if you get anymore, don't bother to read them. Just throw them in there, too."[8]

Although at first Shirley was terribly wounded, offended, and baffled by her husband's unfaithfulness, she ultimately, perhaps to maintain her own equilibrium, adopted a philosophy of resigned indifference that would sustain their marriage. If she could never understand his desire/need for other women, she somehow came to accept it, knowing implicitly that he deeply loved and would always come home to her. Their marriage was very loving and very fulfilling, despite the infidelity which Shirley, for whatever reason, chose to ignore. Others who were aware of Williams's affairs were less tolerant than Shirley, suggesting that he recklessly jeopardized not only his marriage but his career, stupidly putting himself and the NAACP in peril and inexplicably squandering the possibility that he could ever run for public office.

Williams's infidelity is impossible to understand and explain in the context of a man who was, in other ways, a decent person of high moral character, committed to his wife and family. Interestingly, Williams's lovers describe him as kind, honest, and respectful, and never abusive or exploitive; he maintained lifelong platonic relationships with women with whom he'd had romantic encounters. He seemed to have an emotional neediness that could not be fulfilled by just one woman, and at times exhibited the traits of a tribal patriarch holding sway over a large, polygamous family.

Meanwhile, at the NAACP's understaffed Legal Defense Fund, there was no shortage of work. Cases poured in from the local branches and from the public at large, from people desperate for legal representation. The LDF, even if it had a dozen more attorneys, couldn't have met the demand, and had no choice but to pick-and-choose which cases and causes to take. Marshall was primarily interested in cases implicating a fundamental constitutional right, cases that, if they prevailed, would establish a precedent that applied to the entire community and not just one aggrieved individual. Teams of LDF attorneys, including Williams, researched the cases and the law, selected the best and brought them to Marshall's attention. Then, the team would strategize with Marshall and help prepare whichever attorney would argue the case. If the case was going to the Supreme Court, it would almost certainly be Thurgood Marshall at the bar.

With the number of veterans' cases dwindling after the war, Williams was assigned criminal cases that implicated a civil right. He cut his teeth on *Patton v. Mississippi*, the first case he researched, shaped, and briefed almost entirely on his own.[9] The facts of the case were as follows.

In February 1946, Eddie "Buster" Patton, an indigent thirty-four-year-old Black man, was indicted by a Grand Jury in Lauderdale County, Mississippi, for the murder of his white employer. The evidence suggested that Patton was guilty. His hat was found near the body of the victim, and footprints leading away from the scene, from which the police later made plaster casts, matched his shoes. After his arrest, Patton confessed, leading police into some nearby woods where they found a cash box and overcoat belonging to the deceased. Patton pleaded self-defense. He claimed he dealt his victim a deadly blow only after the man refused to pay him his wages and beat him on the head with a soft-drink case. Because no Black in memory had served on a Lauderdale County jury, Patton's attorney moved to suppress the initial indictment. The motion was denied. Later during the trial, he objected that investigating officers obtained Patton's confession with the assistance of blackjacks. His objection was overruled. In a one-day trial, Patton was convicted and sentenced to death by an all-white jury.

For a hundred years, despite the ratification of the Fourteenth Amendment and the passage of the Civil Rights Act of 1875, which guaranteed to all citizens the right to serve on grand and petit juries, regardless of race, color, or previous condition of servitude, southern whites had found effective ways to obstruct the selection process.[10] They achieved their ends by drafting state regulations that kept Blacks' names off voting lists, by ensuring that court officers eliminated them from jury pools, and by creating an environment so hostile and potentially dangerous that intimidated Blacks would simply fail to show up for jury service.[11] And when that didn't work, attorneys used their "peremptory" challenges in jury selection—those for which they did not need to give the court a reason for rejecting a particular juror—to exclude Blacks.

In 1875, President Ulysses S. Grant signed the Civil Rights Act of 1875, making it a criminal offense for state officials to "exclude or fail to summon a qualified citizen for jury service on the basis of race."[12] It took at least twenty decisions in various courts and more than a hundred years before the US Supreme Court, in *Batson v. Kentucky* (1986), finally ended the practice legally if not necessarily in reality. But as early as 1880, the Supreme Court, was crawling toward *Batson*. In *Strauder v. West Virginia*, for example, the justices found the racial stacking of juries constitutionally repugnant: "How can it be maintained that compelling a colored man to submit to a trial for his life by a jury drawn from a panel from which the State has expressly excluded every man of his race, because of color alone, however well qualified in other respects, is not a denial to him of equal protection?"[13]

Regardless, the judiciary struggled for another century to reconcile the principles articulated in *Strauder* with the concept of "peremptory" challenges to prospective jurors. In selecting a jury, attorneys can object to a certain person "for cause"—that is, by persuading the judge that the person would not be objective or had a conflict of interest. For example, if a juror happened to be related to the prosecution's main witness, the defense would seek to have that juror removed "for cause," on the grounds that he or she may not be impartial.

In addition to challenges for cause, attorneys are afforded a certain number of "peremptory challenges" for which they do not need to articulate any reason why a potential juror is unsuitable. That allows attorneys, on a limited basis, to exclude jurors whom their gut tells them are hostile to their case or that they suspect are biased, even if they cannot pinpoint or articulate a reason for that belief. It also allowed prosecutors to systematically keep Blacks off juries and ensure that Black defendants were tried by white juries. Prosecutors could, and did, use peremptory challenges to remove Black jurors, without having to explain themselves.

The courts struggled to balance the two considerations—the principle that a defendant has a right to be tried by a jury of his or her peers, and the time-honored, and important, practice of peremptory challenges. In 1965, the landmark case of *Swain v. Alabama* generally upheld the use of peremptories in a particular case, but said that the systematic exclusion of all Blacks from jury service could constitute a denial of equal protection:[14]

> When the prosecutor in a county, *in case after case* [emphasis added], whatever the circumstances, whatever the crime and whoever the defendant or the victim may be, is responsible for the removal of Negroes . . . it would appear that the purposes of the peremptory challenge are being perverted. If the State has not seen fit to leave a single Negro on any jury in a criminal case, the presumption protecting the prosecutor may well be overcome.[15]

That of course was far from a perfect solution because it saddled the defense with the burden of proving that the prosecutor stacked juries in "case after case." So the practice of keeping Blacks off juries remained both common and legal until 1986 when, in *Batson v. Kentucky*, the US Supreme Court found it unconstitutional. In *Batson*, the Court finally said that if it appears that a prosecutor is misusing peremptory challenges, either the defense or the judge could force him or her to come forth with a race-neutral explanation. Decades before *Batson*, Franklin Williams seized on the issue and become perhaps the nation's foremost expert on race-stacking. His expertise on the topic began with *Patton*.

Patton's lawyer, L. J. Broadway, a smart and clever attorney who was well versed in constitutional law, had a good sense of how that law might evolve and expertly made a solid record for appeal. Broadway differed from most white lawyers handling cases for Black defendants in those years, many of whom did not know constitutional law, were unwilling to argue novel issues, were unconscionable bigots, or were simply lazy. He not only raised the constitutional issues—that the county systematically excluded Blacks from serving on the jury and that Patton's admissions had been coerced—he also meticulously prepared and collected the papers pertaining to the case, including the transcript of the trial, the briefs presented by all sides and the legal written exchanges. Broadway fully understood that an appellate court usually will not consider an issue on appeal that was not first raised at trial or "preserved," and was painfully aware that southern judges precluded Black defendants from taking their issue to a higher court by refusing to allow them to make a record. He fought tooth and nail to preserve the key issues for Patton, so at least he would have his day in court.

After Patton was found guilty and sentenced to die, a verdict and sentence surprising no one, Broadway appealed the case to the Supreme Court of Mississippi. In a farcical interpretation of the law, the Mississippi court ruled that, had a Black been selected for jury duty, the result would have been to *discriminate against potential white jurors*. The Court couched its illogic in the twisted theory that because there were only twelve or thirteen eligible Black jurors in the county as compared with five thousand eligible whites, a ratio of approximately four hundred to one, it would be mathematically improbable to find a Black sitting on a jury of twelve.

> Of the 25 qualified negro male electors there would be left, therefore, as those not exempt, 12 or 13 available male negro electors as compared with 5,500 to 6,000 male white electors as to whom, after deducting 500 to 1,000 exempt, would leave a proportion of 5,000 nonexempt white jurors to 12 or 13 nonexempt negro jurors, or about one-fourth of one per cent negro jurors,—400 to 1. . . . For the reasons already heretofore stated there was only a chance of 1 in 400 that a negro would appear on such a venire and as this venire was of one hundred jurors, the sheriff, had he brought in a negro, would have had to discriminate against white jurors, not against negroes—he could not be expected to bring in one-fourth of one negro.[16]

On the question of the coerced confession, the Court held that because Patton's disclosures had led police to recover the stolen articles, those parts of his confession that turned out to be true were admissible.[17] In other words, since it turned out Patton was guilty, it was okay to beat the confession out of him. Unfortunately for Mr. Patton, the US Supreme Court was more than a decade away from a series of rulings in which it adopted what is known as the "exclusionary rule." Under that rule, evidence obtained illegally—such as from an illegal search or through torturing the suspect—must be excluded.

With no legal options remaining in Mississippi, Broadway turned the case over to the NAACP, with hopes that the LDF could get the Supreme Court to take a look. Williams desperately wanted the case because it perfectly framed the issue that would become his specialty: racial bias in jury selection. He went to Marshall with a handful of cases—*Norris v. Alabama* (1935), *Hollins v. Oklahoma* (1935), and *Smith v. Texas* (1940)—all of which signaled the court was troubled by the issue and searching for a way to address it while preserving the peremptory challenge paradigm, and begged for permission to ask the Supreme Court to review *Patton*.[18]

Marshall was normally reluctant to risk the NAACP's prestige and credibility representing a clearly guilty defendant, and for good reason. As the administrator of the LDF, Marshall had to take into consideration political and economic factors when selecting cases. He could not risk losing the sympathy of those inclined to support the NAACP's efforts by appearing to help career criminals or violent offenders circumvent the law through what some would consider legal technicalities. In 1944, he issued a policy statement entitled "Outline of Procedures for Legal Cases" in which he laid out guidelines for his staff to follow in proceeding with criminal cases. Marshall made clear that the Legal Defense Fund would assist only those defendants it deemed innocent. But in the Patton case, Marshall made an exception and Williams got the green light. Persuading the Supreme Court to hear a case is a long shot—the court rejects about 95 percent of petitions. Williams knew he had to be at his very best to even get the justices to listen.

In crafting his brief to the Court, Williams cited witnesses, none of them sympathetic to Patton, who testified that since 1916 no Black had ever served on a Lauderdale County jury. He presented tax rolls revealing that there were several hundred qualified Black electors who could have served and that their "existence was common knowledge."[19] Williams offered testimony garnered from congressional hearings held in 1946 to show that there was "a state-wide condition of intimidation by state officers of large blocks of negroes [sic] who attempted to register and to vote."[20] On the strength of Williams's brief, the Court agreed to hear the case.

Although Williams wrote the *Patton* brief and likely knew the case better than anyone, including Marshall, he lacked the requisite experience to appear before the Supreme Court. Still, even if he met the criteria, Williams would not have been permitted to present the case to the justices. Marshall reserved the privilege of arguing before the highest court in the land to himself, his Howard University mentors, Charles Houston and Williams Hastie, and outside attorneys who were recruited by the NAACP for just that purpose. Among this group were Spottswood William Robinson III from Virginia, Loren Miller from California, William Robert Ming Jr. from Chicago, and Frank Reeves from Washington, DC. Brilliant lawyers all, these were men who were friends in private practice or academia, and in whom Marshall placed great trust. Williams had not yet earned that level of respect and was not permitted to argue *Patton*, but the underlying legal work was his.

On December 8, 1947, the Supreme Court handed Marshall, and by extension Williams, a unanimous decision written by Justice Hugo Black, a onetime Klansman who observed in *Patton* that although there were 12,541 "adult Negroes" in a county of 34,821 adults there had not been a Black juror in at least thirty years. The *Patton* decision was a vital step toward *Batson*, even though the latter case would not be decided for another forty years, when Marshall was on the Supreme Court. But its reasoning cleared the way for *Batson*: "When a jury selection plan, whatever it is, operates in such way as always to result in the complete and long-continued exclusion of any representative at all from a large group of negroes or any other racial groups, indictments and verdicts returned against them by juries thus selected cannot stand."[21]

From Patton's point of view, despite the important constitutional issues reaffirmed in his case, the Supreme Court's findings only postponed the inevitable. His case was remanded to the Circuit Court of Lauderdale County, where, in May 1949, he was again found guilty of murder and sentenced to death. His appeal to the state court in Mississippi was also denied a second time. Several months later, Williams asked the Supreme Court to review the second conviction, but the court turned him down on jurisdictional grounds. On January 12, 1950, Patton died in the electric chair.

Patton was a watershed moment for Williams, who had just turned thirty. Although he had not argued the case and was not even publicly acknowledged. Williams received only internal, not public, recognition for his work: The opinion credits Marshall only for arguing the case and states, "with him on the brief was Andrew Weinberger." Yet, Williams had played a vital role in a major Supreme Court decision. Relatively few attorneys ever have that experience. Further, Marshall was impressed with Williams's painstaking research and ability to craft a brief that ultimately won over every judge on the highest court in the land. Marshall, although frequently at odds with his underling, described Williams as "the nation's leading expert on the question of systematic exclusion of Negroes from juries."[22]

Williams was eager for his chance to argue before the Supreme Court. But the cases with the best constitutional issues often involved guilty defendants, and while Marshall had relented in *Patton*, he still did not want the LDF defending murderers and rapists. The Indiana case of Robert Austin Watts, a vicious murderer, presented the NAACP with a dilemma.

Watts, a Black man with a long record of violent sexual attacks on women, was working as a municipal truck driver while out on bond. He would gain access to his victims by parking his city-owned vehicle in the driveway, pretending to be lost, and asking permission to use the phone. Once inside, he would assault the woman. True to form, on November 10, 1947, Watts attacked Nancy Stout with a butcher knife. She managed to elude his grasp and ran screaming to a neighbor's house. Undeterred, Watts managed to find another victim, Mary Lois Burney, whose body was found by her husband when he returned from work.

The evidence against Watts was overwhelming. The blood of the victim was on his clothes, his fingerprints were found both inside the Stout and Burney homes, and particles from the Burneys' driveway were embedded in the wheels of his truck.[23] Ms. Stout also identified him as her attacker. When questioned further by police, Watts admitted to the murder of yet another woman in an adjacent neighborhood.[24] He also revealed the whereabouts of the gun used in the Burney shooting.[25] After a thirteen-day trial, Watts was convicted and sentenced to death. Both the conviction and death sentence were upheld in the Indiana appellate courts.

Two court-appointed attorneys, desperate to save their client's life, approached the LDF, arguing that Watts had been denied his constitutional right to a fair trial before a jury of his peers because the deck was stacked: Blacks were kept off the grand jury that indicted him, and the confession came after the defendant was isolated and threatened. Williams was intrigued by the constitutional issues and wrote to one of Watts's trial lawyers seeking more information. He learned of a rigged grand jury process and a confession that resulted from a fifty-two-hour interrogation to which Watts was subjected without legal representation.[26]

Williams wanted to take the case. From his perspective, Watts's clear-cut guilt was beside the point: if not stopped, Williams argued, prosecutors would continue to rig juries and police would continue to coerce confessions, and at least some totally innocent people would find themselves on death row.[27] But the Indianapolis branch of the NAACP did not want to be associated with the case, and Marshall opposed "spending hard-earned dollars of poor Negroes to defend a vicious murderer and rapist."[28] Williams was furious: "Since when are you the judge and jury?" Marshall may not have been "judge and jury," but he was Williams's boss.

A short time later and unrelated to the argument over Watts, Marshall convened one of the weekend meetings he liked to hold when several of his out-of-state lawyer buddies were in town. Usually, the venue was a midtown Manhattan hotel room where, amidst clouds of tobacco smoke, consultants and staff could mull over legal theory, current cases, and whatever else was on their minds. Williams saw an opportunity to maneuver and cornered Robert Ming and Loren Miller, two of Marshall's most respected advisors.

"Bob," Williams said, pretending to speak hypothetically to Ming, "do you think we should take a case to the United States Supreme Court where the question of systematic exclusion of the jury is clear and the question of the use of a coerced confession is equally clear?"

"Of course," Ming replied emphatically. Miller added his own affirmative response, "Hell, yes!" Marshall, feeling boxed in, relented, but not before firing a parting shot at his brash young assistant: "We'll take the case and let you make a fool of yourself."

Williams and Robert Carter (who knew each other as members of the Gaylords social group at Riverton) drafted a petition seeking certiorari on behalf of Watts. In their brief they cited *Patton v. Mississippi* to argue the question of illegal jury selection; witnesses had testified at the trial level that while many qualified Blacks resided in Marion County, none had served on juries in the past 30 years. Regarding the question of coerced confession, they relied on a precedent established in *Haley v. Ohio* (1948) in which the Supreme Court reversed a conviction based upon a confession obtained not from physical duress but from the holding of a defendant without access to family or counsel.[29] On February 1949, the US Supreme Court agreed to hear the Watts case.

Williams felt that he had earned the right to argue Watts; Marshall, however, did not. None of his assistants had ever appeared before the Supreme Court and he saw no reason to change this policy. After turning Williams down, Marshall approached several lawyers, including an obscure Black attorney from Indianapolis, and the white lawyer who had lost the Watts case at the state level. Both declined. Williams, supremely confident in his own abilities, was angered by the fact that Marshall was seeking outsiders, especially outsiders who were not particularly distinguished.

While Williams nursed his bruised ego, Carter incessantly nagged Marshall. Carter knew Williams had spent many tedious hours on the case and knew it better than anyone; he thought his friend should argue the case, and he told Marshall so.[30] Marshall suggested that if anyone earned the right to argue the case, it was Carter, who had more seniority than Williams. "I don't mind wait-ing," Carter said. "My chance will come soon enough."[31] Marshall, worn down, decided to give Williams his chance but neglected to tell him until two days before oral argument: "Frank, get ready to argue the Watts case on Monday."[32]

Giving a young attorney only two days to prepare for an intellectual fencing match with nine of the most brilliant legal minds in the nation was prepos-terous. Equally preposterous was Marshall deciding that he, not Williams, would argue the jury issue—the issue Williams was better equipped than anyone, including Marshall, to handle. Instead, Williams would deal with the question of the allegedly coerced confession. Williams was stunned, but the maneuver—whatever Marshall's motivation—would work brilliantly in Franklin's favor.

During oral argument, legendary Justice Felix Frankfurter was so impressed with Williams that he sent a note to his clerk, William Coleman, the first Black law clerk at the high court, urging him to come in the courtroom and observe Franklin at work. "Bill, take a few minutes off to listen to Franklin Williams. Do you know him?" Coleman replied on a Supreme Court memo, "He is now Mr. Marshall's assistant. . . . I think he studied law at Howard and comes very highly recommended." Frankfurter crossed out Howard, wrote "Fordham," and added "Excellent!!"[33] Franklin would not learn of the exchange for many years. The Supreme Court, in a 4–3 decision, overturned Watts's conviction solely on the issue that Williams argued (coercion), without even addressing the jury issue that Marshall argued (jury stacking): "To turn the detention of an accused into a process of wrenching from him evidence which could not be extorted in open court with all its safeguards, is so grave an abuse of the power of arrest as to offend the procedural stands of due process," Justice Frankfurter wrote for the majority."[34]

The Court sent the case back to Indiana for a retrial, barring the prosecution from using the confession. Regardless, Watts was convicted again. At that point, with the errors of the first trial corrected in the second, there was nothing left for the NAACP. Watts died in the electric chair on January 16, 1951, after a hearty last meal of fried chicken, fried potatoes, brussels sprouts, and a straw-berry sundae.[35] The Watts case was an important milestone toward ending the widespread and unconstitutional use in courts of confessions obtained through emotional duress.

For Williams, the case was a personal triumph: he was the first LDF special counsel ever to argue and win a case before the Supreme Court. He could no longer be held back by Marshall and handled several high-profile cases in 1949. However, neither he nor the LDF had a particularly good year.

Franklin Williams, at the far right and wearing a bow tie, joins Thurgood Marshall (*center*) in arguing *Watts v. Indiana* at the US Supreme Court on June 27, 1949. Standing next to Marshall in this photograph (*third from the left*) was litigator Robert L. Carter, who lobbied Marshall to allow Williams to argue the case, even though it cost him his first opportunity to argue before the Supreme Court. (Enid Gort collection)

In *Taylor v. Dennis* (1949), the US Supreme Court denied Williams's request for a retrial in a rape case in which the victim had originally identified a different man, despite photographs of the imprisoned defendant showing marks of abuse.[36] In *Miller v. Wigging* (1949), the Justices refused to hear the case of a developmentally disabled Black man charged with armed robbery. The defendant claimed authorities beat a confession out of him and never informed him of his right to counsel.[37] A petition for certiorari was also denied in *Dessaure v. New York* (1949).[38] In that case, the defense charged Nassau County, New York, with systematically excluding Blacks from its juries. A great deal of publicity surrounded the case, not because of the nature of the crime, which was simple assault, but because of the involvement of William Kunstler, the flamboyant and confrontational left-wing lawyer whom Williams disliked both for his politics and his personality. Kunstler was bombastic in and out of court; Williams thought a legal argument should more resemble a sober, scholarly discussion than a pyrotechnic performance.

Williams was involved in nearly every major LDF case in 1949, one a novel matter in which the NAACP sued for damages on behalf of a woman whose husband had been lynched.[39] Although South Carolina law specifically made counties liable for damages if they failed to protect a person in custody from being lynched—while at the same time having no law that specifically outlawed lynching—no one had ever brought such an action before.

The basic facts of the case are straightforward. On February 16, 1947, Willie Earle was arrested, charged with the stabbing death of a white cab driver, and imprisoned in the Pickens County jail. The next morning, a mob of thirty-one men, most of them cab drivers, stormed the building and abducted the prisoner to Greenville County, where they lynched him. All of the defendants, including the twenty-six who admitted being part of the mob, were quickly acquitted by an all-white jury.

Two years later, Earle's wife sued both counties under an 1895 provision in the state constitution assessing financial responsibility for a lynching. A trial court dismissed the claim against Pickens County and Greenville County argued that since the actual kidnapping had occurred in Pickens, the murder in Greenville was technically not a lynching. Harold Boulware, a local NAACP lawyer who would later earn his place in history representing Black children in an important segregation case, *Briggs v. Elliott* (1952),[40] was the lead attorney. Williams was brought in to research and raise every cognizable constitutional issue. They won a $3,000 settlement for Mrs. Earle, but far more important, as a result of the negative publicity, Willie Earle's lynching was the last recorded in South Carolina.[41]

Marshall next assigned Williams to the first of a series of cases involving the right to play golf. While golf, in the context of lynchings, may seem trivial, both Marshall and Williams were eager to challenge any form of Jim Crow segregation. The NAACP's goal was to eradicate segregation and use the rule of law to achieve full integration in all societal enterprises—schools, restaurants, buses, and, yes, golf courses and sporting venues.

The golf case began when P. O. Sweeney, a Black dentist from Louisville, Kentucky, was turned away from a public golf course. Sweeney, a fine golfer and president of the Louisville branch of the NAACP, was infuriated, and further outraged that he was barred by race from fishing in the lake, attending concerts in the amphitheater, or using other municipal recreation facilities that he was supporting with his tax dollars. He decided to sue. Williams was sent in as part of the legal team.[42]

The court immediately dismissed the action involving the amphitheater, finding that even though the facility was public property, a private association produced the shows and could discriminate if it so chose. Furious over the judge's ruling, Williams criticized the court's result-oriented decision and attempt to evade the core issue: "There is only one issue," Williams said. "Facilities are available to whites that are not available to Negroes."[43] Still, the legal team pressed on with what remained of the case, and lost on every ground. The Kentucky Court of Appeals said in *Sweeney v. Louisville* (1949) that "to grant the relief which the plaintiff seeks would compel persons to associate with colored persons whether it were to their pleasure or not."[44]

Neither Sweeney nor the NAACP was willing to let it go and appealed to the Kentucky courts, where, as expected, they lost. But by exhausting their state court remedies, the NAACP now had an avenue to federal court and brought an action in the US District Court. By the time the appeal was heard in 1951, Williams had moved on from the LDF, so Robert Carter took over. Carter picked up where Williams left off and won an incremental but important victory against segregation when US District Judge Roy M. Shelbourne ordered Louisville to either open its courses to everyone or build separate golf courses for its Black residents. The result was that the golf course was integrated because the city couldn't afford to build a separate course for its Black population.

By the late 1940s, the NAACP was pushing hard on school desegregation, with the LDF sensing that the climate in the federal courts was slowly but surely growing warmer toward attempts to purge Jim Crow from the public school system, if not the rest of society. One of Williams's cases, out of Kansas, was among the earliest school desegregation cases.

Kansas had a particularly convoluted racial history. The trouble began in the late 1800s when free-soilers defeated pro-slavery forces in the struggle for statehood, but the latter remained firmly entrenched. Consequently, over the years the Kansas schools were alternatively segregated and integrated, depending on the whims of various state legislatures and a succession of superintendents of public education. By the 1940s, an unofficial détente largely integrated high schools and colleges, but left the primary schools segregated, despite the fact that Kansas law forbade such a practice.[45]

Two grammar schools existed in the tiny suburban town of Merriam, Kansas—one for whites, one for Blacks—and those schools had been segregated since the early 1900s. The segregated schools were such a part of the local cultural fabric that even Black parents did not challenge the status quo until 1947, when the school district decided to build a nice, new school for the white kids and pay for it with a $90,000 bond issue that would tax both Black and white parents. Previously, the differences between the Black school and the white school were relatively minimal. But the shiny new South Park School for whites featured the latest comforts, such as indoor lavatories, as well as new equipment, a kindergarten, a music room, and a cafeteria.

On the other hand, the two-room Walker School for Black kids had a dirt playground with broken equipment, outdoor privies, and no cafeteria, and its ancient construction and run-down condition made it a fire hazard. When the Black parents complained, the school district's accommodation was to install a "Stop" sign outside to enhance safety, along with a brand-new mailbox.[46]

In May 1948, the Black parents of Merriam attempted to enroll their children in a school the Black families were helping to pay for, South Park, and were brusquely turned away. They sued, lost in the trial court, and appealed to the Kansas Supreme Court, where they sought an order forcing the school board to admit forty-two Black children into the South Park School.[47] But the legal process moves slowly, and the parents had grown impatient by the fall of 1948 when they refused to send their children back to the deficient and dangerous Walker School. Instead, they hired instructors to teach their kids at various homes in the community, holding bake sales and other fundraisers to pay the teachers.

By the late forties, school desegregation had become a signature priority for the LDF, although the focus was on graduate rather than elementary education. Cases such as *Sipuel v. Board of Regents, Sweatt v. Painter,* and *McLaurin v. Oklahoma State Regents for Higher Education,* in which Blacks had been denied admittance to universities in Oklahoma and Texas, were making their way to the Supreme Court.[48]

Williams was peripherally involved in all of those cases, as were all the LDF attorneys, but he had no special expertise in school desegregation cases. Regardless, Marshall assigned Williams the Merriam cases and sent him to Topeka to assist a local Black attorney, Elisha Scott Sr., with arguments before the Kansas Supreme Court. Scott was a character, an eccentric and frequently inebriated but very competent attorney who quoted scripture and sometimes dropped to his knees in the courtroom, begging for the court to recognize the basic human rights of his clients.[49]

When the case was argued on April 5, parents from Merriam traveled nearly a hundred miles as a show of support. The school board's case relied on the facially ridiculous assertion that race had nothing to do with the segregation. It contended, presumably with a straight face, that the disparity was simply a reflection of residence patterns and racially neutral zoning rules. Williams set the record straight for the judges: "Until May 1948, there had been no such thing as 'zoning lines.' White students walked beyond the Walker School to reach their own. [Now] zoning lines meander up streets and down alleys, zigzagging in such a way as to include every Negro home with school-aged children in the Walker District."[50]

Williams convinced the court, which found that the school board had "for generations" violated Kansas law by segregating pupils on racial grounds and that the newly created district lines had "no reasonable basis." The Court ordered that "the colored pupils and all pupils in District No. 90 must be permitted to attend the South Park District School beginning with the school year 1949–1950."[51]

The Black spectators who had watched Franklin Williams in action were impressed and proud. He was quick on his feet. He spoke with confidence and treated adversaries with the professional respect that he was denied. Yet, when necessary, he could respond with biting irony or dismissive body language to let racist judges and court officers know that he would not be intimidated or demeaned. His natural competitiveness—Franklin hated to lose at anything, whether it was a poker game, a tennis match, or a legal argument—was an asset. When Williams was in the courtroom, he gave the impression that he was in charge.[52]

Within the confines of the Legal Defense Fund staff, Williams was acknowledged as a creative thinker with a razor-sharp analytical mind, an attorney with a remarkable memory who could instantly link the facts of a case to precedents from earlier ones without resorting to notes or digging through stacks of books and journals. He dictated reports, articles for publication, and letters that needed little or no editing. Leaning back in his swivel chair, he would look up at the ceiling and let his words flow, while his secretary struggled to keep up with his pace. Rarely did he strain for a word, fail to complete a thought, or lose sight of his argument. His speeches and articles displayed a clear-headed, pragmatic but principled approach. For example, in the April 10, 1948, issue of *Black Dispatch*, he illustrated the economic folly and stupidity of maintaining parallel, segregated school systems:

> No state in the union is able to support dual schools, but the south, at the bottom of the economic scale, holds segregation its accepted method of keeping the Negro in his place, as paramount to even a good education for its own white children. . . . Southern Negroes have had their honest proportion of federal, state, county and municipal funds stolen from them. But the time is here to talk back through legal battles to obtain equal opportunities all along the line.[53]

In a strict sense, Williams was not a legal "scholar." He did not like to write and was not particularly good at it. The silver tongue that awed judges in court and tormented secretaries trying to keep up with his rapid-fire delivery was accompanied by an oddly leaden writing style. Williams was a great legal orator, although not a great legal writer.

Objectively, Franklin Williams as an attorney was not in the stratosphere of the likes of the legends of civil rights litigation—Thurgood Marshall, Robert Carter, Constance Baker Motley, and Jack Greenberg. Still, he was a highly regarded and highly successful civil rights litigator in what were the halcyon days of the LDF. He was part of a historic era and part of a historic team that passionately fought for justice in the courts—for integration, voting rights, and access to housing and employment.

Yet Franklin Williams was a goal-oriented rather than process-oriented man; for him, the law was a tool, a means to an end. While he had the ability, he lacked the patience or interest to ponder or debate abstract principles of law. His interest in the law was concrete, not abstract, and with his natural impatience he wanted results sooner than later, which is rarely how civil rights law evolves. Williams had little tolerance for Marshall's incrementalism, and increasingly Marshall has little patience for Williams.

Peggy Cooper Davis, a legal scholar at New York University Law School, former LDF lawyer, and former judge, suspects that Marshall and Williams had far more in common than either might admit, but the areas where they differed were perhaps fatal to their relationship.

> From what I know about the two men, I would suspect that their actual differences were not so great, but the conversations might have been very exciting and very intense. It certainly was Thurgood Marshall's strategy to be very mindful of what was achievable with the Supreme Court and to work very carefully, but very consistently and persistently within the range of what he thought was possible. Of course, his sense of what was possible changed over time. . . . I think that Thurgood Marshall did have a very keen sense of what the American people were ready for, but he also had a very crafty lawyer sense of what the Justices were ready for and what their understandings were. I think it was always a matter of playing those things against each other. He was working at lots of levels, and quite brilliantly.[54]

By the late 1940s, Williams's time as an in-the-trenches civil rights lawyer was drawing to a close. But before Williams moved on, the NAACP and Thurgood Marshall would ask him to take on a case that would become transformative, requiring Williams to risk his life and assume the role of a Black Atticus Finch. It was the most significant, and personally dangerous, case of his career, and it nearly got him lynched.

8
Legal Lynching

On the night of July 16, 1949, seventeen-year-old Norma Lee Padgett and her estranged twenty-three-year-old husband, Willie Haven Padgett, went out dancing in Clermont, Florida. What happened next was either the brutal gang rape of a white girl by four "niggers," as they were described in court by the "victim"—or, as the evidence overwhelming suggests, the racist persecution of four innocent young Black men in the Jim Crow South.[1]

Seventy years later, much remains unclear about what history refers to as the Groveland case. But what is plain is that sadistic deputies tortured the suspects to elicit confessions, a sheriff took two of the accused out on a desolate road and shot them, a bloodthirsty mob of Klansmen instigated open warfare against the Black community, the defense was virtually handcuffed and prevented from effectively advocating for the defendants, the trial was flawed to the extent that the convictions were overturned by the US Supreme Court, and all four were posthumously exonerated in 2017 and officially pardoned in 2019. And Franklin Williams was chased by a lynch mob after the sheriff vowed during the trial that "I'm gonna get that nigger lawyer." He barely escaped a high-speed chase out of town with a lynch mob on his tail.[2]

The Groveland Case began in a rural inland town in central Florida, roughly thirty miles west of Orlando. Multiple sources generally agree on the following mix of verified fact and unverified allegations.[3]

Norma Lee and Willie had a stormy marriage—her kin threw him out after he inflicted one too many beatings and threatened him with severe consequences if he did it again—but decided to go to a Saturday night dance together in Clermont. By various accounts, Willie was liquored up, and maybe they both were. Around 1:30 on Sunday morning, the couple claim, they were on their way home when their car stalled on Florida State Road 50 near Groveland. The Padgetts were stranded in an orange grove when a car carrying four Black men stopped to help them. For fifteen minutes the men chatted (Willie never could recall what they talked about) while trying to start the car when suddenly the Black men overpowered Willie, knocked him unconscious and absconded with his wife, bringing her to a secluded location and taking turns raping her in the backseat at gunpoint before abandoning her in the groves. Norma would claim that she could clearly see her assailants by the light of the dashboard.

According to Willie Padgett, once he regained consciousness a driver passing by agreed to push his car, finally starting it. Then Willie drove to a service station in neighboring Leesburg and called the sheriff's office. Moments later, Deputy Sheriff James L. Yates arrived, accompanied by another officer.[4] They drove around the area with Willie in the car, looking for the culprits. Willie spotted a 1942 Mercury sedan parked in front of the home of Henry Shepherd and identified it as the vehicle used by the men who attacked him and snatched his bride.

Around the same time, Norma walked out of the groves to an intersection where Lawrence Burtoft saw her standing nonchalantly near his father's Oka-humpka restaurant.[5] Inviting her to join him inside, Norma told Burtoft over coffee that four Black men had hit her husband over the head and kidnapped her, but that they had let her out of their car, unharmed. She did not mention being raped and said she just wanted to find her husband.[6] After driving a short while, they spotted Willie. Burtoft found it peculiar "that they didn't seem overly excited or relieved to see each other."[7]

Meanwhile, Deputy Yates and other officers convinced themselves that Sammie Shepherd was one of the rapists and brought him to a desolate area, where he was beaten and ordered to reveal the identity of the three men he was supposedly with the night before. But Shepherd revealed only one name, that of his friend Walter Irvin. With Shepherd in the car, police went to Irvin's house, where the young man was getting ready for work, and took him into custody. Shepherd and Irvin insisted they had gone to the movies together the night before and later ended up at a bar. Evidence which the defense was basically precluded from developing indicates the young men were nowhere near the scene of the "crime."[8] But Willie Padgett was adamant that Shepherd and Irvin were two of the four men who had beaten him the night before, and that was good enough for Yates.

Shepherd and Irvin were both brought to a desolate road and tortured by police, who were eager to obtain the names of the other two culprits. They disclosed nothing, probably because they had nothing to disclose. The young veterans were handcuffed together and deputies were preparing to set them on fire when a girl on a horse happened on the scene, ruining the plan by her being an accidental witness.[9] They brought the suspects to the county jail at Tavares where they could torture them in the privacy of their own dungeon.

At the jail, Irvin was dragged into the basement and chained to an overhead pipe so that his feet barely reached the floor. He was pummeled with fists, boots, and clubs but refused to confess to the rape. After Irvin was dragged back to the cell unconscious, Shepherd was brought to the basement. Seeing the condition of his friend, he knew what was in store. Shepherd, who had already undergone two prior beatings that day—one when he was first interrogated and another when deputies had him and Irvin in the woods—couldn't take any more. He finally put an end to the torture by confessing that he raped the girl.

Meanwhile, police were still looking for the final two suspects.

Charles Greenlee was a sixteen-year-old runaway from Gainesville who had left home after his younger sister was run over by a freight train and his mother's grief was more than he could handle. Greenlee had hitchhiked to the Groveland area with a friend, Ernest Thomas, a professional gambler who may have been interested in cutting into the local action, run in part by the sheriff.[10] Thomas went off to pick up some clean clothes and left his friend with an old and unloaded pistol. Charles encountered a night watchman. Since the youth was Black, unfamiliar, and armed—and therefore suspicious—the watchman summoned police. The police decided to hold Greenlee overnight in case there were any crimes reported for which he might be held responsible. Greenlee became suspect number three.

Willie and Norma were brought in to identify Greenlee. Willie was insistent that he was not one of the attackers; Norma was ambivalent. In any case, Charles was brought to the jail at Tavares and dragged to the basement for the same treatment as Irvin and Shepherd. Like Shepherd, he confessed and gave up the name of the youth he had been with the night before, Ernest Thomas. Thomas had heard of the incident and his friend's arrest and fled the area. On Monday, July 18, Lakeland County Sheriff Willis Virgil McCall, a Klansman well familiar to the NAACP, returned from an Elks Convention in Ohio to find his community in turmoil.

Groveland, a hardscrabble sharecropper town of a thousand residents, had a well-deserved reputation for hostility to Blacks, especially returning soldiers under the impression that fighting for their country somehow made them equal to whites. Within that sharecropper community was a large concentration of Blacks who worked for grove owners in the all-white neighboring town of Mascotte, earning fifteen cents a day.[11] Sharecropping had emerged as de facto slavery after emancipation and basically replaced it with peonage. The new economy was an "interlude between bondage and freedom" as the "peons" who left without satisfying a debt could be forcibly returned to service.[12]

The two groups—poor southern whites, barely able to scratch out a living and feeling trapped at the lowest rung of their highly stratified society, and even poorer Blacks—coexisted in a region of plentiful land, fertile soil, and dependable work year after year. That symbiotic relationship worked, more or less, for decades, but it began to unravel as Black veterans returned from World War II wiser and more confident and less willing to accept the status quo. As Black growers began to prosper on their own, without a need to sharecrop or pick oranges for white farmers,[13] lower-class whites bitterly resented that "lowly" Blacks were as or more prosperous than they were. The Shepherd family drew particular wrath from the white community since Sam's father, Henry, owned not only his own house but also a small grove.[14]

Henry Shepherd had cleared thirty acres of woods near Groveland, and his grove and home were the envy of many poor whites—including, quite probably, the Padgetts.[15] He was resented, too, quite likely, by the likes of Willis McCall. As the fully ripened fruit fell to the ground and rotted because fewer Blacks were willing to pick it for fifteen cents a day, the sight of hardworking Blacks harvesting their own crops infuriated their white neighbors. They drove their cows onto Black farmers' fields, ruining the crops and tearing down their fences. And they elected one of their own, McCall, to keep the "uppity niggers" in their place.

McCall, a forty-year-old Lake County native, had served as the region's fruit inspector until 1944, when his network of supporters—growers from across the county—urged him to enter law enforcement, in part to protect their interests from Negro infringement.[16] Once in office, he crushed labor union and civil rights organizers, labeling them godless communists and sympathizers intent on riling up the "niggers" and subverting the southern way of life.[17] A tall man with fleshy jowls, a long pointed nose, and dark, greasy hair, McCall felt an obligation to suppress Blacks, reasoning that a well-timed punch, slap, or kick was necessary to get the "nigra's" attention.[18] McCall, a 1947 inductee into the Georgia Klan's Apopka Klavern,[19] already had a beef with Irvin and Shepherd. He had ordered them to stop wearing their military uniforms and to get back to where they belonged, working in the groves. But they wouldn't listen and dared to think there was life for them beyond the orchards. In McCall's world, that's not the way things worked, and he didn't like that kind of "nigger" challenging his view of the universe.[20]

As news of the "crime" and alleged confessions spread, an angry mob of vigilantes, including Willie Padgett and Norma's father, Coy Tyson, appeared at the jail, demanding that the sheriff turn over the prisoners for a proper lynching. McCall told them, falsely, that the suspects had been transferred to the state prison at Raiford (Irvin and Shepherd were in the process of being moved but were still on the premises), one hundred miles away. "We have got to handle these things in a legal manner," McCall told the mob.[21] "These Negroes are going to be held and tried in court. . . . Let justice be done. Folks, you elected me sheriff, and my job is to uphold the laws of Florida and the United States and to protect my prisoners. This is a crucial moment that could cause a crisis here and throughout the state. Let's let the law handle this calmly." The *Orlando Sentinel Star* reported that many citizens had adopted a hands-off attitude: "We will wait and see what the law does, and if the law doesn't do the right [thing] then we will do it."[22]

But many were not so patient. With its thirst for blood unsatisfied, the mob turned its anger toward the entire Black community, launching war on Stuckey's Still, the African American section of Groveland. Six hundred Klansmen and assorted hangers-on rumbled through the community, firing their rifles and shotguns indiscriminately and lobbing firebombs at the homes of innocent Black people. Henry Shepherd's home and the restaurant owned by the parents of Ernest Thomas were among those burned to the ground. Several prosperous Blacks who had managed to escape received clear warnings to "leave everything and get out now and stay out."[23] Among them were Joseph Maxwell, the owner of a large and profitable farm and a veteran of the D-Day landing at Normandy Beach; his brother Matthew, whose position as foreman on a large plantation infuriated many whites; and Moses Sipline, who on several occasions had the audacity to attempt to exercise his constitutional right to vote, thereby earning a reputation as "a rich and ornery nigger."[24] After two days of rioting, the governor summoned units of the National Guard and the 114th Field Artillery from Tampa to quell the violence.

Simultaneously, police were on the trail of Ernest Thomas and tracked him to the swamps in Madison County, about two hundred miles northwest of Groveland. McCall had a special interest in Thomas, whom he suspected of attempting to horn in on a highly profitable gambling ring that the sheriff operated in secret partnership with Henry Singleton, a Black businessman regarded among his community as an Uncle Tom.[25] The "boleta," a numbers game that generated a fortune in illicit profits, and the prospect of losing revenue to a potential interloper made the hunt for Thomas a high priority.[26]

McCall pulled together a posse of a thousand lawmen from three counties, along with assorted bloodhounds, to scour the swamps in search of Thomas. Nine days into the hunt, the posse found Thomas asleep under a tree and riddled him with hundreds of bullets.[27] A coroner's jury investigated, but when vigilantes testified that Thomas pulled a gun on them, they concluded the executioners had no choice but to kill their prey in self-defense.[28]

While Groveland was coming apart at the racial seams, Franklin Williams was 1,100 miles away, sweltering at his desk in New York City and uncharacteristically bored. It was July, and everyone else was either on vacation or out of the office. Although Williams frequently complained about the noisy and overcrowded office he shared with Constance Baker Motley and Annette Peyser,[29] in truth he did not like being alone.

When the telephone rang, Williams leaped for it and heard the atypically frantic voice of Harry Tyson Moore, executive secretary of the Florida State Conference of the NAACP. Williams knew that Moore was not easily frazzled and not one to panic. A battle-scarred veteran of the civil rights movement who had lost his teaching job, as had his wife, for urging Blacks to register to vote and for suing to equalize teachers' pay,[30] Moore hurriedly told Williams the harrowing story of four young Black men accused of rape.[31] He noted that Klansmen from as far away as Georgia were circling the jail where the suspects were held, pillagers were burning Black homes and businesses, and Blacks were fleeing into the surrounding woodlands and swamps. He reported that some disgusted whites were risking their own safety in attempting to truck their Black neighbors to Orlando or anywhere other than Groveland, and that the American Legion Post had set up army cots, Salvation Army employees and concerned citizens of both races were putting aside social conventions to contribute food and offer words of comfort to the terrified victims, and even R. I. Williams, the acting mayor, was among the whites providing emergency relief.

Williams sprang into action and tried, unsuccessfully, to locate Thurgood Marshall. When he couldn't reach Marshall, he reached out to Roy Wilkins, then acting executive secretary of the NAACP, who immediately dispatched Williams to Florida. Before departing, Williams issued a terse, cautionary press release announcing that he was headed to Florida to investigate the Groveland case. He wanted a public record of the fact, in case he disappeared, and authorities claimed he never arrived. At the time, it was standard operating procedure; NAACP lawyers knew their lives were on the line. On Friday, July 22, 1949, Williams was met at the Orlando airport by John P. Ellis, president of the local NAACP chapter, who offered Williams a room in his home.

Ellis updated Williams on the latest goings-on, including the fact that Sheriff McCall was doing his level best to poison the jury pool by pronouncing the defendants guilty, announcing they had confessed and manipulating a pliable and corrupt press. The *Orlando Sentinel Star* was already calling for the death penalty. On the front page was a gruesome drawing of four electric chairs with straps hanging from the seats and hoods placed over the backs. Written across the seats were the words "THE SUPREME PENALTY." Above the picture was a headline that read: "NO COMPROMISES."[32] In a direct response to Williams's press release, the editorial warned, "If smart lawyers or agents of different organizations seek to hamper justice through the employment of legal technicalities, they may bring suffering to many innocent Negroes."[33]

Williams first met Irvin, Shepherd, and Greenlee at the Raiford prison two weeks after their arrest. He was horrified at the story they told and flabbergasted at their appearance. Irvin's story chilled Williams to the bone:

> They handcuffed me, over a pipe, so that my feet could not touch the floor, then they started beating me again with a rubber hose. I was bleeding all the time around my head. They kept saying that I was the one that picked the girl up last night and said they would beat me until I told them I was the one. I don't know how long this went on, but in my estimation, it was more than five minutes. I don't remember very well because I was very dizzy. They hit me in my nose with their fist and beat me across my back and chest and they beat me all over.[34]

When that didn't elicit a confession, Irvin endured a second round of beatings in the basement, with one deputy repeatedly "kick(ing) me in the balls."[35] Still, Irvin would not confess. Shepherd and Greenlee, who did succumb, told strikingly similar stories about what occurred in the courthouse basement. What's more, some fifteen days after their arrest, the young men sported ugly bruises and scars, their hair was matted with blood, and they were in the same blood-stained clothes they wore when they left McCall's jail. According to Williams, "All three had lash scars on their bodies and cuts on their heads and wrists, inflicted when they were hung with handcuffs from the ceiling pipe. The sole of Greenlee's left foot was cut with glass and Shepherd had three broken teeth and a possibly fractured jaw."[36]

Williams wanted independent medical reviews, but it took several days to find a physician and dentist to examine the prisoners. When they finally were seen by a doctor more than three weeks after the beating, their injuries were still raw. Nelson Spaulding, a physician from Jacksonville who examined the three men twenty-two days after the beatings, stated in his report: "Those boys were subjected to tortures capable only by Nazis."[37]

The more Williams learned, the more he was convinced of the young men's innocence and the more intent he was to help them. But that would require an investigation and an adequate defense at trial, both of which cost money. Williams spent the coming weeks attempting to collect evidence and organizing the defense while simultaneously trying to raise money; unlike the prosecution, he did not have a team of investigators at his disposal. Racing around the state with Horace Hill, a Howard University Law School graduate who had volunteered his help and his black Chevrolet, Williams spoke at rallies, protest meetings, and church services to large and small crowds, eager for every last dollar to fund a suitable defense. He picked up $500 from a man who happened to be a housemate at Pinky Price's, a rooming house in Orlando that catered to Blacks: former heavyweight champion Joe Louis, the "Brown Bomber" of yesteryear. Louis, down on his luck, past his prime, and resigned to taking whatever local exhibition fights he could, was hardly in a position to donate $500—the equivalent of more than $5,000 as of 2022—to the cause.

Coincidentally, Louis and Williams had become the unlikeliest of friends during the Isaac Woodard matter a couple years earlier, when the veteran was blinded by the Batesburg, South Carolina, sheriff. Williams was an urbane, well-educated, quick-thinking, silver-tongued northern lawyer; Louis was the undereducated sharecropper's son from Alabama who was more persuasive with his fists than his voice. Yet, they shared an innate passion for justice. Louis had been a generous supporter of the NAACP with his time and money. But more important, Louis had a cache of prestige and credibility left from his glory years. In 1938 at Yankee Stadium, Louis was the "American" fighter, not the "Negro" fighter, who knocked out Hitler's symbol of white, German supremacy, Max Schmeling, in just over two minutes. He brought a certain gravitas to the fundraising effort. Ultimately, Williams raised $4,600 (roughly $50,000 today).[38]

But money was less than half the problem. The bigger problem was finding a competent Florida attorney to take the case. Horace Hill, who had not yet been admitted to the Bar, drove Williams from city to city, from one law office to the next, looking, begging, for someone to defend Shepherd, Irvin, and Greenlee. Williams knew of two Black lawyers in Florida, but neither was a viable choice: L. E. Thomas in Miami was in poor health and could not travel, and William Fordham in Tampa, a member of the Bar for only three months, was far too inexperienced.[39]

In Daytona Beach, a prominent white criminal defense lawyer admitted that he was just too scared to take the case.[40] "Surely you realize that those corn-eating crackers would just as soon shoot me as they would you with one of their high-powered rifles," he told Williams.[41] In Miami, a well-known attorney—a labor lawyer, not a criminal defense attorney—assured Williams that he could put aside his fears for $25,000 payable before the trial, an astronomical sum that the NAACP could never raise. An attorney in Inverness said he would do it for $10,000, an amount that the NAACP might be able to solicit.[42] But before Williams could get Marshall's consent, the attorney backed out on the grounds that his wife would not allow him to participate in a rape case where the victim was white and the defendants Black. "My wife is the epitome of the flower of southern womanhood, so I cannot take this case," he explained.[43]

Spessard Holland Jr., a young white attorney in Vero Beach, listened intently as Williams read the statements of the three Groveland youths and the report of the doctor who examined them at Raiford.[44] As Williams spoke, he thought he detected genuine sympathy on Holland's part for the three men, so he agreed to remain until the following day to allow Holland time to make his decision. This was a hardship for Williams and Hill because an unscheduled stay in an unfamiliar place posed special problems for Black travelers, who could seldom find suitable hotels willing to accommodate them. Williams could usually rely on the hospitality of some local NAACP member, but he resented the Jim Crow restrictions that kept Blacks and whites separate and forced him to impose on strangers. Nevertheless, he agreed to remain overnight so he could meet with Holland in the morning. The next day, Holland dejectedly turned him down. The attorney was the son of Spessard Holland Sr., a former Florida governor who was planning to run for the US Senate. His son wanted desperately to defend the accused men but could not be the cause of his father's defeat.

Growing more desperate, Williams returned to Groveland to offer the case to Harry Gaylord, the court-appointed attorney for the Groveland defendants. But Gaylord told Williams that he would do no more than go through the motions and perform his duty as required by law. In other words, he wouldn't do anything more than the bare minimum; he would be nothing more than a cardboard cutout, not a real lawyer. He refused to even ask for a change of venue when he had to know that Shepherd, Irvin, and Greenlee couldn't possibly get a fair trial in a community where they were prejudged by the press and a citizenry that attempted to lynch them.[45]

Time was running out. Eleven lawyers had already turned Williams down, and unless motions were filed by August 24, Gaylord or another uninterested court-appointed attorney would take charge of the case.[46] Williams and Hill returned to Orlando in a last-ditch effort to persuade Alex Akerman Jr., a white attorney who had been one of Williams's first choices, to argue the case for the defense. Originally, Akerman had turned Williams down because of a suit he had pending against the University of Florida on behalf of several Black students who had been denied admittance. At first, he felt his clients' interests might be prejudiced if he took the Groveland case. By this time, however, Akerman realized that if he did not take the case, no one else would, and he fully appreciated the implications: If he lost the university case, some Black kids might not get to go to college, or at least that college; if he left the Groveland case to an incompetent or indifferent attorney, some Black men would likely die in the electric chair. The decision was obvious, and Akerman agreed on August 22 to take the case. Motions were due two days later.

Akerman, whose blue eyes, sandy hair, and toothy grin gave him the look of a mischievous choirboy, came from a family of distinguished lawyers and judges who had courageously stood up to racism for decades.[47] His grandfather, Amos T. Akerman, had prosecuted members of the original Ku Klux Klan during his tenure as Georgia district attorney. Later, as attorney general of the United States under President Ulysses S. Grant, the first southerner appointed to the cabinet after the Civil War, he brought more than thirty suits against Klansmen. Akerman's father, Alex Akerman Sr., who had died the previous year, was a US District Court Judge, and Akerman himself had been a municipal court judge before his election to the Florida legislature as the only Republican in state government. Williams knew that Akerman was a competent attorney, if somewhat lacking in trial experience, with a sincere passion for justice, a sound moral compass, and the backbone to stand up to the bullies in the Klan.[48]

The day after Williams convinced Akerman to take the case, the two men, accompanied by the ever dependable and endlessly patient Horace Hill, drove from Orlando to the Lake County Court House in Tavares. The five-story building with a classical facade sat near the shore of Lake Dora, a tiny jewel of sparkling blue water. They were there to discuss trial procedures with the prosecuting attorney, Jess Hunter, who maintained an office in the courthouse. Hunter was a tall, seventy-one-year-old square-faced man who nurtured an unassuming image of a country boy, a hayseed lawyer. Williams took one look at the red suspenders and shirtsleeves and quickly wrote off his opponent as a "dumb backwoods cracker."[49] In truth, Hunter was a crafty lawyer who Williams would belatedly admit was "one of the smartest sons of bitches I ever ran up against."[50]

On August 24, 1949, Williams and Akerman returned to the Tavares Court House to present pretrial motions before Judge Truman G. Futch, the circuit court judge known as the "whittling judge" for his penchant for obsessively carving cedar sticks while presiding over trials.[51] Futch stymied the defense at every juncture in the crucial pretrial stage. He refused to grant an extension to give Akerman reasonable time to prepare, rather gratuitously delaying the trial from August 29 to September 1, 1949. In the judge's mind, apparently three days was plenty of time to prepare for a capital trial, especially since Williams had been on the case for two months. Besides, the judge sarcastically noted, the defense had publicly proclaimed their clients innocent; therefore, they must already have had all the evidence they needed.[52]

Of more importance to Williams and Akerman than getting more time to prepare, however, was allowing local outrage and passion over the "crime" to subside before their clients went on trial. There was considerable legal precedent for their position. In both 1923 and 1932, the Supreme Court expressed grave concerns over public passions dictating legal proceedings.[53] One of those cases, *Moore v. Dempsey* (1923), spoke to a "trial dominated by a mob so that there is actual interference with the course of justice" and the danger that occurs when the "judge and jury were swept to the fatal end by an irresistible wave of public passion."[54]

When they couldn't get a delay, Williams and Akerman argued for a change of venue, observing that the local juror pool was hopelessly contaminated by incessant and inflammatory newspaper articles. They presented Judge Futch with a packet of articles from the three Lake County papers widely read in the community—the *Mount Dora Topic*, the *Clermont News-Topic*, and the *Groveland News-Topic*—and raised the question as to whether, in an area where Blacks had to be driven away in trucks to be assured of their safety, the defendants could be treated justly. But since a couple of locals, including a sixty-three-year-old Black dentist, testified that race relations in Lake County were just swell, Judge Futch denied the motion.[55]

Williams and Akerman next moved to quash the indictment on the grounds that Blacks had systematically been excluded from Lake County juries for the past twenty-five years—the same jury-stacking issue that Williams repeatedly raised in the courts.[56] Judge Futch merely noted that there had been a Black on the grand jury that indicted the youths, hence there was nothing with which to be concerned. Futch made it virtually impossible for the defense to find and interview potential alibi witnesses or challenge physical evidence.

On the opening day of trial, security was unusually heavy, and the third-floor courtroom was uncharacteristically full; every seat was taken, even those relegated to the gallery customarily reserved for Blacks. Judge Futch made clear that he would brook no disruptions or distractions from "agitators or agents . . . sent in to purposely start trouble . . . . [and give] critics of the south . . . something to base [their] criticism upon."[57] To forestall that possibility, he prohibited any "bag, basket, bottle, jar, bucket," or other such items in the courthouse, and required inspection of "crutches, canes, walking sticks, and any other aids to locomotion."[58] Signs were posted admonishing: "No Weapons are Allowed in the Courtroom."[59]

The all-important process of jury selection consumed the first morning, with the defense hamstrung since they were allowed to exclude only those prospective jurors unwilling to agree that "Negro lawyers should have the same rights in Lake County courts as white lawyers, even to the cross-examination of all witnesses, including white ladies."[60] The prosecutor, Hunter, sat by making snide remarks within earshot of the sweaty and impatient jury pool, such as, "We could get the proceedings over in just one day if only we can get a jury."[61] Williams generally ignored Hunter's remarks, but when the prosecutor referred to the defense attorneys as "boys" he jumped to his feet in anger: "We're not 'boys!'" he thundered defiantly. "We're men, and we're lawyers, and we're here to defend these young men."[62]

The prosecution called its first witness: Willie Padgett, a slight, blondish farmer who was called to confirm what he had told the police, and to set the stage for what Hunter viewed as crucial physical evidence: a bit of lint on Norma that was allegedly traceable to Shepherd's car.

It was time for the star witness, Norma Lee Padgett. Wearing her Sunday best, a floral print dress trimmed with lace, and clutching a little black purse, Norma had presumably never had this much attention in her life. A reporter covering the trial noted that the young woman seemed neither embarrassed nor deterred by the "red-faced, leathery-necked hillbillies [who] leaned forward eagerly as she took the stand." Her testimony struck one reporter in the courtroom as "rehearsed."[63] Norma openly displayed her brazen racism, repeatedly and casually referring to the defendants as "nigger."

"Did the defendants stop anywhere along the way?" Hunter inquired.

"Well, they pulled into the side of the road . . . and that Thomas nigger, he got in the back with me. And that Shepherd nigger, he drove then."

"Who had the pistol?"

"The first time I seen it, the Thomas nigger, he had it. . . . And then the Greenlee nigger took it."[64]

During Akerman's cross-examination, it was clear, if only to the defense, that Willie Padgett's recollections and those of his wife conflicted in many ways. For example, in answer to a question about whether their car had broken down anywhere else that night, Willie said it had, while Norma had no such recollection.[65] When asked what they did after their car got stuck, Norma stated that she and her husband had tried to push it off the road. Willie said that they did nothing.[66]

Hunter's third witness, Deputy Sheriff Yates, testified that plaster casts of footprints and tire tracks left at the scene of the crime matched Irvin's shoes and the tires of Shepherd's Mercury sedan. When Akerman objected on the grounds that the deputy had illegally confiscated Irvin's shoes without a warrant—and thus had ample opportunity to manufacture footprint evidence—his objection was instantly overruled. Years later, it would become crystal clear that Yates was quite capable of manufacturing evidence. In March 1960, Yates again used plaster casts to prove the guilt of two Black men charged with rape in Fruitland Park, Florida. By analyzing soil samples in that case, the NAACP and FBI determined that the casts had not been produced at the crime scene. Yates and his accomplice were indicted in December 1962 on charges of perjury and conspiracy, crimes carrying a life sentence. Incredibly, their case was delayed until the statute of limitations expired and both men were reinstated by Sheriff McCall, who provided them with back pay.[67]

Strategically, Hunter declined to introduce medical testimony that, if in fact she had been raped, presumably would have corroborated Norma's claims. Although Norma had been examined by a doctor, the prosecution declined to put him on the witness stand (and subject him to cross-examination) and Judge Futch refused to allow the defense access to his report. If Norma had been gang-raped, a physical exam would likely have revealed evidence of an attack, such as scratches and presence of four distinct sperm deposits. Hunter did not introduce medical testimony into the record because the medical evidence did not support Norma Padgett's claim that she had been raped.[68]

Hunter also opted against introducing the confessions; there was no need to since, thanks to McCall, the entire community (including the jurors) already knew about the confessions. Further, since the confessions were clearly the product of coercion, if Hunter used them at trial he would provide the defendants with a gift-wrapped issue on appeal. As it was, he had his cake and ate it, too. He got all the benefit of the confessions, prevented the defense from making the alleged admissions an issue during trial, and eliminated the confessions as an avenue of appeal.

Thus, the prosecution relied on several factors: the testimony, albeit somewhat inconsistent, of the Padgetts; "physical proof" in the form of shoe and tire tracks that Deputy Yates linked to Shepherd and his vehicle; and the lint on Norma's clothing that supposedly matched lint from Shepherd's car. With that, Hunter contended he had proven the defendants' guilt beyond a reasonable doubt, as required under the US Constitution.

The defense had little with which to work. Akerman and Williams were not afforded the time to build an alibi defense (later, it would become evident that witnesses placed all of the defendants far from the scene of the alleged crime), could not bring up the torture since Hunter had skillfully kept the confessions out of the trial, and lacked adequate resources to effectively attack the physical evidence—the plaster casts Deputy Yates said he made at the crime scene allegedly proving that Shepherd (or at least his shoes) and his car had been at the scene of the crime. Williams was certain that Yates had manufactured the evidence, but he had no proof. Further, the defense could not question the examining physician; Hunter didn't put him on the stand, so he could not be cross-examined, and the judge wouldn't permit Akerman and Williams to call him as their witness. It wasn't a trial but an ambush.

The defense had no choice but to put the defendants on the stand, knowing that the word of three African Americans against that of a white woman and white police officers would hardly influence and would more likely alienate an all-white, all-male jury. Still, it was their only shot, and while they knew the white jury could never exonerate the young men, they hoped it would do the next best thing and vote for a sentence of life in prison rather than death in the electric chair.

Shepherd and Irvin, appearing "disdainful and unbroken,"[69] swore they had been barhopping in Orlando until 12:30 a.m. and then drove directly to Shepherd's home, a distance of approximately forty miles. Both insisted they never encountered the Padgetts; both maintained that they met Greenlee for the first time in the Tavares jail. Greenlee's testimony was full of wide-eyed youthful earnestness and naivete. One reporter noted that the unschooled but well-spoken sixteen-year-old seemed to believe "if you just tell the good white folks the truth and make them understand, then everything will be all right."[70]

Greenlee told the jury he had arrived in Groveland with Thomas around 5:00 p.m., had spent the night in the shack behind the railroad depot, and had gone nowhere except to a corner gasoline station for drinking water. He testified that several whites had seen him, including a handicapped man and a woman driving a two-tone 1948 Chevrolet, and he hoped they would come forward to confirm his story. Without enough time to investigate and prepare their case, the defense attorneys had no opportunity to ferret out those witnesses and put them under oath. Hunter strategically declined to cross-examine any of the defendants, a subtle way of signaling to the jury that he didn't care what they said, and neither should they.

The trial seemed to be going perfectly for the prosecution. Hunter, with Judge Futch's acquiescence, got in the evidence he wanted in, kept out the evidence he wanted out, and had the local newspapers—the *Mount Dora Topic*, *Leesburg Commercial*, and *Orlando Sentinel*—functioning as cheerleaders for the prosecution and sheriff, and protectors of the image of the south. One reporter, Mable Norris-Reese, owner of the *Mount Dora Topic*, was particularly biased and displayed a hostility toward Williams that bordered on hatred.

Despite Judge Futch's order barring cameras in the courtroom, Reece obnoxiously brought hers, getting in the face of Williams and his clients and maliciously popping flash bulbs in their eyes, temporarily blinding them.[71] When Williams confronted her and accused her of "trying to out-southern the southerners," in order to sell newspapers, Reese (who had grown up in the north) used her newspaper for revenge:

> Historians will not have been on hand in the Lake County Court-
> house last week when the facts of the story were first related. . . . They
> will not have seen the complete bitterness . . . of Franklin Williams.
> . . . [They] will not picture him with his eyes filled with hatred as they
> were in the courthouse, of his picking at every incident as a discrimi-
> nation against his race. . . . Williams personified to Lake Countians
> the racial question—as they have never known it with the peaceful
> colored people who live and let live and are happy in the South. More
> than that, his attitude could be likened to that of Paul Robeson whose
> outlook on the world is that of a man whose sole existence is for the
> purpose of fanning hatred.[72]

Years later, Reese continued to write angry diatribes about Williams, even to the point of printing false statements: "It was one person who did damage to Lake County in the first place. That one person was Attorney Franklin Williams, the hate-dominated Negro, who has been censured by the NAACP for his actions in Lake County, his untruthful statements and his venom."[73]

Any reader of any of Franklin's speeches or articles or any quote attributed to him in any newspaper would be hard-pressed to ever find evidence of "hate" or "venom." That simply was not his style, his demeanor, or his nature. Further, he was never censured by the NAACP for anything. That was a flat-out lie. Williams fought back in the press, to the extent that he could, with the help of two friendly reporters: the *New York Post*'s Ted Poston, the "Dean of Black Journalists" and one of the first African American reporters to write for a mainstream, white-owned newspaper;[74] and Ramona Lowe, a Black journalist with the *Chicago Defender*, who regularly scooped other outside press, likely because she hitched a ride to and from court each day with the defense attorneys and had access to inside information.[75]

Poston, who had long been friendly with Williams, came to Groveland with the experience of having covered a very similar trial in Alabama, the infamous Scottsboro matter in which two white women accused nine young Black men—one only thirteen years old—of raping them on a freight train passing through the town. All but the youngest were sentenced to death, even though one of the accusers admitted she made up the story to avoid prosecution for vagrancy and prostitution. After years of legal wrangling and two trips to the US Supreme Court, charges against the four youngest were dropped altogether and the others received reduced sentences. Groveland would come to be known as "Little Scottsboro" because of the many similarities. Both involved the charge of rape; the rescue of defendants from vigilantes by local sheriffs; the white community's outrage over the involvement of the NAACP and other "outsiders"; the defenses attorneys' attack on the all-white jury system; and an attempt by communists to exploit the cases for their own agenda.

In Scottsboro, the defendants were persuaded to dump their NAACP representatives and hire the International Labor Defense, a Communist Party front, to defend them. The party threw substantial resources behind the effort to get new trials for the accused and mounted an effective worldwide publicity campaign for its own aims. Similarly, the Civil Rights Congress, also a Communist front, attempted to weasel into the Groveland case. Williams, all too familiar with communist shenanigans from his days with the American Veterans Committee, wanted nothing to do with them for several reasons: for one thing, he didn't trust them, and for another, the communists were anti-American while Williams and the NAACP were not. They firmly believed that the Constitution, if properly applied by the courts, provided all the rights and protections that Blacks needed. The NAACP had enough problems without being linked to communists in the Red Scare era.[76]

From his experience in Scottsboro, Poston knew that the Groveland defendants "would have no chance at all if they didn't get some publicity,"[77] and he took up their cause, as did Ramona Lowe.

McCall, his henchmen, Judge Futch, and his court attendants did their part to bully the Black reporters, to no avail. Poston and Lowe were removed from the press area of the courtroom and relegated to gallery with the other African Americans after Norris-Reese put up a stink about sitting in the company of Blacks.[78] When Poston vigorously objected, Judge Futch grudging relented and, with Hunter's consent, agreed to set up a special, segregated press desk. But Poston was placed next to a hostile court officer, who spent much of the trial jabbing the reporter with the tip of an umbrella when he thought no one was watching. That was hardly the only sign that Poston—the outside, agitating, northern, "nigger" reporter"—was unwelcome in those parts: when Poston dropped his glasses, a white man "accidently" stepped on them, and then added insult to injury by grinding them into the floor; when he tried to wire his articles, he discovered the operator was forwarding them to Hunter instead; when he called his office, the eavesdropping operator cut him off, saying, "That's enough Ted, you've been talking too long."[79] Poston was irritated but not intimidated. He had experienced worse. Once, he was the victim of a blackmail attempt over a false rape allegation.[80] Lowe endured similar indignities yet refused to be intimidated.

The attempted intimidation extended beyond the Black reporters to Williams. On the first day of trial, Shepherd whispered to Williams: "Mr. Williams,

Franklin Williams. (Photo
courtesy of Franklin H.
Williams Judicial
Commission)

when the trial is over, be careful. The sheriff said he's going to 'get that nigger lawyer' when the trial was over."[81] It was not the last time that Williams would hear through the grapevine that McCall pledged vengeance.

The jury deliberated only two hours before announcing its verdict at around 9:00 p.m. on Wednesday, August 3, 1949: Guilty as to Shepherd. Guilty as to Irvin. Guilty as to Greenlee. The men of the jury showed no mercy for Shepherd or Irvin and recommended the death sentence. But apparently because of Greenlee's young age, they recommended what passed for leniency: life in prison. That show of "mercy" did not sit well with some locals who were disgusted that the young "nigger" had charmed the jury and gotten "off"—as if a sentence of life in prison amounted to "getting off."

Williams was nervous as he and the defense team prepared to leave the courtroom into the dark night. While the governor, during the course of the trial, had assigned a special representative to the court proceedings, and the room was filled with deputy sheriffs and state highway patrolmen, once the judge pronounced the trial at an end, these officers were suddenly nowhere to be found. Williams and Hill were escorted only to the doorway by a state highway patrol lieutenant and his officer and left to fend for themselves. The officers were not about to get between two Black lawyers and the makings of an angry white mob.[82]

The two men rushed down an alley to Hill's black sedan, which was parked on the side street next to the courthouse. Hill hopped behind the wheel and Williams jumped in, noticing smoke coming out of the cigarette lighter. It had been jammed in the socket—apparently someone's attempt to short-circuit the car so the attorneys couldn't escape. Williams grabbed the lighter and dislodged it, causing flames to shoot out and burn his finger. Fortunately, that was the extent of the damage, to either the car or Williams.[83]

With the knowledge that the car had apparently been tampered with, Williams and Hill were all the more eager to bolt, but they couldn't leave without Poston and Lowe, who were in just as much danger as the lawyers. The spectators had been released from the courtroom and were coming up to the car, menacingly. Meanwhile, the reporters were in the lobby of the courtroom, doing their job and attempting to conduct interviews with Samuel Shepherd's father and others as the crowd milled nearby, growing more and more agitated and more and more ferocious. Finally, an elderly Black man's gesture—a signal to run for it, now—prompted Poston to grab Lowe and escape through a side door and run to Hill's car.[84] As soon as Poston and Lowe jumped in the car, Hill raced off. Williams looked out the back window and saw two vehicles in pursuit.

They raced down a country road where a man in the middle of the road was waving a white handkerchief and motioning Hill to stop. Hill knew it was a setup and swerved around the man, pushed the gas pedal to the floor, turned off his headlights and glanced in the rearview mirror. Two more vehicles had joined the chase, and they were coming to an intersection and a red light in the tiny town of Apopka. Poston recalled: "And suddenly you open your eyes to find yourself hurtling forward in a stygian blackness, lighted only by the reflection of pursuing headlights in your own rearview mirror. You are on a long straight stretch of highway and Hill has cut off his own lights, trusting only to the light of the Florida moon."[85]

Hill raced through the red light, and sped through the intersection, narrowly missing a truck. The chase continued all the way to the outskirts of Orlando, roughly thirty miles. Poston wrote:

> Hill sent the car hurtling through the light and the country town at 80 miles scattering a few pedestrians . . . and missing by inches a pickup truck which crossed our path at the third traffic light. Williams reported that the lead car, still on our tail, had almost crashed into the

sidewalk . . . it had straightened up now, though, and again was trying to close the gap.

"I guess this is it, then," Williams said. "No cracker would endanger other crackers . . . just to put a scare into a bunch of Negroes. I guess they really intend to take us."[86]

Once they were near Orlando, Hill was at an advantage. He knew his way around, and a deft series of quick turns brought them into the Black section of town. They had lost the posse, but for how long, nobody knew. The three men and Lowe dispersed. Williams mingled with a crowd in front of a movie, hoping to go unnoticed if the mob got near. Eventually, he found his way back to Pinky's Price's rooming house, where the reality of what had just about occurred struck home. Sweat seeped from every pore. His heart raced, and he wanted nothing more than to get out of Florida as fast as he could.

By morning, Williams had calmed down and began plotting his next move, fully expecting that the Florida appeals courts would uphold the convictions but hoping he and Akerman had made enough of a record to persuade the US Supreme Court to hear the case. If not, Williams knew, Walter Irvin and Samuel Shepherd would die in the electric chair and a sixteen-year-old boy would spend the remainder of his days in prison. He was committed to preventing those injustices, eager to get started with the appeals and, in his mind, already preparing for the next chapter, not knowing that the tension with Thurgood Marshall was about to uproot his career and his family.

9

Passion and Power Plays

Franklin Williams returned from Florida to find the New York office in a state of barely contained chaos. Assistant Counsel Marian Wynn Perry had moved on. A brilliant but raw twenty-five-year-old recent law school graduate named Jack Greenberg had joined the staff, his intellect and exuberance overcoming his total lack of experience. The overworked, underpaid staff was generally content to put up with long, tedious hours and meager compensation because, in their gut, they knew they were on the brink of making history. It was an exhilarating, groundbreaking era in the legal battle for equality, and Williams was at the vortex.

The US Supreme Court was signaling an interest in novel civil rights litigation and Thurgood Marshall's core legal team—Williams, Constance Baker Motley, Greenberg, and Robert L. Carter—was working feverishly to strike while the Supreme Court iron was seemingly hot. They truly thought they could relegate Jim Crow to the dustbin of history—the elusive goal of the NAACP from day one—and pursued various school desegregation cases that, in retrospect, paved the way for *Brown v. Board of Education* in 1954 and the end of legally sanctioned public school segregation. Among them were two 1950 cases, *McLaurin v. Oklahoma State Board of Regents* and *Sweatt v. Painter*.[1] In *McLaurin*, the Supreme Court struck down an Oklahoma statute mandating segregation in education. *Sweatt* was a nail in the coffin of "separate but equal," and a key stepping-stone toward *Brown*. Under Marshall's leadership of the Legal Defense Fund, virtually all the lawyers on staff collaboratively worked on all the briefs, fine-tuning the product and prepping the director, who most times argued the matter in Washington. They were grueling yet energizing years.

In writing and rewriting portions of briefs, Williams was tasked with not only preparing the Groveland appeal for presentation to the Florida Supreme Court but also helping raise the $20,000 necessary to take the matter to Washington. No one expected to prevail in the Florida courts, but until exhausting their state court remedies the Groveland defendants could not petition the US Supreme Court. Williams had proven his fundraising prowess in the Isaac Woodard matter, and did so again in the Groveland case, raising $4,600 (the equivalent of about $49,000 as of 2022).[2] His poetic oratory was such that people wanted to hear him speak, and his calm persuasion encouraged them to open their wallets.

Williams was surely aware that neither his rhetoric nor legal reasoning was likely to sway the Florida Supreme Court, where he argued the Groveland appeal. He knew his case was dead on arrival in the state where the injustice had occurred, and the decision by Justice Roy Chapman and the state's highest court came as no surprise. The court rejected the argument that the trial should have been moved to a different location because "our study of the record reflects the view that harmony and good will and friendly relations continuously existed between the white and colored races."[3]

The court clearly overlooked the fact that if there was an insufficient record it was because Judge Futch did everything he could to prevent the defense from making an adequate record. It similarly brushed aside the various other defense arguments—such as a racially stacked jury—and unanimously affirmed the convictions. Any other decision would have undermined a society and culture the court needed to protect. However, the court did issue a ninety-day stay of execution, giving Williams and the defense team a chance to petition the US Supreme Court. At least the court didn't rush Shepherd and Irvin off to the executioner, which outraged Mabel Norris-Reese, the local newspaper editor and reporter who had been hostile to the defense from the start. She urged the NAACP to "let well enough alone,"[4] implying the NAACP should not bother the good justices in Washington with such a trivial matter as the lives of young Black men.

Of course, Marshall immediately directed Greenberg to begin preparing a petition in hopes of persuading the Supreme Court to hear the appeals of Irvin and Shepherd but not Greenlee, a strategic but difficult choice. It was entirely possible that Greenlee could win the battle—securing a new trial—only to lose the war, being convicted anew and this time being condemned to the electric chair. It was too big a risk to take.

Greenberg's petition to the Supreme Court was nothing short of masterful. He focused primarily on jury selection, contending that the "long and continued absence of any Negro from a grand or petit jury in Lake County" was by "design," not coincidental. But he also raised several other issues, such as that of venue and the rush by the prosecution and judge to get the trial started and finished to end the demonstrations and rioting that were disturbing the tranquility of the town (the petition noted that at a pretrial hearing, Norris-Reese testified that the prosecutor confided that he wanted to hold the trial as quickly as possible to put an end to the demonstrations and violence in Lake County).[5] Remarkably, the newly minted attorney persuaded the US Supreme Court to hear the case. The Legal Defense Fund (LDF) was encouraged: The Supreme Court doesn't take cases simply to rubber-stamp the courts below. Usually, if the Court takes a case it's because it sees a problem or because there is a novel issue of law that it wants to examine and address. If nothing else, Greenberg bought Irvin and Shepherd a little more time and gave them a fighting chance.

Meanwhile, the old tensions and rivalries that had long infected Williams's relationship with Marshall exploded in the hot New York City summer of 1950. Greenberg, new to the office, was taken aback by the "yelling and screaming and carrying on . . . [Williams] and Thurgood clashed constantly."[6] Part of it was the clash of personalities and egos, part of it was the disagreements over strategy and part of it was pure resentment. Both seemed to begrudge the growing prominence of the other, and Williams in particular was irked that after he did all the groundwork on Groveland, Marshall intended to be the one arguing it at the Supreme Court if they were granted leave. Williams, who had handled the trial, argued the appeal, raised the funds for both and was already working on the briefs for the Supreme Court, thought he had earned the right to argue the case in Washington. Marshall had other ideas.

Beyond their personal difficulties, internal NAACP politics infected the Williams-Marshall dynamic as well. In Williams's view, Marshall and Roy Wilkins, acting secretary of the NAACP, had conspired to wrest all control of the organization from Walter White, his mentor and rabbi. In the view of others, Williams, Jackie Robinson, and several other dissidents tried and failed to wrest control of the NAACP from Wilkins. White, who perhaps could have successfully mediated the tensions, was wounded by both health issues and a controversy in his personal life. He suffered a heart attack in 1948, and during his time off he divorced his longtime wife, Gladys Powell White, and married Poppy Cannon, a white woman and the well-known author of popular cookbooks.[7]

The interracial marriage "did not sit well with the Black press" and "all hell broke loose" within the NAACP.[8] Wilkin and other members of the board tried to block White's return to the NAACP. But a particularly persuasive board member, Eleanor Roosevelt, came to bat for White and he kept his job.[9] Regardless, the ill will and distrust remained. The board reinstated White as executive secretary but made Wilkins comptroller, giving him control over the purse strings, and named Marshall the special counsel and Henry Lee Moon the director of public relations—and then declared that all four had equal authority. Williams found the managerial structure both unworkable and "ridiculous."[10] His mentor, friend, and protector Walter White was essentially nullified. Williams, who remained White's close friend (and when others abandoned him over the marriage to Poppy Cannon, Franklin and Shirley welcomed Poppy into their social circle), was outspoken in support of his mentor and against the new structure.

There are multiple accounts of what occurred next. One story has Marshall firing Williams, or at least telling him he was fired.[11] Gloster Current, the National Director of Branches, insisted he was the one who sent Williams to California. Current said the West Coast director, Noah Griffin, was "quiet, a former schoolteacher from Florida who did not raise much recognition for the association. He was just an easy-going person. We needed someone out there like Frank."[12] Nathaniel S. "Nat" Colley Sr., a leader in the NAACP who served as western regional counsel, said Williams was the victim of "petty jealousies . . . Frank was brilliant, good looking and dedicated. Some couldn't deal with that without feelings of insecurity. . . . A lot of people in the NAACP were very happy to see Frank end up on the west coast, in the Siberia of the association, out of the way. But Frank was too good to be exiled and forgotten."[13]

Williams claimed that he asked for a transfer, partially because he "was getting very restless working with Thurgood. It was clear that he and I were not on the same wave length . . . I was unhappy working for him" and partially for reasons related to the education of his older son, Franklin Jr., who was about to enter preschool.[14] Franklin and Shirley cared deeply about education and they had hoped to send young Frankie to the Ethical Culture Lower School in Manhattan, a private school that emphasized racial equality, social justice, and intellectual freedom—values at the core of their own beliefs. But there were no school buses that would bring Frankie from Harlem to midtown Manhattan, and the school frowned on the idea of such a young child traveling twice a day on public transportation. Also, there was the question of tuition. With Franklin Sr. earning only $3,000 yearly, unless they could be certain of a scholarship, it was doubtful whether little Frank would be able to attend. Thus, Franklin and Shirley were open to exploring opportunities elsewhere.

In August 1950, White formally advised Williams of his transfer to California and the responsibility he would have "for the implementation, stimulation and coordination of the NAACP's program and policy on the West Coast, both branch and legal, throughout that region."[15]

Before 1941, the NAACP seemingly gave little thought to the Communist Party and virtually no thought to the idea that communists might try to exploit the NAACP by latching on to its credibility and cases. A *Crisis* magazine editorial written in 1941 made the point that the Communist Party did "constitute a political party [that has] rights under the Constitution as do other parties" and "that these rights must be maintained."[16] In other words, from the NAACP perspective the Communist Party was just another political party. That naivete betrayed a stunning lack of institutional memory. In the 1930s, through the establishment of the National Negro Congress, the communists attempted to take control of the NAACP, an effort that "collapsed in the welter of communist ineptitude and double dealing," according to Williams.[17]

But that changed during the Red Scare era, when the NAACP was struggling to build standing in all communities—Black and white—and grew increasingly concerned about being connected to an organization that was viewed as "un-American." A marked change in the organization's attitude toward communism and other far-left ideologies was brewing based on "the pervasive aura of anti-communism—a new Red Scare—so powerful that many social causes identified with liberal principles could be tarred by opponents with the fatal brush of being subversive."[18] Williams, already distrustful of the communists after his experiences with the American Veterans Committee, was perhaps tapped for the West Coast because of concerns of Walter White and others of communist infiltration.[19]

While the exact conditions of Williams's move to the West Coast remain unclear, what is abundantly obvious is Marshall wanted Williams out of his sight—if not out of his life altogether—and created an environment where it was virtually impossible for Williams to remain in New York. In the end, it seemed that everyone got what they wanted: Thurgood Marshall rid his office of an overly ambitious challenger, Gloster Current got the help he wanted on the West Coast, and Franklin Williams got out from under Marshall's thumb, saved face, and moved his family out of Harlem and what he viewed as a substandard school situation.

Days after receiving the transfer memo, Williams bought himself a two-year-old Chevrolet, eagerly anticipating his first cross-country road trip and planning to fly Shirley and his sons (they now had two little boys: Franklin Hall Williams Jr., born on February 14, 1946; and Paul Anatole Williams, born on June 7, 1950) once he got settled. Franklin and a friend, Lewis Thompson, set off in early September 1950 on a leisurely adventure. Williams made a point of meeting with, and often staying with, leaders of NAACP branches in Davenport, Omaha, Denver, Colorado Springs, Salt Lake City, Reno, and Sacramento, building relationships, networking, and learning about the different as well as common problems encountered by the various divisions.[20] Finally, on

Franklin, Shirley, and their son Paul arrive in California, where he would do his best work. (Photo courtesy of Franklin H. Williams Judicial Commission)

September 15, he arrived at the West Coast Regional Office on Kearny Street in San Francisco where, waiting to greet him, was the man whose position he was taking: Noah Griffin.

Griffin, who had briefly taught at Lincoln University around 1930, more than a decade before Williams enrolled in the school, was the son of former slaves and a prominent figure within the NAACP. In 1942, Griffin became the first director of the West Coast Reginal Office.[21] He was essentially put out to pasture by a brash young upstart. While Griffin "disliked being demoted," he graciously took a "back seat" to Williams, according to a 1974 interview with his widow, Terressa E. Ballou. "Apparently the "tall, handsome, and glib Williams, who had rubbed shoulders with Walter White and earned his admiration, was ideal for this position."[22]

Williams found a fully furnished, three-bedroom apartment in Codornices Village, a temporary veterans' housing project in Berkeley with an extraordinary reputation for interracial harmony. Blacks, whites, and Japanese Americans lived together in harmony with "little ruffling of the racial water."[23] Williams was impressed, signed a lease, and quickly flew Shirley and the boys to California. Meanwhile, he quickly got to work, found nicer and less expensive accommodations for the NAACP ($80 a month compared to $100) and took measure of the challenges he was inheriting.[24]

It was a critical time for African Americans and an opportune time for the NAACP. During the late Depression and war years, Blacks flocked to the west in search of jobs in factories, shipyards, and mines. The Black population of San Francisco jumped 798 percent, while in Los Angeles it increased 168 percent; in Las Vegas, the African American population exploded from 178 to 2,888, an increase of 1522 percent, between 1940 and 1950.[25]

Although their labor was sorely needed and vital to the war effort, and jobs were plentiful, Black workers were hardly welcomed with open arms. Both employers and all-white labor unions resented Black "encroachment" on the status quo,[26] prompting President Roosevelt to issue Executive Order 8802 on June 25, 1941, banning "discrimination in the employment of workers in defense industries or government because of race, creed, color or national origin" and establishing the Fair Employment Practices Committee (FEPC) to enforce the order.

The FEPC was established as part of the order to give teeth to its enforcement. Still, the guarantee of employment did not guarantee equal treatment. As the numbers of Blacks in western cities increased, "Whites Only" signs "suddenly appeared in restaurants, theaters, motels, and recreational areas for the first time."[27] Despite Williams's positive experience at Codornices Village, other Blacks faced daunting and blatantly discriminatory attempts to deny them decent housing. Collusion between realtors and mortgage lenders kept Blacks "in their place," which meant "in the ghetto." Race restrictive covenants were inserted into property deeds prohibiting the sale or occupancy of homes to African Americans and members of other minorities.[28] The covenants were difficult to challenge because they relied on private contracts rather than government action to ensure that the color line held. When the covenants were challenged, "homeowner associations" functioned as cartels, ensuring that members had the money to fight off any challenges.

Williams had more than enough on his plate, but to him Groveland remained a nagging bit of unfinished business. On December 4, 1950, Williams wrote to Marshall expressing his strong desire to argue the case before the Supreme Court, suggesting it would be a "logical conclusion" to his involvement with the case.[29] Marshall responded dismissively and condescendingly: "To pull you out of the west coast for a week or two would certainly deprive the Association of your services during this period. I think you will agree that it will be better to leave things as they are." It was nothing short of a tit-for-tat slap at Williams. But Marshall had a problem.

Although Robert Carter was a more than able litigator, he admittedly didn't know the case nearly as well as Greenberg, who had written the petition. But Greenberg was still young and inexperienced, and Marshall did not think he was quite ready to argue before the Supreme Court.[30] Perhaps concluding that the lives of Irvin and Shepherd were more important than his differences with Franklin, Marshall summoned Williams back to the East Coast in the winter of 1951 to argue *Shepherd v. Florida*, but got in one last dig by assigning Carter the issue Williams knew better than anyone—the matter of excluding Blacks from juries. Williams, on the other hand, would deal with the venue question (whether the defendants could receive a fair trial from any jury in riled-up Lake County) and the impossible task of finding jurors who were not familiar with and had not already prejudged the case.

At the Supreme Court on March 9, 1951, Carter quickly pointed out that the state of Florida openly admitted it used a racial proportion scheme to select jurors; one Black would be included in the jury pool for every eighteen whites because that was the proportion in the voter registration rolls. With that alone, Associate Justice Robert H. Jackson had heard enough. He interrupted Carter, commenting that the NAACP attorney really didn't need "to say anything more" to prove his point.[31] Jackson had made up his mind.

The state's attorney, Assistant Attorney General Reeves Bowen, knew his argument was weak and privately confessed that he expected "to be slaughtered,"[32] and basically he was. The prosecutor seemingly only made matters worse when he attempted to justify the racial proportion system on the grounds that, without such a system, Florida jury commissioners wouldn't think of putting a Negro on a jury panel "any more than on a list for a social function."[33] Justice Harold Burton asked Bowen if there were any reason jury commissioners couldn't simply put names of white and Black prospective jurors in a box and draw names randomly. Bowen, thoroughly boxed in, had to admit that there was not.

On the venue issue, Williams spoke from firsthand experience of the racial tension and hostility in the region at the time of the trial and the trial judge's refusal to move the proceeding to a more neutral location. His argument was convincing, as Bowen likely knew as he lamely attempted to deny those conditions existed and stressed the efforts made by the court to prevent bias. But he was quickly cut off by Justice Jackson, who told the state that "the hardest thing for you to overcome" was the notion that a trial could be rammed through quickly in an effort to quiet the public.[34]

Just a month later, on April 9, 1951, the Supreme Court issued a terse, two-sentence, unsigned unanimous opinion reversing the convictions of Irvin and Shepherd based on the court's year-old decision in *Cassell v. Texas*.[35] In *Cassell*, the court reversed a Texas murder conviction because the grand jury that indicted the Black defendant was composed solely of whites. While the Court as a whole said little, Justice Jackson wrote a powerful concurrence, joined by Justice Felix Frankfurter, expressing grave concerns over the issue that Williams had apparently argued so persuasively: prejudicial publicity. In Justice Jackson's view, the case "presents one of the best examples of one of the worst menaces to American justice." He wrote:

> The conclusion is inescapable that these defendants were prejudged as guilty and the trial was but a legal gesture to register a verdict already dictated by the press and the public opinion which it generated . . .
>   Newspapers published as a fact, and attributed the information to the sheriff, that these defendants had confessed. No one, including the sheriff, repudiated the story. Witnesses and persons called as jurors said they had read or heard of this statement. However, no confession was offered at the trial. The only rational explanations for its nonproduction in court are that the story was false or that the confession was obtained under circumstances which made it inadmissible or its use inexpedient.[36]

Jackson excoriated McCall for leaking the supposed "confessions," and the lap dog press for reporting it:

> If the prosecutor in the courtroom had told the jury that the accused had confessed but did not offer to prove the confession, the court would undoubtedly have declared a mistrial and cited the attorney for contempt. If a confession had been offered in court, the defendant would have had the right to be confronted by the persons who claimed to have witnessed it, to cross-examine them, and to contradict their testimony. If the court had allowed an involuntary confession to be placed before

the jury, we would not hesitate to consider it a denial of due process of law and reverse. When such events take place in the courtroom, defendant's counsel can meet them with evidence, arguments, and requests for instructions, and can at least preserve his objections on the record.

But neither counsel nor court can control the admission of evidence if unproven, and probably unprovable, "confessions" are put before the jury by newspapers and radio. . . . It is hard to imagine a more prejudicial influence than a press release by the officer of the court charged with defendants' custody stating that they had confessed, and here just such a statement, unsworn to, unseen, uncross-examined and uncontradicted, was conveyed by the press to the jury.[37]

It was a huge victory for the LDF, not to mention the two young men on death row, and LDF grasped the case and decision as a fundraising tool. It issued a flyer in 1951 titled "Freedom Is Possible" for "two of the three victims who had been sentenced to death by an all-white jury—a jury whose prejudices had been whipped into fury by inflammatory editorials, cartoons and news stories published in the local papers. . . . But freedom requires faith and money as well as legal skill before the bar."[38] It asked for monetary support for Shepherd, Irvin, and "other victims of brutal injustice."[39]

Sheriff McCall, reportedly livid with the Supreme Court's meddling in local "justice," dispatched himself to the Florida State Prison at Raiford to retrieve Samuel Shepherd and Walter Irvin and bring them back to Lake County for retrial. It seems preposterous that a lone lawman would take charge of two allegedly violent rapists and transport them a hundred miles alone, with no other officer nearby. In any case, along State Route 19 near the Ocala National Forest, McCall claimed he got a flat tire and ordered his prisoners to change it. He alleged the prisoners, who were handcuffed together, attacked him with a flashlight and, in self-defense, he shot both of them before summoning Deputy Yates for assistance. Shepherd died at the scene, but Irvin survived and told a far different story.

Irvin denied that he and Shepherd attempted to escape and denied they attacked the sheriff. Rather, he claimed the sheriff simply attempted to execute his prisoners before they ever got to the retrial. According to Irvin, when Yates arrived and realized that he—Irvin—wasn't dead, he shot him again at close range, a claim that was later supported by an FBI investigation. The bullet, which went through Irvin's neck, was found in the clay precisely below Irvin's blood spot. Indeed, everything Irvin said that was verifiable was indeed verified. Regardless, a Lake County coroner's inquest exonerated Sheriff McCall, and Judge Futch saw no reason to convene a grand jury.[40]

To the local press, the shootings represented just another peculiar twist in the case; Mabel Norris-Reese's *Mount Dora Topic* dismissed Irvin's story as "bizarre."[41] But *The Crisis* and the national press quickly pounced on the incident, and the outspoken chairman of the Florida branch of the NAAP, Harry T. Moore, relentlessly pressured the governor to remove McCall from office. He paid a fatal price for speaking out. On Christmas Eve of 1951, Moore and his wife, Harriette, were killed in their Brevard County home when a bomb went off under their bed. The FBI investigated thoroughly, but no one was prosecuted.

Many years later, in 2005 and 2006, forensic evidence and a state investigation linked four Ku Klux Klan members to the bombing—and implicated the same four in the attempted lynching of Franklin Williams as he was chased out of Lake County following the first trial. All four were dead by the time they were identified by the Florida attorney general in 2006; one of them committed suicide the day after the FBI interviewed him about the case.[42] Historian James C. Clark argues that Moore was murdered on orders from Sheriff McCall, but that speculation—while entirely plausible—remains just that, speculation.[43]

With two of the original four Groveland suspects, Shepherd and Ernest Thomas, killed and Greenlee fearing that a retrial could result in a one-way trip to the electric chair, Irvin was left to face the second trial alone. This time, Alex Akerman would lead the defense, with Thurgood Marshall, Jack Greenberg, and Paul Perkins, a Black attorney from Daytona Beach, on the defense team. (Williams returned to California after arguing at the Supreme Court and had no involvement in the retrial.) Judge Futch agreed to a change of venue, but it was a meaningless one, since the trial would simply be moved over the border to neighboring Marion County. The trial lasted only three days, and the jury was out only two hours before unanimously finding Irvin guilty. On Valentine's Day 1952, Judge Futch once again sentenced Irvin to death.

Irvin was saved from the electric chair in 1954, when Florida Governor LeRoy Collins issued a last-minute stay of execution and commuted the sentence to life in prison. Walter was paroled in 1968 and moved to Miami to be near his sister. A year later, he returned to Groveland to attend his uncle's funeral and was found dead in his car, apparently of natural causes. He was forty years old.[44] Greenlee, paroled after twelve years, lived a relatively long life, dying in 2012 at the age of seventy-eight. All four were pardoned in 2019, shortly after Republican Governor Ron DeSantis took office. Before doing so, DeSantis said publicly: "Seventy years is a long time. And that's the amount of time four young men have been wrongly written into Florida history for crimes they did not commit and punishments they did not deserve."[45]

By the time of the second Groveland verdict, Williams had fully moved on from the case and that chapter of his life and was completely engaged in his work on the West Coast—where he was in charge, where he wasn't under the shadow of Thurgood Marshall, where he could do things his way. And in California over the next decade, largely answering to no one but himself, Williams did perhaps the greatest work of his life.

10

California Deliverance

After arguing the Groveland appeal in Washington, Williams returned to California, three thousand miles removed from Thurgood Marshall and the NAACP politics that had stunted his career. He felt both liberated and energized and immediately faced two crises that he was eager to address: communist infiltration in the NAACP and a byzantine, balkanized organizational structure that doomed the western region to mediocrity and near irrelevancy. From his experiences with the American Veterans Committee, Williams was well prepared to deal with the communists. But the administrative trials would test—and ultimately vindicate—leadership qualities that enabled him to successfully battle Jim Crow.

Part of the rationale for transferring Williams to San Francisco apparently involved his prior experience dealing with communists, and the nagging concern of Walter White, Roy Wilkins, and other NAACP leaders that the leftists were trying to take over branches of the organization.[1] Before World War II, the NAACP leadership was not particularly concerned about the communists or their ulterior agenda and viewed the Marxists as "tolerable" additions to the struggle for civil rights, so long as the NAACP remained "in the vanguard."[2] But by the 1950s, with the Cold War surging, Senator Joseph McCarthy quick to brand as un-American anyone even remotely associated with the Communist Party, and segregationists eager to link the civil rights movement to godless communism, the NAACP came to view the Marxist element as a threat to its own legitimacy. Even the mere hint of an appeasement of communist ideology would derail fundraising and discourage membership at precisely the time when the NAACP was poised to have its greatest impact. Philosophically, some Black leaders, including Williams, strongly rejected communist dogma; with its inherent disdain for individual rights and, consequently freedom, communism was inconsistent with the NAACP mission.

At the 1950 national convention, the NAACP national office was empowered to "expel any unit that had come under communist or other political control."[3] The following year, the NAACP amended its constitution to actually ban communists from the organization. A year later, at its forty-second annual convention, the NAACP again amended its constitution, this time to prevent communists from joining the organization in the first place.[4]

During his AVC days, Williams diplomatically attempted to remain neutral or agnostic in the battles between the communists and anticommunist factions, partially due to his commitment to the principles of the First Amendment (even though, as private organizations neither the AVC nor the NAACP, is subject to it). But Williams viewed the threat to the NAACP as so great that he thoroughly embraced and sought to enforce the sentiment of the organization, even to the extent of rooting out and banishing communists. He had seen how the communists had ultimately undermined and neutered the AVC, and he was not about to permit them to do the same to the NAACP.

Several months into his tenure in San Francisco, Williams wrote to Gloster Current, the National Director of Branches, reporting that he had "substantial reason to believe" that branches in San Pedro, Santa Monica, Pasadena, Marysville, Monrovia, Long Beach, and Marin City were influenced or even dominated by the Communist Party.[5] Williams aggressively and often abrasively discouraged any connection between the NAACP and the Communist Party or its alleged sympathizers and front organizations, such as the National Negro Labor Council, the Civil Rights Congress, and the California Labor School. Left-wing publications such as the *Daily People's World*, *Political World*, and *Militant* were shunned as "subversive." After the Christmas Eve assassinations of Harry T. Moore, the founder of the Florida chapter of the NAACP, and his wife, Harriette, card-carrying Communist Party members as well as their more discrete allies planned a fundraising parade in Oakland. Williams quickly fired off a press release suggesting the communists were exploiting the death of an NAACP martyr for their own agenda, not the mission of the NAACP:

We wish the public to know that the NAACP is in no way connected with any parade or public demonstration on Saturday, February 2nd, eulogizing Harry T. Moore or his wife, Harriet [sic], or the Groveland Florida case. Information has come to our office that certain groups consisting of Communists and communist sympathizers are holding such a demonstration and parade on Saturday, Feb 2nd [in] the City of Oakland . . .

The NAACP is the only authorized organization to solicit and collect funds for the case. Harry T. Moore was an NAACP official and it
is an NAACP case—the Groveland case, which precipitated this murder. While we are calling on organizations interested in action against
the terrorist murders of Mr. Moore, we cannot afford to have linked
with our protest left-wing organizations which seek to use this issue for
purposes contrary to those of [the] NAACP. We are working only with
organizations approved by the NAACP.

Williams expressed to Walter White and Roy Wilkins his certainty that the
western region could control communist and communist-front organizations,
and confidently reported that he was "fortunate enough to have a fairly reliable
pipeline into communist plans for [the] NAACP here in the West."[6] That
seems to have been the case. In a March 19, 1954, letter to Wilkins, Williams
reported that the western region was presenting civil rights activist (and socialist) A. Philip Randolph at a mass meeting in Oakland expected to draw
up to ten thousand African Americans, adding "WE KNOW" that the communist-
backed Negro Labor Council and the Civil Rights Congress planned to be
there to "mislead" the African American community: "We broke up one such
front group here a few months ago by taking the initiative and we shall continue to do so."[7]

Eleven days later at a "Fight for Freedom" rally organized by the North
California Area office of the NAACP, Williams told the six thousand attendees to be on the lookout for, and to reject, subversive groups and subversive
newspapers:

We denied a seat at our press table to a reporter of the People's World,
because he was here to distort and subvert the objective of this rally.
The representatives of these communist-front groups have been
attempting to sell you literature and newspapers as you approached
this auditorium; if you have not already thrown this subversive material
away, I suggest that you toss it in the wastebasket as you leave this
meeting.[8]

In 1955, after fourteen-year-old Emmett Till was murdered and mutilated
and his body was dumped in the Tallahatchie River, allegedly for whistling at
a white woman, Williams and the West Coast Region NAACP quickly contracted
with the boy's mother to participate in a variety of protest meetings and rallies.
Although the contract required Mamie Till Bradley to speak only at NAACP
events, Williams learned from his newly hired field secretary, Lester Bailey, that
the Civil Rights Congress had invited her to speak at its own event to raise

money surreptitiously for the communist cause. He quickly alerted the NAACP board to a 'MOST SERIOUS SITUATION!" with regard to communist infiltration: "As you know I am not given to being hysterical about Communism—if anything, my fault has been in the direction of being too lax. This is not the reaction of a hysterical or frightened field person—I know what's happening and we are preparing to meet the problem as best we can out here with what limited power we have."[9] In a late 1950s speech, Williams told an audience in Virginia at the First Baptist Church of Suffolk that "there is no difference between a Dixiecrat and a Communist—both are guilty of subverting the United States constitution and both should be treated as enemies."[10]

In hindsight, some scholars argue that the NAACP's zeal to disassociate itself from anything that smacked of communism ultimately delayed the progress of civil rights and prevented alliances where there was common ground. That is questionable. The NAACP was already fighting an uphill battle and struggling to attract and maintain the support of middle America—white *and* Black. It seems more likely that a "the-enemy-of-my-enemy-is-my-friend" posture would have achieved little and cost much. In his later years, Williams acknowledged that the threat of an actual takeover of the NAACP by communists was small, but he insisted that even the perception of an NAACP-communist connection would have been devastating to the credibility he was working to establish for both the association and himself. With his magnetism and eloquence, he was a popular advocate and an effective bridge between the national organization, the western section, and the populace. That image would have suffered, and he likely would have been constantly on the defensive, if the NAACP hadn't so strongly, and some say stridently, disavowed the Communist Party and its sympathizers.

In the early 1950s, Williams, thirty-three, spent countless hours traveling the region, speaking wherever he could find an audience and captivating the hearts and minds of Blacks and whites. At the time, long-distance telephone calls were expensive, and email didn't exist. Letters moved slowly. Telegrams were available for terse communications, and Williams quickly learned that, despite the size of the region he was running, face-to-face communication was the only real way to communicate. He did a lot of driving and developed a habit of keeping a bag of golf clubs stashed in his trunk. Stopping en route to hit a few balls at a driving range became a pleasant part of his routine until he came to view it as a waste of time. One day, while driving along the coast, Williams stopped the car, walked purposefully across the beach with his clubs and, one by one, tossed them into the Pacific Ocean. He had no time for fun and games and saved his time and energy for the cause. He was business, all business.

Administratively, Williams, who had grown impatient with the methodical and sometimes plodding approach of the East Coast leaders, eagerly grasped the opportunity to restructure the western region to increase its effectiveness, cohesiveness, and efficiency. While the state-based structure perhaps made sense with the geographically smaller but denser eastern states, it made no sense to Williams in the expansive western region that encompassed such a vast and diverse area. In his view, it was both unproductive and counterproductive to have, for example, Idaho and Utah, states with only a few branches, compete against each other for programming and funding. The smaller states lacked influence, and that lack of influence fueled a lack of interest. The western region was moribund and somewhat overlooked by the national organization, but it was an ideal setting for an ambitious man of action to take charge and make changes without worrying about the organizational bureaucracy.

Williams split the West Coast region into five units, consolidating all branches in Idaho, Oregon, Washington, and Alaska into a new Northwest Area Conference.[11] Branches in northern California west of the San Joaquin Valley and north of Monterey were combined into the Northern California Area Conference. The Central Area Conference merged all branches in the San Joaquin Valley from its northern to southern points and encompassed Reno, in northern Nevada, and two branches in Utah. And the Southern Area Conference unified all branches in Southern California south of the city of Carmel and in the southern valley area and combined them with all the Arizona branches. Each branch elected a local president, and together the group comprised a regional board of directors, with Williams as chairman of the board. Suddenly, the western region had an identity and a cocky pride that did not sit well with the status quo leaders on the East Coast. At the NAACP national convention in Dallas, the first Williams would attend, he led his boisterous delegation into the event, wearing cowboy hats and chanting, "California, here we come, we are region number one!" Roy Wilkins, incensed at the lack of what he deemed proper decorum, yelled, "Cut it out! Cut it out!"[12] Wilkins was flatly ignored, and a strong message was sent that Region 1 belonged to Franklin Williams. What had been a region with a stagnant membership was now the unit with the fastest growing membership in the entire NAACP.[13] With his new power base and the unbridled support of western region leaders who had long felt rudderless and neglected, there was no stopping Williams.

When Franklin learned the NAACP was sending Thurgood Marshall to Asia in 1950 to investigate the treatment of Black troops, with a layover in California, he extracted every benefit he could from the brief appearance of his former boss/nemesis/friend/adversary, who by then was the most renowned civil rights attorney in the nation. Marshall's trip to Asia was an important step, especially since General Douglas MacArthur sent word that he would not allow the civil rights attorney to interview court-martialed infantrymen (MacArthur, out of step with the mood of the country and President Truman, ultimately backed down). Williams organized huge fundraising rallies in Oakland and Los Angeles, attracting more than six thousand people, and printed petitions and leaflets imploring Truman to make good his promise to desegregate the armed forces. The petitions were shared with NAACP branches throughout the region, and those branches took them to community events, shopping centers, and anywhere they could find a crowd. Williams's aim was to rally the troops, make all the units and unit leaders feel as if they were an integral part of the NAACP's national strategy, recruit new members, and, of course, raise funds. Because of Williams's vision, what could have been an unnoticed flyby became a wildly successful fundraising/membership-raising/consciousness-raising event.

Franklin challenged Black professionals to risk their relatively comfortable existence and fight for the cause of equal rights. He recruited Loren Miller, a noted journalist as well as an extraordinarily tenacious and talented litigator who had likely argued more racial covenant cases in the Supreme Court than any other attorney in the nation, to head a lawyers committee that would aggressively pursue civil rights litigation.[14] In short order, nearly every young, Black lawyer in the region affiliated with the NAACP in one way or another.[15] Williams himself became such a draw with his powerful oratory that Walter White invited him to speak at a major fundraising appeal at Madison Square Garden, which irritated Marshall and Roy Wilkins to distraction; they thought they had rid themselves of Williams by sending him to California, and there he was at one of the most prominent venues in Manhattan, just blocks from their office, stealing their thunder.

Williams fearlessly took on the segregated San Francisco Fire Department, the Southern Pacific Railroad, and any other entity that had long practiced a quiet, previously accepted/tolerated segregation. He reached out to religious leaders, organizing a regionwide conference of ministers, led by Rev. Hamilton Boswell, a prominent minister in San Francisco who was among the first wave of southern Blacks migrating to California after World War II, as an indirect way to enlist the faithful.[16] Although Williams was not religious, he understood the importance of faith and the influence of clergy in the Black community. In 1952, he held a region-wide conference of ministers, and won many of them—and likely their flocks—over to the newly energized NAACP.

Williams was particularly incensed with retail establishments that welcomed the dollars Black customers spent in their establishment but refused to employ them. He encouraged Blacks to apply to businesses he suspected would discriminate, and if a qualified Black applicant was passed over, the NAACP would organize boycotts and picket lines, brandishing signs that read, "Don't Buy Where You Can't Earn." Marchers peacefully picketed, urging would-be patrons to shop elsewhere. The tide was beginning to turn, and businesses that deserved shame could be shamed.

On one occasion, Williams enlisted the help of an internationally acclaimed celebrity, Josephine Baker, an American-born entertainer who after relocating to France became active in the French resistance during World War II. Known as a civil rights activist, Baker attracted large adoring crowds wherever she went. When Williams learned that Baker, who had been named the NAACP "Woman of the Year" in 1951, would be visiting San Francisco, he set up a sting on the City of Paris, a fashionable store that sought to bring French culture to California.[17] With Williams and the press corps accompanying the glamorous celebrity, Baker spent thousands of dollars in the store—and then confronted the manager and demanded to know why he had no Black salespeople. She accused the manager of discrimination, promised to bad-mouth the store throughout France and threatened to return the merchandise she had just purchased. Overwhelmed, and with a horde of journalists and press photographers capturing the moment, the manager backed down on the spot and agreed to promptly hire a Black salesperson. The color barrier at City of Paris was broken.

Williams understood the importance of enlisting the young. In 1953, in concert with the University of California branch of the NAACP, Williams established the first regionwide conference for college-aged students. In May of that year, the First Annual Youth Conference on Civil Rights was held at Asilomar, California. More than 150 young people, representing all racial groups, attended. As youth groups obtained power and influence, a permanent seat on the national Board of the NAACP was set aside for a student representative.[18]

Like any smart and self-secure leader, Williams surrounded himself with talent and went so far as to raid other NAACP offices to bring the best and brightest to the western region. He persuaded Lester P. Bailey from New York to move across the country to serve as his field secretary. Bailey became a force in one of Williams's priority objectives, fighting housing discrimination, taking the lead in 1957 in pushing Stanford University to include antidiscrimination clauses in its property lease contracts.[19] Williams recruited Tarea Hall Pittman, a well-educated woman who a decade earlier organized protests to force Kaiser Shipyards to hire African Americans. Pittman played a key role desegregating the Oakland Fire Department, became the first president of the Northern

California Area Conference and later succeeded Williams as West Coast Regional Director.[20]

Internally, the organization had long been hindered by an internecine battle between Carlton Goodlett and attorney and later federal judge Cecil Poole, who had been vying for control of the San Francisco branch. Goodlett wanted the branch to work closely with the waterfront unions, which were reportedly the realm of communist sympathizers; Poole wanted nothing to do with the unions. When Goodlett and Poole couldn't get along, Williams brought in attorney William Bradford Reynolds and got him elected president.[21]

The NAACP was not the only game in town, and a number of other civil rights organizations formed during or after World War II were already actively working to address the concerns of Black migrants and Japanese Americans who had been unjustly interned. The most prominent was the Council on Civic Unity (CCU), an interracial organization founded by a branch of the Society of Friends. It would seem that those organizations were natural allies of the NAACP, but Williams was leery. First, he resented that those groups were siphoning support from West Coast liberals that Williams thought should have gone to the NAACP.[22] Second, it could not escape his notice that most of these organizations were run by whites, with Blacks holding less then predominant positions. Finally, he feared that the leaders of some of those groups, particularly Edward Howden, executive director of the CCU, were too willing to compromise on issues of vital important to the NAACP, such as housing policy, fair employment practices, and aid to education. Williams was seeking victory on those issues, not coexistence with his opponents.

For example, both the NAACP and the CCU had long turned a blind eye to a policy enforced by the San Francisco Housing Authority that perpetuated the "separate but equal" doctrine that, while still legal, Williams found repugnant. The Housing Authority policy was designed to prevent new public housing projects from altering the racial composition of the neighborhood. So, when the Housing Authority built a project in the heart of Chinatown, it generally restricted occupancy to people of Chinese ancestry. In that instance, the policy worked to the benefit of a minority group, and consequently both the NAACP and the CCU were content to look the other way, afraid of creating a schism between the Chinese minority, the Black minority, and other racial minorities.[23]

Williams saw that policy for what it was—a sellout. He argued that segregation was wrong—period—even if, as in this case, it benefited a minority group. He was adamant that the NAACP never abandon its values simply to avoid conflict. He was fed up with appeasement, compromise, and incrementalism, all of which he viewed as an evasion of responsibility. He'd had enough of sage white intellectuals and social theorists, such as the author William Faulkner, urging Blacks to "go slow," take a "long view," be "patient," and "calm."[24] Williams felt that Blacks had been too patient for too long and expressed his frustration regularly:

> I'm 36 years old and I've been colored since the day I was born. I have two sons and because I'm their father, they're colored boys. They're handicapped because of that and that makes me mad. . . . I'm tired of being studied. We want equality and we want it now.[25]

> The patience of Job is put to shame when one considers that the Negro awaited the end of slavery for 244 years and has been patiently pursuing full citizenship rights for 93 years.[26]

One of those he persuaded was Branch Rickey, the part-owner of the Brooklyn Dodgers who signed Jackie Robinson. Rickey, somewhat surprisingly, had urged patience. But after hearing Williams speak at an NAACP dinner in Pittsburgh, Rickey had his epiphany; he told the audience that the time had come for the Negro to "do everything in his power short of violence to get what he deserves."[27]

Williams was convinced that the "West Coast has not kept pace with the rest of the country in improving the conditions of civil rights."[28] He advocated and implemented a more aggressive, proactive strategy, one that often involved the courts. He encouraged the NAACP to litigate cases, even if they might offend an ally.

> When the day comes that the Negro ever compromises his just demands, then the National Association for the Advanced of Colored People should close its doors in shame. The organization was founded by dedicated men who never compromised, and we welcome to our ranks those people who will stand with us.[29]

In the San Francisco Housing Authority (SFHA) case, Loren Miller, Terry Francois, and Nat Colley—three of the attorneys on Williams's lawyers committee—demanded that the SFHA apply the same eligibility standards, regardless of race, color, or religion. Since the US Supreme Court had yet to outlaw segregation (as it would do in 1954 in *Brown v. Board of Education*), the housing authority proffered a "separate but equal" argument, consistent with *Plessy v. Ferguson* (1896). But the California court, in *Banks v. Housing Authority of San Francisco* (1953),[30] ruled against the housing authority. The Supreme Court declined to review the case, thereby leaving intact an important precedent.[31]

Banks, both the final ruling and the fact that it was brought to court in the first place, sent notice that under Williams's leadership there would be no more walking on eggshells to avoid offending the liberal elite or forcing them to face the truth, no more pretending that the race situation was any better than it was. The western region NAACP became more dynamic, more aggressive, and more willing to litigate cases they might lose.[32]

Williams and Howden butted heads over federal education aid. Howden's relatively modest goal was to ensure that every state received education aid. He would have left for another day the discussion of whether that aid should be denied to states that practiced racial segregation. Williams had no intention of waiting for another day. He went around Howden's back and over his head to Rep. Adam Clayton Powell, the Harlem congressman, who sponsored bills denying aid to any state refusing to desegregate.[33]

Williams sought to establish the NAACP, and himself, as the leader in civil rights advocacy. He insisted that all Bay Area groups clear news releases and announcements of protests or other events with *his* office (notably, *not* the national office).[34] He sought to distance the NAACP from a natural ally, the Urban League, a highly regarded civil rights organization that predated the NAACP and dedicated itself to economic empowerment and social justice.[35] In Williams's view, while the Urban League had a noble purpose, it was primarily a "social work organization," while the NAACP was a "direct action and propaganda organization." He did not think the NAACP chapters had any business "trying to be employment agencies," and he did not think the Urban League had any business "running membership drives in the Negro community."[36] Additionally, the League was financially dependent on the Community Chest, a philanthropic organization whose agenda did not always align with the NAACP's. Nonetheless, some years later Williams joined the board of the Urban League when he could not get on the board of the NAACP.

Around the same time, Williams's friend and mentor, Executive Secretary Walter White, died suddenly on March 21, 1955, and Franklin saw an opportunity to take over the NAACP. A group of NAACP members, dubbing themselves the "Young Turks" and made up largely of World War II veterans, unionists, and students, had long held the view that the organization needed to become more activist, staging boycotts, sit-ins, and marches, and were looking to install a more aggressive leader. While some of the Young Turks had become dissatisfied with the leadership provided by Walter White as executive secretary, they viewed Roy Wilkins, the assistant secretary, as even more ineffectual. Quiet, genteel, and reserved, Wilkins "took a detached, intellectual approach to the fight for equality" and strongly believed that "the only rational and effective way to address inequality . . . was to ensure that rights were protected through legislation and court rulings."[37] The Young Turks wanted to thwart the natural succession of Wilkins, and they strenuously lobbied for Williams. But they failed to take into account the culture of the NAACP's old guard. Williams was steamrolled, and Wilkins won a unanimous vote. It was clear to Williams that both his present and future with the NAACP existed in the fiefdom he was building in California, and nowhere else.[38]

Despite Williams's less-than-collegial and often dismissive attitude toward West Coast organizations that refused to play by his rules or meet his standards, his eagerness to challenge racial discrimination wherever he found it made him a wildly popular leader in the various states that comprised the western region and, in the past, had felt forgotten and neglected. Utah, for example, was a small state with a tiny Black population. The first African Americans were a few fur trappers who arrived in the early nineteenth century; the second wave included freedmen who had converted to Mormonism, as well as a handful of slaves belonging to white converts.[39] Utah had willingly desegregated its schools. It surely did not have the pressing issues confronting California and Nevada, but Williams made a point of promoting his mission in Utah and filed a protest at the University of Utah when he learned students were planning to perform in blackface at an annual event. In the 1957 NAACP annual report, Williams wrote that the "color-bar in Salt Lake and some other areas has been relaxed"[40] due to the ongoing protestations of the association. The Utah delegation heard the message clearly: Williams has our back.

Oregon was a different dynamic. In 1849, white settlers in the Oregon Territory enacted the Black Exclusion Law, prohibiting Blacks and mulattos from settling in the region and barring those who had managed to slip through from owning property, voting, or seeking redress in the courts.[41] Almost immediately, two hundred whites signed a petition on behalf of Abner H. Frances, a Black merchant, demanding that the territorial government repeal its exclusionary law. Although that effort was unsuccessful, it was a hopeful sign that a sizeable number of white settlers were willing to stand up for the rights of a tiny, powerless (and unthreatening) minority. Throughout the nineteenth century, the small community of Blacks aligned with progressive whites, and consequently African Americans in Oregon avoided banishment to ghettos and segregated schools that were the norm elsewhere.[42]

Still, Blacks in Oregon did not fully escape the yoke of racism. The Exclusion Law was rendered unenforceable by the Fourteenth Amendment (which was ratified in 1868, nine years after Oregon achieved statehood), but it reflected local sentiment to a large extent and remained on the books until 1926. Around the turn of the century, Blacks were barred from service at white-owned hotels, restaurants, and other places of public accommodation, and the Ku Klux Klan felt emboldened to organize local klaverns. But the Blacks did not accept those indignities lying down, and the inspired leadership of Edward and Beatrice Morrow Cannady kept their hopes alive for a fairer society. The Cannadys started Portland's first Black newspaper, *The Advocate*, in 1903, and a decade later were instrumental in establishing the Portland branch of the NAACP.[43]

The World War II years altered the demographic significantly. Some 22,000 African Americans migrated to Portland during the 1940s in search of work in the burgeoning defense industry, dramatically increasing the number of Blacks in the state. More and more of them were willing to speak out against labor unions promoting Jim Crow restrictions and against local governments all too happy to look the other way in the face of undeniable evidence of rampant discrimination. Blacks increasingly found support in the Urban League and the NAACP, and the memberships of those organizations mushroomed. During the 1950s, the years of Franklin Williams's leadership, Oregon's legislature passed laws concerning public accommodation (1953) and fair housing (1957) that augured well for civil rights in the state, and in which he took great pride.

One of Williams's flaws, the tendency to take things personally, was also one of his strongest assets as an NAACP leader. He often viewed racial slights to anyone as a personal affront to himself and responded aggressively and re-flexively. For example, when Oregon State Senator William Gill, who had opposed the state's civil rights bill, was nominated for US Attorney, Williams took it as a personal insult. Gill's stance on the bill didn't directly impact Williams any more than it directly impacted any other individual, but he reacted as if he alone was the target of the bill. He could not sit by and allow a bigot to become the top federal prosecutor in the state of Oregon and mounted a ferocious effort to deny Gill the prestigious appointment. As a result of the NAACP pressure, then–US Attorney General Herbert Brownell Jr. refused to appoint Gill. It was an unlikely show of force for the NAACP; its voice was heard, and it prevailed,[44] largely because Williams was so personally invested. Only a few years earlier, the NAACP lacked the numbers and clout to garner attention, and even if it had, it's unlikely that anyone, much less the attorney general of the United States, would have cared. Franklin Williams, however, was hard to ignore.

Arizona and Nevada presented distinct challenges. African Americans first arrived in Phoenix and its environs in the late nineteenth century, eager to escape the racist brutality of Arkansas, Louisiana, and Oklahoma. All they escaped, though, was a southern culture that embraced lynching as a means of keeping Blacks in their place.[45] Arizonians were more subtle. Initially, Blacks were so overwhelmingly outnumbered that they could be ignored; most people in Arizona could go weeks or months without encountering an African American. But in the early decades of the twentieth century, the number of Blacks in Arizona became noticeable, and therefore troublesome, and whites began to take notice, segregating the "coloreds" in decrepit neighborhoods where they would ostensibly be happier with their "own kind," relegating them to substandard schools. They worked as domestics, laborers, and agricultural workers, doing the chores deemed below all but those they considered to be "white trash." Many worked in the cotton fields, an assignment painfully and insultingly familiar to Black families.

Regardless of their status as second-class citizens, African Americans living in Phoenix created a culture fostered at first by the tiny number of Black professionals and businesspeople who broke out of the racial mold. They established churches, fraternal groups, self-help associations, women's clubs, and political groups. They joined art and literary clubs, and they cheered and booed at Negro League baseball games. Very slowly, their numbers grew. The tide was turning, ever so subtly. Liberal whites were starting to join with Blacks in organizations such as the NAACP, the Greater Phoenix Council for Civic Unity (GPCU), and the National Urban League. Suddenly, a cadre of leaders, Black and white, was ready to fight for civil rights. They were looking for a forceful, aggressive presence, someone who could capture the hearts and minds of Blacks, and whites, in the Grand Canyon State. Franklin Williams arrived just in time. He promptly visited all the branches and consulted with NAACP leaders in Phoenix, Flagstaff, Winslow, Tucson, and Yuma. He visited the East Lake Park Community Center in Phoenix, lambasting authorities for allowing the George Washington Carver High School to continue as a segregated school.[46] The school had made considerable improvements to facilities for Blacks, but if it expected applause it was sorely disappointed. In the Williams era, good enough was no longer good enough. Williams's appetite for justice would not be satisfied with crumbs and scraps.

Williams turned to the courts, announcing that the Southwestern Area Conference, which included all branches in Arizona, would underwrite a federal lawsuit, spearheaded by the GPCU, challenging school segregation in Arizona. In that case, *Phillips vs. Phoenix Union High Schools and Junior College District*, Maricopa County Superior Court Judge Fred C. Struckmeyer decided "a half century of intolerance is enough" and held unconstitutional an Arizona law permitting school boards to segregate pupils.[47] Fittingly, the case was filed by Hayzel B. Daniels, the first African American to pass the

Arizona bar examination.[48] A year later, the Hon. Charles Bernstein, a Superior Court Judge who was the first Jewish jurist in Arizona history, struck down elementary school segregation in *Heard v. Davis*.[49] Both Arizona state court rulings came before the US Supreme Court rejected "separate but equal" in *Brown v. Board of Education*.

Williams praised the Yuma and Tucson school boards for quickly implementing the *Phillips* and *Heard* decisions, giving credit where credit was due. But he made quite clear that the NAACP would not be satisfied with half a loaf. He publicly excoriated cities throughout the state for allowing local businesses to display "Colored Trade Not Solicited" signs in their windows, a form of "unabashed bigotry" he rarely encountered outside the Deep South.[50]

In Nevada, the state and many of its businesses were systemically and unapologetically racist; one restaurant openly displayed a sign that read, "No Indians, dogs or Negroes Allowed."[51] From the start, Nevada discriminated against Blacks in the public sphere as a matter of law. Blacks were barred from voting, holding office, or serving in the militia. They were banned from the legal profession and could not serve as jurors or on cases involving whites. Intermarriage was a criminal offense.[52] In the 1930s, in the wake of a large-scale migration that brought segregationist southern whites to Nevada in search of jobs, laws were enacted allowing individuals to segregate themselves socially. While Las Vegas welcomed the taxes that acts like Lena Horne, Sammy Davis Jr., and Harry Belafonte brought to its economy, it wasn't about to let lowly "coloreds" stay in their fancy hotels and relegated them to seedy trailers. Similarly, Blacks were generally barred from the gambling casinos. Williams came to the defense of Black entertainers, daring the casinos to roll the dice with the NAACP.

Two of Williams's best lawyers, Nat Colley and Loren Miller, devised a scheme to see what would happen when two lighter-skinned African Americans who weren't obviously Black—Williams and Miller—and one who was—Colley—attempted to gain admission. Williams was at first resistant, according to Colley:

> It required great effort on our part to make Frank go first because he didn't want to pretend not to be Black, because Frank was very Black within himself. When I say he was very Black within himself I mean that he was very much a part of the struggle and he understood that in America it didn't make much difference what you looked like if you're Black. He didn't want to be treated as anything other than Black.[53]

Colley, however, would never be mistaken for anything but Black. The three thought they could trick the casino into discriminating and force a confrontation, but the casino, which had been tipped off, decided it wasn't up for the negative publicity a racial battle would entail, allowed all three in, immediately renounced its prior policy, and promised to accept all customers regardless of race.[54] The victory strengthened Williams's resolve and his base of support in the western states. With his power intact and his support growing, Williams was finally able to focus on his main policy objectives—open housing, school desegregation, and civil rights—and quickly targeted residential segregation, an issue that personally impacted his family.

When Williams first moved to California, he met a white real estate developer named Joseph Eichler who was active in the NAACP. Eichler, a liberal Democrat, was philosophically committed to racial equality and fairness, but he would not build homes in his housing tracts for Blacks out of fear that it would jeopardize his financing though the Federal Housing Agency. In other words, he wasn't willing to put his money where his mouth was. Eichler initially told Williams there were no homes available in his tract—a flat-out lie.[55] Then Eichler agreed to sell Williams a house, but only if he first obtained permission from his prospective white neighbors. Williams refused to even acknowledge such a demeaning and insulting suggestion. Then, Eichler offered to build a housing tract exclusively for Blacks, so long as the NAACP sold the houses. It was a ridiculous demand; the NAACP was not going to become a real estate agency, and Williams rejected the proposal instantly. Worn out, Eichler agreed to sell Williams a house—and then promptly caved to pressure and reneged, as Williams recalled:

> That Saturday night the salesman came to our house. He said Joe had changed his mind and couldn't sell us the house, that his sister-in-law had seen me in the sales office and she was a major stockbroker and she objected to Joe selling to a Black family, and so he was calling off the deal. Well, I went through the ceiling and I said that I was going to file a lawsuit for breach of contract. I was going to smear his name up and down Northern California.[56]

Before it got to the litigation/reputation-smearing stage, the two men talked heart-to-heart. "Look," Williams pleaded, "you know me. I'm an ordinary guy. I just happen to have a different color of skin."[57] Eichler, out of excuses, relented and agreed to build a home for the Williams family, but outside of his white-only development. While building that house, the two men got to know and understand each other and became lifelong friends. Through Williams—a bright, energetic, hardworking Black man who shattered stereotypes—Eichler learned to view Blacks in a different light and was transformed from a limousine liberal who talked the talk but didn't walk the walk to an outspoken and courageous advocate for fair housing. And through Eichler, Williams gained an understanding of the courage it took for even the best-intentioned whites to stand up to society as a whole, their families, and the values and prejudices that were part of the larger culture. Eichler adopted a progressive nondiscrimination policy at a time when he was under no legal obligation to do so and when there was a real chance his business would suffer. He became a minor hero in the civil rights movement, and when his business not only survived but flourished, an object lesson for other business owners. In the end, Eichler went with his conscience rather than his wallet, and came out on top both morally and financially. Williams came to view Eichler as a courageous pioneer in the struggle for housing equality: "Joe Eichler, on his own initiative, and saying nothing to me . . . adopted a policy of non-discrimination. . . . Throughout all of Northern California [he was selling] beautiful modern homes to Hispanics and Blacks and Japanese Americans without any discrimination."[58]

The day the Williams family moved into the Eichler-built home, a delegation of white neighbors visited and "politely" asked the newcomers to leave. Rather than slam the door, punch them in the nose, threaten to sue, or rant, Williams invited them in and sent his boys out to play. He spoke with and reasoned with the neighbors, convinced them that he was a decent, hardworking family man who had no intention of leaving a beat-up Cadillac on blocks in his driveway (a concern that was actually expressed to him). By the time the evening was over, a group of antagonists became a group of friends. Williams, understanding that they were driven not so much by racial hatred as fear, won them over with reason, not force.

> "Dad told us, my brother and I, to go outside and play because he didn't want us to hear," recalled Franklin Williams Jr. "They had a long, long, long discussion. When the discussion was over—it started in the afternoon. It was well past dark when it ended—they left saying, "Welcome to the neighborhood!" I think that if he had, as we say today, copped an attitude, it would have had a very different ending. He was accommodating because he knew that people who can accommodate can be accommodated. . . . We wanted to integrate ourselves into society, and become a part of society, and bring along the things that we had to contribute and hoped that those things would be accepted.[59]

Still, Williams bitterly resented having to audition for the privilege of living in a white neighborhood and was more eager than ever to combat housing discrimination.

At the same time, the NAACP and other groups were pushing California to create a Fair Employment Practices Commission to deal with complaints of discriminatory employment practices. However, to win over opponents, many—including, according to Williams, Terry Francois, the chair of the NAACP Legal Committee[60]—were willing to compromise and accept a commission that could only act after receiving a complaint. Williams thought individuals had too much to lose by coming forward and successfully pressed for a commission with the authority to initiate and investigate complaints on its own.

When the legal route seemed too tedious, Williams went beyond the court of law and argued his case in the court of public opinion, publicly calling out the banks and government financial agencies that were discriminating against Blacks by holding them to a higher and often impossible credit standard. Williams knew that to gain public support he needed not only a good legal case but also a sympathetic example that would raise eyebrows. San Francisco, supposedly liberal and accepting of all, provided a perfect example when a popular young baseball prodigy named Willie Mays was denied the opportunity to buy a home in an upscale neighborhood purely because of his race.[61] Around the same time, the great Jackie Robinson, the man who broke the Major League Baseball color barrier in 1947, was looking to become more involved in the civil rights struggle.

Robinson was a complex, intelligent, often misunderstood man who in many ways was unfulfilled as an athlete. Although he opened the big leagues to Black players—and constantly endured racial taunts from fans and players (and frequently had 90 mph pitches aimed at his head)—Jackie was looking to advance the cause in ways that he could not on the ballfield. In 1954, Robinson became involved in the National Conference of Christians and Jews (NCCJ), and remained active throughout his life, lecturing at schools and other venues, feeling a sense of satisfaction he didn't find at the ballpark.[62] But the Black struggle was just a small part of the NCCJ agenda. By 1956, Robinson was becoming more and more concerned. Particularly in the South, Martin Luther King's message of love and peace perversely seemed to spark hatred, and *Brown v. Board of Education* had energized, frightened, and galvanized those intent on keeping Blacks "in their place." Jackie decided to become more active in the NAACP which, according to his widow, Rachel Robinson, was "the only organization at the time that gave him a sense of hope."[63]

Roy Wilkins, then executive director of the NAACP, knew that Robinson could be a powerful force for the organization, but the ballplayer lacked the polish, oratorical skill, and experience that the NAACP needed. In January 1957, Wilkins somewhat surprisingly summoned Williams to New York to serve as Robinson's speaking coach and guide.

Wilkins and Williams did not care for each other and had often locked horns, but—similar to the Williams-Marshall tension—the differences were largely a matter of style, strategy, and personality, not substance. Wilkins, a southerner, thought northern Blacks were too brash, and Williams certainly fit the New York City stereotype. For his part, Williams thought Wilkins was too incremental, too willing to compromise, and basically weak. But if their means diverged, their goals were parallel, and it is likely that Wilkins recognized that Williams would bring out the best in Jackie Robinson.[64] What he could not have foreseen is that the two men and their families would become lifelong friends.

Robinson agreed to serve as the NAACP national chairman of the annual Fight for Freedom Campaign, and Williams agreed to serve as temporary director of the Freedom Fund. Their respective tasks would bring them close. Jackie had little experience speaking to large groups and less experience asking for money. That's where Williams came in. When the two men met in New York City at the start of the tour, Williams came with a packet of index cards he had prepared for Robinson, cue cards, in effect, to which Jackie could refer to for help in content, tone, and style. Together, they traveled to Baltimore, Pittsburgh, Cleveland, Detroit, Cincinnati, St. Louis, Oakland, and Los Angeles, racking up some eight thousand travel miles in the first three months. They spoke to small groups, large groups, and huge groups. At the Oakland Auditorium, Jackie spoke to ten thousand people.[65] Franklin capitalized on Robinson's fame, devising novel ways of raising money—including selling kisses from Jackie for those willing to pitch in. The tour was a great success, and by the end of it, Shirley Williams and Rachel Robinson had become as close as their husbands. When Jackie died in 1972, Shirley comforted Rachel after the funeral in a way she never forgot:

> I had a little porch outside my bedroom. I was seated out there and I didn't want to talk to anybody. I was deeply grieved. Shirley came back, kneeled by my chair and said, "I wish we could take you home with us." She got right through to what I was feeling, [like] an abandoned child or someone who had lost everything. The sensitivity of her. . . . In just a few words she said everything that I needed to hear and I just felt comforted, so Shirley's very special to me. . . . I just love her.[66]

Williams had begun to grasp the potential of political activism during the buildup to the 1956 presidential election. The likely Democratic nominee, former Illinois governor Adlai Stevenson, issued what Williams viewed as an "extremely wishy-washy" position on implementing *Brown v. Board of Education* and on employment discrimination.[67] Williams's patience, never a strong point, was at the end of its rope, as evidenced by a speech he delivered in Los Angeles in 1956:

The Negro and NAACP are under virtual attack by frightened liberals and self-styled civil rights experts whose greatest fear seems to be the fact that the law of the land is inevitable. Their arguments that the "deep seated emotions of the south" must not be pushed too fast sound strangely like personal unreadiness of the "go slow" advocates themselves. . . . The biggest lie of the century is found in the regularly repeated charges that the NAACP stirs up racial trouble and that the association, not the south's hoodlum element, is guilty of violence. Even our so-called friends are giving credence to this great lie by cautioning us on the "hot-headedness" they find in our continued use of the courts, legislation, protest and other phases of universally accepted democratic processes.[68]

Williams sent Stevenson and Senator Estes Kefauver of Tennessee (then, opponents in the Democratic primary, but later running mates against the Eisenhower-Nixon ticket) telegrams, demanding that they take a position. The point was made: No candidate *and no party* could take the Black vote for granted. He was adamant that the NAACP remain politically independent. Shortly after the Stevenson matter, Williams reprimanded Frank Barnes, president of the NAACP Southern California branch, for inviting only Democratic candidates to a forum for state office seekers. One of the candidates invited was Stanley Mosk, who would go on to a storied judicial career. Williams made a stink over the fact that Mosk, and not his Republican opponent, had been invited to an NAACP event in Southern California.

Mosk won a landslide victory in 1958, and shortly thereafter Williams wrote to the new attorney general, urging him to establish a civil rights section in the Department of Justice. Rather than ignore Williams or send him a form letter, Mosk called Franklin and asked to meet him face-to-face. At that meeting in Mosk's office, the new attorney general revealed that he was already planning to set up a constitutional rights section and asked Williams who he would recommend to run it. Williams suggested first Loren Miller and then Nat Colley, but Mosk figured both were too entrenched in their own legal practice to take a full-time government job. Williams was caught completely off guard when Mosk offered him the position:

So, then he turned to me and said, "Well, how about you, Franklin, would you consider it?" Well, I was quite flattered that he thought positively of me in view of the fact that I had been critical and had almost embarrassed him in Southern California. In retrospect, I guess what happened was that my honesty and objectivity in criticizing Frank

Barnes for inviting the Democrat and not the Republican impressed him positively rather than negatively, and apparently he had developed a respect for me.[69]

Williams was intrigued. For nearly nine years, he had fought an intense legal and public relations battle throughout the western third of the country, achieving the "status and hegemony that he desired" and maintaining an exhausting schedule.[70] The 1956 NAACP annual report, for instance, shows that in that year Williams fulfilled 103 speaking commitments, appeared on radio or TV 52 times, and logged 41,010 miles traveling for the organization.[71] Regardless, he was feeling restless. He knew he had risen as far as he could in the NAACP. He knew Roy Wilkins would never bring him back to the east. He was tired of living on the $9,600 the NAACP was paying him and found the $12,500 Mosk offered quite enticing. He felt the western region, under his leadership, had achieved the status it deserved.[72] Mosk's proposition was the right offer at the right time, and Williams accepted the appointment as assistant attorney general and chief of the constitutional rights section—apparently the first such unit in any state Department of Law in the nation.[73] His job in California would be fourfold: to investigate and report on alleged infringements of civil rights; to intervene on behalf of the state of California as amicus in both civil and criminal cases; to serve as a mediator to prevent civil rights violations; and to work with the new fair employment practices commission to help achieve legislative goals. For the first time in his career, Williams had the force of government behind him, and for the first time in his life he held a political post.

It was not long before his independent streak got him in trouble. Williams knew that the all-white musicians' union discriminated against Black artists and, without telling Mosk, fired off a letter to the president of the union, a very powerful Democratic labor leader, and at the same time sent it to the press. Mosk was livid, according to Williams:

> Mosk called me in, and this was my first introduction to what happens when you're in a politically sensitive appointive job. All my professional life, I had been with the NAACP, had been completely independent. . . . I was in effect my own boss. . . . I was free to determine strategy and how to implement it and I was running the show. Suddenly I was caught up short. Here I had done what I would have done over the prior years—I wrote the letter and let the press know about it. And suddenly I'm on the carpet with Stanley Mosk, who is very upset because he's a politico [and a gubernatorial aspirant]. This was a political goof, and I

was rather shaken by that and made a little bit insecure, because I had never had that experience before.[74]

Lesson learned, Williams knew to go through appropriate channels henceforth. He quickly realized with appreciation that Mosk was behind him all the way, so long as he knew in advance what his deputy was doing.

As head of the constitutional rights section, Williams—with Mosk's approval—took on the Professional Golfers Association (PGA), which had banned a Black golf pro named Charlie Sifford. Williams threatened to seek an injunction barring the PGA from functioning in the state of California, and traveled to Washington, DC, to discuss the matter with the PGA lawyers, liberal attorneys like Thurmond Arnold, who had run President Franklin Roosevelt's antitrust division. "Well, why do colored people want to go where they're not welcome anyhow?"[75] Arnold asked. Williams was dumbfounded, at first:

> It suddenly struck me as I sat there on this cold December night in 1960 . . . that the Roosevelt liberals were economic liberals and that the issues of the '50s and '60s were social issues and they had no conception of those. And then I remembered very vividly as I sat there how Roosevelt had had advisors on Negro affairs . . . [but] he never appointed Negroes or Blacks to these positions. I also recalled how the public housing projects, which grew out of the New Deal, were all segregated by government fiat, as were the various government mortgage lending programs. They were imposing patterns of racial segregation on newly created residential areas. Rather than resisting them or destroying them, they were creating them. So, the Roosevelt New Deal liberal image was truly an economic perception and not a social perception at all.[76]

Williams flew back, discouraged and angry, and after meeting with Mosk advised the PGA that the state intended to file an injunctive lawsuit that would have put the organization out of business in California. The PGA couldn't take that risk and capitulated, amending its bylaws.[77] Charlie Sifford became the first Black golfer on the PGA tour.[78]

Meanwhile, Williams had become intensely interested in the 1960 presidential campaign and, again with Mosk's approval, took a two-month leave of absence to return east and head up the National Campaign to Register One Million New Negro Voters. Working out of the NAACP offices, Williams sent petitions throughout the country and recorded soundbites of Roy Wilkins, Thurgood Marshall, A. Phillip Randolph, Muhammad Ali (then known as

Cassius Clay), and others, sending them to rhythm and blues stations from coast to coast.

In the fall of 1960, Harris Wofford, a Notre Dame law professor and early supporter of the civil rights movement, invited Williams to lecture to his class on constitutional law. Wofford, who had met Kennedy in 1947 at a party at Clare Boothe Luce's home in Connecticut and was working with Sargent Shriver to deliver the "Negro vote," was impressed with Williams's lecture on the changing legal status of the Negro in America.[79] He recruited Williams to speak in favor of Kennedy in Newark, New Jersey; Baltimore, Maryland; Richmond, Virginia; Tampa, Florida; and Portland, Oregon.

The timing was ideal. The Kennedy opposition research team had just learned that Vice President Richard Nixon, JFK's opponent, had a restrictive covenant on his property in California prohibiting the sale or occupancy of the property "by Mongols, by Negroes, by Africans."[80] Williams printed and circulated copies of the covenant far and wide and used it repeatedly in his appearances on behalf of Kennedy.[81]

While Williams was campaigning for Kennedy, Jackie Robinson was supporting Richard Nixon. Robinson had become friendly with the vice president several years earlier and thought Kennedy was "insincere" in his commitment to civil rights.[82] Jackie remained a Nixon supporter until 1968, when Nixon embraced the segregationist Senator Strom Thurmond of South Carolina. That was the last straw, and Robinson endorsed Vice President Hubert Humphrey in the 1968 election. Although Robinson was a strong Nixon backer while Williams was campaigning for Kennedy and then worked in the Kennedy administration, there is no indication that the men allowed their political differences to get in the way of their friendship. Their mutual respect transcended politics.

Williams's growing respect for Kennedy was cemented with JFK's legendary inauguration speech, and he took literally the new president's call: "Ask not what your country can do for you; ask what you can do for your country." Like so many others, Williams was inspired by Kennedy. At the same time, he felt he had accomplished as much as he could in California and was "quietly hoping that I would get a bid to come east to the administration."[83] His phone rang several times as Wofford urged him to consider joining the Kennedy administration. Williams traveled to Washington in the spring of 1961 and was interviewed by G. Mennen "Soapy" Williams, the former governor of Michigan who had been appointed assistant secretary of state for African affairs. Franklin Williams knew Soapy Williams from his AVC days, and he learned when they met that he was under consideration for assistant counsel. But after speaking with Soapy, Franklin decided he did not want the position and headed over to the cafeteria at the Executive Office Building, where he met Wofford and Louis E. Martin, a Black newspaper publisher and activist who was deputy chairman of the Democratic National Committee. Martin, called the "godfather of Black politics,"[84] was a liaison between African Americans and presidents from Franklin Roosevelt to Jimmy Carter.

Williams somewhat dejectedly told Wofford and Martin that he wasn't interested in working for Soapy Williams, and the job he really wanted—assistant director of the US Civil Rights Commission—was already taken. Martin suggested Wofford introduce Williams to Sargent Shriver, Kennedy's brother-in-law, who was putting together a senior staff.[85] Shriver and Williams hit it off immediately; in fact, Shriver picked up the phone and called Williams's boss—loyal Democrat Stanley Mosk—and told him the Kennedy administration needed his deputy attorney general in Washington. He offered Williams $16,000 a year. Franklin called Shirley and told her to start packing.

As time went on, Williams's admiration for Shriver only grew, and he developed "tremendous respect for Sarge's integrity and decency."[86] He and Shirley often associated with the Shrivers, and that association brought them into contact with the Kennedy clan on occasion.

One day, while driving home from a gathering at the Shriver's home, Franklin asked his nine-year-old son why he hadn't been playing with Bobby Kennedy Jr., the son of Robert F. Kennedy. The answer stunned him: Young Bobby, who would have been about nine years old, had asked Paul Williams if he was a "nigger." Shocked at first, Williams figured the Kennedy boy was probably repeating something he had heard from his grandfather, the family patriarch Joseph P. Kennedy, who was known to use racist language. The incident was a reminder of the deep racial divisions in the country and a culture of bigotry that was too often handed down from generation to generation.

11

The Washington Years

Three weeks from the election and after a long day of campaigning, John Fitzgerald Kennedy arrived at the University of Michigan in Ann Arbor at 2:00 a.m. on October 14, 1960, planning to get some sleep, not to deliver a speech. But when thousands of students at the university greeted Kennedy, he spoke with them from the steps of the student union and, for the first time, shared publicly an idea he'd been contemplating for at least a year:

> How many of you who are going to be doctors, are willing to spend your days in Ghana? Technicians or engineers, how many of you are willing to work in the Foreign Service and spend your lives traveling around the world . . . not merely to serve one year or two years in the service, but on your willingness to contribute part of your life to this country. . . . I think Americans are willing to contribute. But the effort must be far greater than we have ever made in the past.[1]

It was something that had been on Kennedy's mind for quite some time. In 1959, Kennedy expressed to Harris Wofford his interest in establishing a "new relationship" between the United States and the developing world.[2] The response was overwhelmingly positive, and Kennedy built upon that theme two weeks later during a speech at the Cow Palace in San Francisco where, on November 2, 1960—less than a week before the election—he proposed "a peace corps of talented men and women" who would dedicate themselves to the progress and peace of developing nations.[3] But Kennedy's motive was not purely humanitarian or even economic. Rather, it was in large measure a Cold War initiative antidote to communist expansion.[4] Kennedy was concerned that the Soviet Union "had hundreds of men and women, scientists, physicists, teachers, engineers, doctors, and nurses . . . prepared to spend their lives abroad in the service of world communism," and he wanted Americans more actively involved in the causes of freedom, peace, economic development, and democracy.[5]

Within days of taking office as the thirty-fifth president of the United States, Kennedy asked his sister Eunice's husband, Robert Sargent Shriver Jr., to lead a task force to design and structure this new entity. Reluctantly, Shriver agreed to head the new agency, and went about the task of building a team that shared his vision for the Peace Corps. Shriver had no desire to preside over a do-nothing bureaucracy, and he was particularly concerned that Americans not appear as arrogant missionaries claiming to have all the answers. Instead, he viewed the Peace Corps as a hub that encouraged the entire Western bloc to assist developing nations, preferably under the sponsorship and auspices of the United Nations, not the United States.[6] Williams was one of Shriver's first hires, and one of his few contemporaries; both were in their early forties, while most of the other top executives were in their thirties. Shriver and Williams sought to create a culture and mindset where the Peace Corps was viewed as a service, not a job with the usual emoluments of a public sector career.

Williams crafted an "in-up-and-out" policy which Shriver adopted. The idea was to bring in bright, ambitious, energetic young professionals, and empower them to move up in the organization—and then get them out before they settled into a bureaucratic mindset. In a March 6, 1963, memorandum, Williams expressed his concern over "careerism":

> Unless we permanently build in some protections, it is inevitable that the Peace Corps . . . will eventually become so bureaucratic, hidebound, and "the-way-we-did-it-yesterday-is-the-way-it-should-be-done-today" . . . that all the wonderful vigor, originality, flexibility, etc. that we talk about will slowly disappear. . . . This kind of bureaucratic hardening of the arteries can be avoided. The secret is staffing. I propose an "in-up-and-out" procedure for the Peace Corps.[7]

Williams, who was dealing with such arcane issues as whether Peace Corps volunteers could wear beards and how and if to accommodate married volunteers, was tasked immediately with persuading the UN to either set up a voluntary service akin to the Peace Corps or forge volunteer relationships among the various nations. Shriver had greased the wheels just weeks after taking office, arranging a meeting between Assistant Secretary of State Harlan Cleveland and Adlai Stevenson, the US ambassador to the United Nations, in April 1961.[8] Stevenson agreed to promote a two-part Peace Corps initiative that would permit the agency to appoint volunteers directly to UN programs while the UN provided "comparable opportunities" to volunteers from other member nations.[9]

The US resolution to "use volunteer workers in the operational programmes of the United Nations" passed the thirty-second session of the Economic and Social Council (ECOSOC) over the opposition of the Soviet Union. One week later, Williams visited Paris, where he met with senior officials of the secretariat of the United Nations Educational, Scientific and Cultural Organization (UNESCO), which had been established to promote international collaboration in education, science, and culture with the goal of increasing universal respect for human rights, justice, the rule of law, and principles of freedom proclaimed in the UN charter.[10] The visit was extremely fruitful, according to a staff member of the US Embassy in Paris, who wrote that Williams was "very successful in engendering interest and enthusiasm in the Peace Corps and in stimulating serious thought by the Secretariat on possible U.S. Peace Corps–UNESCO cooperation."[11] The reaction abroad was unprecedented, with US embassies in Austria, Britain, Cyprus, Denmark, Egypt, Ethiopia, the Netherlands, and Sweden promptly reporting enthusiastic reviews.[12]

The Peace Corps initiative earned Kennedy a reputation in Third World nations, such as Nigeria, Ethiopia, Guatemala, and Gabon, as the friend of the colored man everywhere, and the administration was eager to capitalize immediately on that goodwill. In the spring of 1961, Williams joined Shriver, Wofford, and Ed Bayley, a former Wisconsin newspaperman who was brought

Williams (left) was second-in-command of the newly established Peace Corps to Sargent Shriver (center), President Kennedy's brother-in-law. Williams and Shriver developed a deep mutual respect and friendship. (Enid Gort collection)

in to handle press relations, on a whirlwind tour that took them to Ghana, Nigeria, Turkey, Pakistan, Burma, Malaya (now Malaysia), Thailand, the Philippines, and Singapore. Only Williams was Black. "I thought it would be good for the people in Africa to see that this was not some crowd of white, Western, colonialist types who were out there trying to do to Africa what hundreds of other people had done in times past," Shriver said in a 1991 interview.[13] "I thought the very fact that he was Black would help minimize suspicions that might lie in people's minds, and also I thought that he would have sensitivities about political personalities that we would meet, who were Black, that I would not have."[14]

For his part, Williams felt at home in Africa in a way that he'd never felt before. When he was growing up, he never quite knew where he fit in. He was raised in a white neighborhood and initially questioned if he was more African or American Indian. As a young man and young adult, he still lacked the full cultural connection; he was light-skinned, could be mistaken for Mediterranean, Mexican, or even Asian, and lacked the southern roots and vernacular that defined others, such as Thurgood Marshall. In Ghana, Williams fully came to terms with who he was: an African American. The mannerisms and mores of the Ghanaians reminded him of some of his relatives. He found that he spoke the same language as the people of Ghana—a different dialect, to be sure, but the same language. They understood each other on an ancestral level. His Lincoln University classmate, Prime Minister Kwame Nkrumah, greeted Williams as if he were an old friend when in reality, they barely knew each other.

Nkrumah viewed himself as a prophet of pan-Africanism and chieftain of an emerging African continent. His worshipful followers referred to him as "Osagyefo," or "Victorious Leader."[15] The American delegation, however, was leery, suspecting that Nkrumah "was going to be very anti-American and would reject the idea of young college graduates coming to his country to teach Ghanaians."[16] Indeed, a leading newspaper, the Ghanaian Times, had denounced the Peace Corps as an "agent of neocolonialism" and an "instrument for subversion and bluntly rejected "all twaddle about its humanitarianism."[17] But Nkrumah, although suspicious of the Central Intelligence Agency after its disastrous attempt to overthrow Fidel Castro in Cuba, was cautiously amenable. He told Williams their volunteers were welcome, so long as they did "not propagandize or spy or try to subvert the Ghanaian system."[18] Nkrumah said his country could benefit from science, math, and English teachers, but he wanted nothing to do with social scientists who might try to influence local opinions. He specifically requested plumbers and electricians. He even

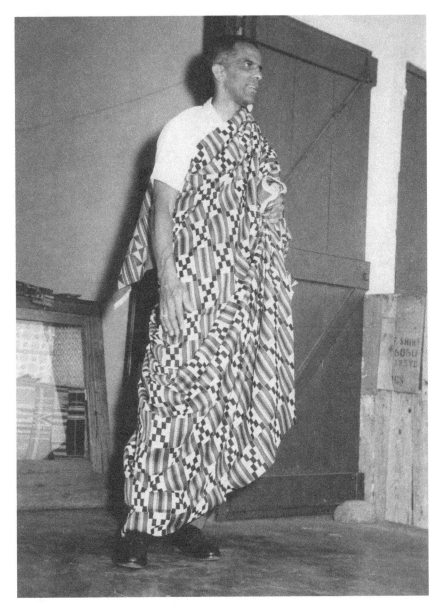

As ambassador to Ghana, Williams discovered his roots and fully embraced the African culture. Here he is wearing a kente cloth. (Enid Gort collection)

Williams pays his respects to Otumfuo Nan Sir Osei Tutu Agyeman Prempeh II, the fourteenth "Asantehene," or king of the Asante. Prempeh II reigned from 1931 to 1970. (Enid Gort
collection)

proposed a reciprocal agreement in which Ghanaian students would come to
the United States.[19]

In Nigeria, Williams and Shriver encountered an American couple who
had volunteered under a different program and were living in poverty and poor
health. The male was clearly suffering from malaria, the female was sickly
thin, and their baby was covered from head to toe with mosquito bites. Shriver
was so alarmed at their condition that he immediately sent a cable back to
Washington, directing that each country where a Peace Corps volunteer was
sent would have to have a volunteer doctor on staff.[20] Each stop was a different
and new experience, and Williams relished the diversity of the African nations,
each with its own identity and customs.

When Williams returned to Washington, eager to finish the deal with the
UN, he was stunned to learn that the idea was no longer viable, largely because of an unrelated issue over whether to send a UN peacekeeping force
into the Congo. The Soviet Union, which opposed the measure, refused to pay

its dues to the UN in violation of the charter, which at least temporarily turned Congress sour on the UN in general. In that atmosphere, the Peace Corps no longer sought UN affiliation, the State Department was in opposition, and even Shriver threw down his cards. "The Peace Corps didn't want it. The State Department didn't want it. Nobody wanted it but me," Williams later said.[21] "That was a lesson I learned of both politics and bureaucracies: You don't get wedded to a position and an idea. If it doesn't work, if it doesn't fit today's needs in terms of strategies to reach the ultimate goal, you just drop it." Williams was disappointed but had his eye on Africa. He voluntarily took a demotion just so he could return to what he had come to view as his ancestral homeland and become director of the African regional division in 1963—the position he would hold for the remainder of his Peace Corps days.[22] Williams's brief tenure as African regional director proved an invaluable opportunity to further explore and grasp his own heritage.

While Williams was in Kenya, President Kennedy was assassinated in Dallas. Williams had bought into the "ask what you can do for your country" atmosphere and viewed Kennedy, first and foremost, as a "man of ideas and ideals," but also a "man of action who knows how to use power and when not to use it."[23] He knew relatively little about Lyndon Johnson but intended to remain on the job until and unless asked to leave to take another position. In 1964, a new opportunity arose with the United Nations Economic and Social Council (ECOSOC), a group of representatives from eighteen countries tasked with promoting higher standards of living and providing a central forum for discussion on international economic and social issues.

The vacancy arose when Jonathan Bingham, the US representative on the council, resigned to run for a New York congressional seat. Bill Moyers, a former journalist who was serving as a special advisor to President Johnson, recommended Williams, whom he knew from the Peace Corps. Johnson agreed and nominated Williams for ambassador to the ECOSOC, a position requiring Senate confirmation.[24] However, Adlai Stevenson was quietly working against him, leading Williams to assume, wrongly, that the senator's opposition was race-based. It was neither the first nor last time that Williams would wrongly assume a racial slight. But to his credit, he was quite willing to revisit his presumptions as the evidence warranted, as it did with Stevenson. "His antagonism towards me was not based on race at all," Williams readily confessed in 1990.[25] "It was based on economics. . . . It was based on the fact that I was of no economic service to him."

According to Williams, Stevenson was a notorious cheapskate.[26] Still, Stevenson liked to surround himself with millionaires such as Francis T. P. Plimpton, partner in a major Manhattan law firm (Debevoise & Plimpton), whom he designated second-in-command, and socialite Marietta Tree, who was on the UN Human Rights Commission. Wealthy people could pick up the tab for the fancy dinner parties where diplomats often did their business; less wealthy people like Williams could not, and they either didn't host those important events or charged them to Stevenson's office.[27]

Stevenson, however, did not aggressively oppose Williams, and he was confirmed by the Senate after Senator Thomas H. Kuchel, a California Republican, praised his "wealth of imagination and concern about social and economic problems." In the *Congressional Record*, Kuchel added: "We think his effectiveness will be enhanced by the fact that he happens to be a Negro who has always worked and spoken forcefully for the cause of human equality. And we think his appointment will contribute to the world's recognition that human equality is finding full realization in the United States. The President deserves congratulations on so felicitous a nomination."[28] Williams was sworn in during an emotional ceremony attended by Shirley, both of their sons, and May Chinn, his godmother.

Williams is sworn in as ambassador to Ghana. (*Standing from left*), May Edward Chinn, Franklin's godmother; Miguel Augustus Rubiero, Ghana's ambassador to the United States; George Ball, undersecretary of state; and Shirley Broyard Williams. (Enid Gort collection)

Within a few days, Williams was on his way to Geneva as ambassador to ECOSOC, with a stop first in Stockholm for duty with the Third UN Congress on the Prevention of Crime and Treatment of Offenders. He found the position rewarding, although in what appears to be a diary entry, Williams wrote that "working with Stevenson is very unsatisfactory."[29]

> One does not get the feeling of being involved in any of the political decision-making. In many ways that is OK with me—for the positions we take are too frequently wrong in my opinion—but Stevenson seems to do very little to soften our stance. He is not at all vigorous or strong in his relationship with Washington. One day he got in the elevator with me and never even said "hello"—this thoughtlessness, or better said this self-ceteredness [sic] is felt by the delegates from the lesser-developed countries especially.[30]

Williams had an opportunity to leave in the spring of 1965, when Bill Moyers called and said LBJ wanted to know whether he would be interested in returning to Washington to take the number two spot at the Department of Health, Education and Welfare. He told Moyers he would do whatever the president requested but felt he had not yet had an opportunity to make an impact in his post with ECOSOC. A few days later, Williams's diary shows, he was back in Washington with other senior appointees for dinner at the White House, where LBJ mistook him for Carl Rowan, a noted Black journalist who at the time was serving as director of the US Information Agency. "Carl," the president mistakenly said to Williams, "you're going to have a helluva time tomorrow morning. I just ordered the Marines into the Dominican Republic." In the diary, Williams wrote, "The president's action seemed wrong and precipitous to me."[31] Perhaps it was. The next day, Johnson sent 22,000 troops into the Dominican Republic to restore order and forestall a communist takeover, only to provoke loud protests throughout Latin America and skepticism back home.[32]

It is unclear what happened during Williams's brief return to Washington, but it appears he was looking to get away from Stevenson. In June, he returned to California as ambassador to ECOSOC to attend the UN anniversary celebration. Williams's scrapbook contains a very flattering article on his visit published in the *San Francisco Chronicle*, but that included what he deemed a "rather funny headline." It read: "Ex-S.F. Negro Returns to U.N. Envoy."[33] He apparently used the trip to do some personal politicking and made an effort to oust Roy Wilkins and get on the NAACP board. But his attempt a decade earlier to take over the organization with the "Young Turks" likely left an enduring impression that he was too brash, too arrogant; if the NAACP didn't want him in a leadership position, well, he'd find another outlet for his energy and commitment. According to a diary entry from July 1965:

> After my failure to get elected to the NAACP board—I was determined to lend my time and talents to some civil rights organization. Bob Mangum [chairman of the Urban League Board] indicated that he would get me on the UL (Urban League) board if I wanted to serve. I would have preferred the NAACP. On the other hand, Whitney Young proved to be such a "big man" without so many of the petty insecurities that Roy [Wilkins] has—I thought it would be nice to support his organization.[34]

Meanwhile, Williams seemed to be using every avenue available to preach his gospel of social justice, which by the mid-1960s had expanded well beyond Blacks. In an impassioned address to the thirty-ninth session of the UN Economic and Social Council in July 1965, Williams spoke eloquently in favor of women's rights:

> Of the three and one-half billion humans who populate this earth, more than one-half are women. Among the 700 million illiterates, a disproportionately large number are women. In far too many areas of the world women occupy a status lower than that of men and at birth—not unlike some racial and religious minorities—have severe limitations set upon the level of their aspirations by law, customs, practice and usage. . . .
>
> We can hardly speak seriously of the development of humankind without reference in specific terms to raising the present depressed status of more than half of the human race. This is not simply a question of human dignity—fundamental as that is—it is as well a question of good judgment and good sense.[35]

Around the same time, Stevenson suffered a heart attack and died in London on July 14, 1965. He was replaced by Arthur Goldberg, who surprisingly gave up a lifetime appointment (by Kennedy) to the US Supreme Court in exchange for a temporary job. In his memoir, Goldberg claimed he left the court because he thought he could persuade Johnson to get out of Vietnam.[36] Williams, as protocol demanded, tendered his resignation to his new boss and flew to New York to meet with Goldberg, who warned Williams that "higher up in the State Department you have some enemies."[37] In his papers and in interviews, Williams gives no clue that he knew anything about "enemies" and proclaimed to simply be surprised by the remark:

He said, "Franklin, tomorrow we're announcing a whole new team here." My heart went down to my stomach. He said, "But I want you to know the President said to me"—and I'm quoting him now—"you're the only one up here he gives a damn about and that you can stay on until such time as we can find something to give you that you can accept with dignity." I went home and I wept. I was fired, in effect.[38]

Newspaper articles from the time made clear that Williams was dumped. A banner headline in the *Bay Area Independent* of September 11, 1965, read, "Franklin H. Williams Ouster." An undated column in the *New York Herald Tribune* by syndicated columnists Rowland Evans and Robert Novak said Williams had been "quietly shelved" and would become acting director of the Peace Corps.[39]

James Roosevelt, eldest son of Franklin Delano Roosevelt, replaced Williams, who was left to ponder his professional future. Williams was recruited by radio pioneer R. Peter Strauss, the media executive who turned WMCA in New York into one of the top stations in the nation, and rejected various government positions, holding out for an ambassadorship.[40] He was offered Guinea, but rejected it, in part because Guinea is a French-speaking country and Williams didn't speak French. He lobbied instead for an open position in Ghana. Ghana made sense: it's an English-speaking nation; the premier, Nkrumah, had been Williams's college classmate; Williams's best friend and college roommate (Bobby Freeman) ran an insurance company there; and another classmate, K. A. B. Jones-Quartey of the class of 1949 was a prominent professor at the University of Ghana. Johnson was receptive. The president, however, had a second thought. LBJ had created the Office of Economic Opportunity and tasked Shriver with leading the "War on Poverty" while simultaneously running the Peace Corps. But Shriver wanted to focus exclusively on the antipoverty effort. Before Williams departed for Ghana, the president and his solicitor general—Thurgood Marshall—discussed how to handle the situation, according to a furtive Oval Office recording that emerged years later:

LBJ: "I'm giving thought to another fellow that's not for this place at all, but for another rather top spot that has to be confirmed by the Senate. And he's this boy that's just named Ambassador to Ghana, Williams. . . . What's your evaluation of him, just between us two, what's his strength and weakness?"

Marshall: "He's got all the imagination and brain that you want. His ambition is a little too much for him. When he was with me, I . . . just explained to him as a Dutch uncle, I said, 'Frank, I know what you're shooting at. You're shooting for my job or Roy Wilkins'. So far as I'm concerned, you better start shooting for Roy's because you can't take mine. You're not man enough.' [Johnson laughs]. He's that kind of operator and he somehow fouled up with the Peace Corps. I don't know how, but he did over there. But as for ability, he's really tops. He's very good."

LBJ: "Well now, can I tell you something without your discussing it with another human?"

Marshall: "Why, certainly."

LBJ: "What would you think about his taking Shriver's place at the Peace Corps?"

Marshall: "Terrific."

LBJ: "The boys that know him over there . . . like him because he's imaginative, and he's attractive, and he's acceptable to Latin America and to Africa and to the non-aligned and he's personable and he's got an attractive wife, and he works at it. And Shriver's . . . begging every day to get out. And I want somebody that will give me a good image and . . ."

Marshall: "I would put Frank there without any hesitation. . . . He can come up with more ideas in a minute than most people I know of, and they're darn good ones. Once he gets what he wants, I think from that he'll drive like mad. And he'll drive everybody under him, too, 'cause he puts in a real day's work. He's terrific. I think he'd be good. Yes, sir."[41]

It is unclear whether Shriver's position at the Peace Corps was ever offered to Williams—and it's doubtful he would have taken it. In any case, former professional boxer Jack Vaughn of the State Department got the job. It is also unclear to what Marshall was referring when he said Williams "fouled up with the Peace Corps." Regardless, on October 10, 1965, while recovering from gall bladder surgery at Bethesda Naval Hospital, LBJ publicly announced Williams's appointment. Franklin and Shirley made plans to move to Ghana after the first of the year, without either son. Their older son, Franklin Jr., had just entered college at Amherst, Massachusetts, and the younger son, Paul, was in a New Jersey boarding school. However, they had to wait for the *agrément*, or approval of a diplomatic representative, and, ironically, there was some question whether Nkrumah would accept a Black man; in the past, the United States had sent Black diplomats only to what some viewed as second-tier states, such as Haiti and Liberia, and Nkrumah did not want the newly independent state of Ghana treated as a second-rate nation.[42]

But Nkrumah signed off on Williams rather readily, and Franklin and Shirley made plans for their first-ever cruise. They sailed to London, first-class, hob-nobbing with celebrities such as the actor Keir Dullea and screenwriter Sidney Lumet. After disembarking in southern England, Franklin and Shirley traveled to London, meeting with diplomats before boarding an Air Ghana flight to Accra the night of January 14, 1966. They were met by a large, welcoming delegation, and whisked to a palatial residence where lush plantings adorned gleaming marble terraces. About ten miles away, to the east of Tema, they had a beachfront getaway. Franklin and Shirley had never imagined such extravagance.[43]

Williams prepared for his first official visit with Nkrumah. He knew it was customary to bring a gift but wasn't sure what to bring. He consulted with an American businessman and the assistant secretary of state for Africa, both of whom had paid official visits to the prime minister and brought gifts. The former brought a remote-control dirigible and the latter a cork remover. Williams found the gifts insulting and brought him a gift befitting the leader of proud nation: a beautifully framed reproduction of a petition signed by

Williams enjoys a toast with his Lincoln College classmate Kwame Nkrumah, who became prime minister and president of Ghana. (Enid Gort collection)

Lincoln University students and faculty calling on the US Senate to adopt the Fourteenth Amendment, which granted citizenship to former slaves and guaranteed them "equal protection of the laws." Nkrumah was delighted. But if Williams and Nkrumah got off on the right foot, their relations soured within weeks.

Williams did his best to maintain friendly relations but could not come through on the first major request from the Nkrumah administration. President Kennedy had helped Nkrumah secure funding for the Akosombo Dam, a hydroelectric dam on the Volta River in southwest Ghana, and Nkrumah was eager to have either former First Lady Jacqueline Kennedy or Attorney General Robert F. Kennedy, the late president's younger brother, present for the dedication. Williams tried, but was rebuffed: "There was no desire or willingness on the part of the Johnson Administration to have Mrs. Kennedy or Bobby Kennedy do anything. It was made very clear to me that neither one of them would come to the dedication, which was creating some unhappiness for me, and it was almost a test of whether or not I could deliver as ambassador. And I couldn't."[44]

Then, just weeks into the job, Williams was summoned to Flagstaff House, the presidential palace in Accra, for a private meeting with Nkrumah, who stunned the new ambassador. Nkrumah asked Williams to alert President Johnson that he planned to go to North Vietnam in an effort to settle the war but was awaiting clearance from North Vietnam and was concerned that his "enemies"—the Chinese Communists—not find out. Williams dutifully cabled Washington, only to be called back to another meeting with Nkrumah, this one in the presence of aides. In the second meeting, Nkrumah said he was planning to travel to Vietnam at the end of February and wanted assurance that LBJ would suspend the bombing of Hanoi while he was there. Williams agreed to relay the message, and Nkrumah said he would go as soon as he got the word from Johnson and *approval from the Chinese Communists*, the same group that days earlier he had identified as his enemy. Williams had told the administration that Nkrumah considered the Chinese Communists his enemies and did not want them to know of the planned trip; now Nkrumah was asking him to tell LBJ the exact opposite.

> My head was spinning. I thought, "Oh my God, is he trying to make a fool out of me? Is he trying to make me look silly to the State Department, or is he just playing me like a monkey on a string?" I cabled that back to Washington with great trepidation, thinking that Washington's going to think, "What kind of ambassador is this? What's going on

here? He can't report accurately on all these fairy tales. Nkrumah, the great anti-Western African leader didn't want our common enemy Communist China to know about this trip, and now he's saying that clearance from Communist China . . . is the only thing that's standing in the way of confirming the date."[45]

Nkrumah had been under attack for at least a year, was wildly unpopular in some quarters, and had survived assassination and coups attempts. Williams's directive from Secretary of State Dean Rusk was to avoid doing anything that might destabilize the regime, and he obeyed the directive.[46] But Williams was constantly hearing rumors that Nkrumah's regime, and life, were on borrowed time. On the morning of February 24, when Nkrumah was in China—not Vietnam—a group of dissident army officers took over the government. Nkrumah was convinced that the Americans, and by extension Williams, were behind the coup, and in fact called him an "Uncle Tom" in his book *Dark Days in Ghana*. Williams was deeply hurt and offended, and he prevailed on the president of Lincoln University, Marvin Wachman, to write a personal letter to Nkrumah sharing Franklin's insistence he was in no way complicit.[47]

While Williams was certainly aware of, and reported to Washington, persistent rumors that Nkrumah's life was in jeopardy, it is unclear whether he had any direct prior knowledge of the coup.[48] He had been in Ghana only a couple of weeks. Williams's second-in-command, John W. Foley Jr., the deputy chief of mission, recalled persistent rumors of a coup, saying, "we quite often had the expectation that we might wake up the next morning and find that a coup had taken place. . . . Franklin just felt he had to keep out of it completely."[49] Yet, this one felt different, and Foley slept in the embassy office the night of February 23. "Franklin, I think, went to bed that night knowing a coup was probably going to take place."[50]

Foley was confident Williams did nothing to instigate or support the coup and was equally confident that the CIA did play a role, or at least take advantage of the discord. Years later, documents indicated that the CIA advised and supported the dissidents, but nothing implicates Williams.[51] In an interview late in his life, Williams revealed that he did know that the CIA—regardless of whether it played an active or passive role in the coup—was eager to exploit the rebellion *after* it took place.

> During the day of the coup—the coup occurred early in the morning—Howard Bane [the CIA station chief in Accra] came to me and said he would like to put together an operation to invade the Chinese embassy as if it was a mob and get whatever intelligence they could.

I told him, "No way." Howard Bane was very pissed off and angry at
me. He said I was naïve and missing a great opportunity. I said,
"Absolutely not."

Some weeks later . . . after the new government was in place, Bane
came to me and said the internal security of Ghana had asked the CIA
for help in training some of their personnel, who they would place in
Ghanaian missions around the world. . . . I said, "No, we can't do
that," and a big disagreement developed. . . . I needed State Department support, which I got . . .

Kermit Roosevelt [grandson of President Theodore Roosevelt and a
career intelligence officer who had engineered the overthrow of the
leader of Iran in 1953] actually came to Ghana . . . and demanded that
I give approval. . . . I absolutely refused. . . . Roosevelt got really pissed
off at me, extremely angry. He charged me with being naïve, a poor
ambassador, not knowing what I was doing, and not having any con-
ception of the Communist threat that America faces around the world.
I still refused.[52]

Only a year later, Ghana endured another coup—this one aborted—when
Major General Emmanuel Kwasi Kotoka, a member of the National Liberation
Council that overthrew Nkrumah, was murdered by a small contingent of
junior officers. The dissidents were promptly captured and executed, which
shocked and disturbed Williams. In his view, Nkrumah had been an oppressive
dictator who was not above jailing his political opponents. But he did not view
Nkrumah as a cold-blooded murderer. The National Liberation Council showed
no such restraint.[53]

The Nkrumah affair remains an unfair stain on Williams's legacy, and some
continue to insist that he sold out an African hero, even though Nkrumah
himself ultimately conceded there was no evidence of Williams's involvement.[54]
It was a sore point with Williams for the remainder of his life and placed him
in the hopelessly frustrating position of attempting to prove the unprovable—
that he did not know in advance of the coup.

In the early 1970s, Williams was attending an international conference in
the Caribbean when he was caught completely off guard and verbally attacked
by a man he did not know, Tanzanian novelist and diplomat Peter K. Palangyo.
Palangyo called Williams a traitor to his race and blamed him and his "imperialist" government for the removal of Nkrumah. Williams saw that Palangyo
was surrounded by a coterie of supporters and knew he would be shouted down
if he attempted to defend himself, so he quietly but angrily walked out. He

never forgot the incident or forgave Palangyo, and in fact kept his name Scotch-taped to his office wall. It was an odd action since Williams was not ordinarily one to harbor a grudge. But this slight got and stayed under his skin.

Incredibly, more than a decade later Palangyo had the gall, or ignorance, to approach Williams at the Phelps Stokes Fund, seeking scholarship money for his son. Palangyo had apparently forgotten the incident; Williams had not. In a calm, even-tempered tone, Williams reminded Palangyo of what had transpired in the Caribbean. At first the flustered visitor claimed he had no recollection of the conference or of Williams. Then, when Williams refreshed his memory, Palangyo apologized profusely, claimed a friend put him up to it and that he had no knowledge of anything that transpired or didn't transpire in Ghana vis-à-vis Nkrumah, and that he did it on a dare. In other words, Palangyo admitted that he had no idea what he was talking about when he publicly insulted and sullied the reputation of a man he did not know and had never met, but did it to appease his friends. Regardless, Williams treated Palangyo like a gentleman and, after accepting his apology, agreed to help his son find scholarship money.[55] It was an elegant act by a statesman; Williams was not going to punish the son for the sins of the father—and he quietly taught the father, by example, a poignant lesson about integrity and decency and grace.

By 1968, Franklin and, especially Shirley, were ready to come home. While Shirley enjoyed traveling and meeting interesting people, Franklin knew that, at heart, she was a homebody whose fondest wish was to return to New York. During their married life, they had moved constantly: from the Brooklyn brownstone to Harlem to Berkeley to Palo Alto to Washington to New York City to Ghana. During all those years, Shirley stayed at home, raised their children, and cared for the household. She joined PTAs and involved herself in charity work, particularly for the NAACP. Shirley was her husband's fashion stylist; she bought his clothes and kept them well maintained, a quiet intellectual, content to be in Franklin's shadow, dutifully attending and hosting social events that she tolerated more than enjoyed. But she'd had enough, needed a nest, and prevailed upon Franklin to purchase a five-story brownstone on West Eighty-Ninth Street even before they left for Africa. In truth, it was a slum building with a leaky roof and tenants nestled in decrepit cubby holes. They bought the building through a Federal Housing Authority program providing money to those willing to buy and renovate distressed buildings and turn them into rent-controlled apartments. Shirley traveled back and forth from Africa for the next three years, working with architects and contractors to ensure that at last, she would have a permanent home.

Williams in his home on West Eighty-Ninth Street in Manhattan, probably in the mid-1980s. (Photo courtesy of Franklin H. Williams Judicial Commission)

From his travels around the globe, Franklin had come to view his own country through a different lens, and came to believe that he could best serve the interests of justice and equal rights by returning to the United States:

In every country, on every continent where I have traveled, I have been asked in a hundred ways, "How can America claim democracy, while it denies equality to its citizens of color?" This is a hard question to answer . . . for it is a sad and disgraceful fact that a hundred years after the Emancipation our country is still far from being the land of the free. . . . On the pernicious issue of color, both our friends and enemies will insist that we practice the democracy we preach.[56]

But perhaps the turning point came on a beach in Ghana when his seventeen-year-old son, Paul, asked how he could serve as ambassador for a racist country. At first, Franklin was angry. And then he looked back. He thought of his childhood, recalling his years at PS 23 in Flushing and how he wasn't allowed to use the public swimming pool. He recalled the opening of the RKO Keith Theater on Broadway and Main and how Blacks were not allowed to sit in the orchestra seats. He thought of the YMCA and YWCA in Flushing, and how Black boys and girls could not join. He remembered the few opportunities for Black high school graduates, and how at the five-and-ten on Thirty-Ninth Street and Fifth Avenue in Manhattan "we colored boys were permitted only to be dishwashers and bus boys." He thought back to 1952 when he was denied the right to buy a house in Palo Alto. He recalled the military segregation that had opened his eyes to racial injustice during World War II. And he knew it was time to fight his battles at home.[57]

Columbia University in Harlem had just received a $10 million grant from the Ford Foundation to help ameliorate the long-simmering resentment between the school and the Harlem community that surrounded it. Williams notified the administration of his resignation effective June 1, 1968, to become director of the Columbia University Center for Urban and Minority Affairs: "I resigned from the employ of my government—not out of hatred or anger or even disillusionment, but in an effort to re-identify with the forces . . . that were at work back home among my own people, influencing my own family, and, in the final analysis, shaping the nature of our society."[58]

The academy seemed like a good fit. Williams was increasingly troubled with the state of higher education and in various speeches implored the academy to embrace its obligation to teach students to think, as Lincoln University had taught him. Williams had grown concerned that American students were woefully ignorant of history and thought "it would be a disaster if our educational system was geared to turning out an endless parade of mindless stereotypes with 'safe' political views, who will fit without complaint into pre-built niches society has waiting for them."[59]

But Williams had been out of the country for a long time, and he was not prepared for what awaited him at Columbia.

12

After Washington

Franklin Williams returned to a nation in turmoil, reeling from the assassinations of Martin Luther King and Bobby Kennedy and violently divided over the Vietnam War. He found the students at Columbia so thoroughly immersed in the politics of the day that he was uncertain the university would even be open in the fall.

Williams sympathized with the cause of the student protestors, totally agreed that the time for patience had long since passed, and reminded them of the evolution of the Black movement vis-à-vis Booker T. Washington and W. E. B. Du Bois: While Washington urged accommodation to the existing order, the latter "advocated political activity, agitation and protest, and for the first time placed the blame for the Black man's plight squarely on white prejudice and conduct."[1] Yet Williams strongly disagreed with their tactics and those of the more militant and separatist Black leaders. Williams pleaded with the students and the community to take the moral high road, but without compromise or appeasement.[2] One of his first tasks was to bridge the cultural divide between Columbia University and the residents of Harlem.

Columbia students—both Black and white—were incensed with the university's plan to commandeer a section of Harlem called Morningside Heights for the construction of a new gymnasium, to be used exclusively by students and completely off-limits to the people whose community would be disrupted. Williams was quite willing to listen to the concerns and attempt to mediate a resolution but was unprepared for the raw tensions that developed. He had been out of the country for three years and did not fully appreciate how deep the racial divide had grown, how militant Black activists had become, and the depth of the schism over fundamental issues of integration and racial cooperation versus Black Nationalism and racial separation. Lloyd Johnson, whom Williams hired as his assistant at the Urban Center, found his new boss relatively out of touch, accustomed to the deference customarily shown to diplomats and stunned when the Black Panthers and other militants on and near campus dismissed him as an outsider.[3] Williams had landed in a minefield, with a university lazily going through the motions, and overbearing community "leaders" with their own agendas:

> Roy Innis, who was then the Deputy Director of the Congress of Racial Equality (C.O.R.E), came to see me at my home with four or five men that I can only describe as thugs. [He] threatened me, actually told me that I would spend that [Ford Foundation] money in Harlem in a fashion that he and "the barons," I think he called them, would dictate to me. I told him that I had no such intention of doing that . . . but the threat was overt and very clear; my son Paul was there at the time and he was in shock and quite afraid.[4]

Another time Williams was confronted by a well-dressed stranger in Harlem, who put a gun to his chest, called him a "fink," and warned that "we're going to get you."[5] Williams suspected that Black Nationalists, who blamed him for the downfall of Kwame Nkrumah, were behind the incident.

Despite the threats, Williams attempted to sensitize the university to the needs of the community and to encourage the school to share its resources with its neighbors. He recruited highly qualified Blacks to teach or lecture, including civil rights leader and political scientist Charles Hamilton.[6] He used Ford Foundation money to hire Black associate deans and got them assigned to the schools of medicine, journalism, and architecture, to the business school and the school of arts, and then he added to their academic responsibilities the task of serving as role models for African American students. He examined the curriculum and found ways to integrate urban issues, and he actively supported programs such as the "Broadcast and Print Journalism for Minorities" initiative at Columbia that helped launch the careers of talk show host Geraldo Rivera and Michele Clark, the first Black female news correspondent at CBS.

The Urban Center initiated projects in the Harlem community, establishing an employment agency to encourage neighborhood people to apply for jobs at the university, and assigned students from the business school to advise small business owners in Harlem. It commissioned a major study entitled "The Uses of the University" to chart its course and serve as a model for other universities willing to create departments of urban and ethnic affairs. Yet Williams was perpetually disappointed and felt that the university and the Ford Foundation paid only lip service to his goals. It seemed that both the school and the foundation wanted to create a perception they were "doing something," but were unwilling to roll up their sleeves and actually do something: "It was probably one of the most difficult and disillusioning positions I had ever taken on. I had the feeling from the time that I went there that Columbia University was really just irritated by the creation of the center and what we were trying to do. There was no commitment at Columbia, there was no commitment at Ford."[7] After only two years, he quit.

Meanwhile, Williams was discovering that the title "Ambassador," which he was entitled to carry for life, was valuable not only socially but also financially. A number of corporate boards were slowly but sincerely integrating and were eager to include a highly respected Black man who came with an impressive title. It started with URS Corp., a small computer software company in San Mateo. The position paid only $100 a meeting, but it included quarterly junkets to California, so Williams agreed to serve. Typically, he took an active role on the board, which captured the attention of another board member who was president of a savings and loan and recruited Williams for the board of United Airlines. Around the same time Consolidated Edison was dealing with picketers complaining that the utility had no Blacks on its board and few on its management staff. Williams was the response, but he was not about to sit idly on the board as the go-along-to-get-along token Black. He intended to be a contributing member of the board, and not just on racial issues.

Franklin was aghast that Con Ed was writing off millions of dollars in losses every month (and passing the losses along to consumers), claiming the uncollectible accounts were largely a result of welfare recipients who couldn't or wouldn't pay their bills and transients who moved around just enough to keep the bill collectors at bay. He pestered Con Ed to take a hard look at uncollectible bills and discovered that it wasn't the welfare class at all to blame, but small businesses that shut down under one corporate name and reopened under another, as well as large not-for-profit institutions such as hospitals and foundations that knew Con Ed would never risk the public relations disaster of shutting off their power. Remarkably, many of the deadbeat nonprofits were beneficiaries of Con Ed's philanthropy. Ultimately, Con Ed adopted what became known as the "Williams Policy," in which it refused to fund any organization or entity in arrears on their utility bills.[8]

From there, Williams's service on corporate boards snowballed, and he ended up on multiple boards, including Borden Inc., Chemical Bank, and the American Stock Exchange. Most were paying an annual retainer of up to $25,000, plus roughly $500 for attending meetings. Many would continue to pay the annual retainer for up to twenty years after the board member retired, on the dubious theory that the individual remained available to provide counsel and advice. Williams considered it a "rip-off of the stockholders," but he gratefully took the money and the perks to build a very attractive retirement nest egg.

These corporate boards are composed of essentially chief executive officers of corporations who serve on one another's boards. It is sort of an old-boys club. The chairman of Chemical Bank always serves on Con Ed's board, the chairman of Con Ed always serves on Metropolitan Life's board, the chairman of Metropolitan Life always serves on Con Ed's. It was that kind of thing. And Blacks, of course, not being corporate chairpersons, were having difficulty in breaking through this network, as were women.

My point in telling this story is twofold: one, once you broke in, the process became quite easy, because you met others who observed you and realized you weren't crazy, you had something to contribute, you had a viewpoint, and that it was important for people such as yourself to serve on these boards and bring to their deliberations a different angle and different viewpoint; secondly, from a purely personal and selfish viewpoint, I deferred all my fees, and these fees are quite handsome.[9]

While serving on the Chemical Bank board, Williams became friendly with Lawrence Rawls, the chief executive officer of Exxon. One night over drinks, Rawls bemoaned the sparsity of minorities in the upper echelons of his corporation and asked Williams to investigate. Williams spent two years meeting with the human resources staff and visiting facilities in Dallas and New Jersey, and ultimately he drafted a proposal for an ambitious scholarship program with the Stevens Institute, an engineering school in New Jersey that would fund the educations of exceptional minority students and guarantee them a position at Exxon when they graduated. Rawls was so impressed with the proposal that he not only adopted it but also created the Ambassador Franklin H. Williams Minority Scholarship Program.[10]

For the remainder of his life, Williams used the contacts he made on the corporate boards to raise funds for various causes dear to his heart, such as the NAACP, the Barnes Foundation, the Boys Club of Harlem, the Caribbean Cultural Center, the African Student Aid Fund, the Bishop Desmond Tutu Scholarship Fund, and the Jackie Robinson Foundation. He used the same contacts to raise money—a lot of money—in his next professional role as head of the Phelps Stokes Fund, a philanthropy.

Under other circumstances, Williams could have used those sources to help fund a political campaign. But Franklin had learned late that too many people in power were aware of, and disapproved of, his extramarital affairs. At one speaking engagement at the Schomburg Center for Research in Black Culture, Williams spoke about the civil rights movement, stressing his favorite theme—that the movement did not start with Martin Luther King but with those who had escaped from slavery, and that organizations such as the NAACP, which fought for justice in the courts, deserved credit as well. During a question and answer period afterward, a woman in the audience confronted him: "Why haven't you run for public office? Why haven't you served in government, fighting for our rights?" Franklin responded simply: "I have too many skeletons in my closet." He understood that his days in the public sector were over, and that elective office would never be in the cards.

In 1970, Williams agreed to head the Phelps Stokes Fund, a fifty-nine-year-old philanthropy established with an $800,000 bequest from one of America's first woman philanthropists, Caroline Phelps Stokes, to advance educational opportunities for Africans and African Americans, Native Americans, and needy whites, and to create housing for the poor. Stokes, the heir of a family with a long history of philanthropy—her great-grandfather had been a founder of the London Missionary Society—left $1 million in a trust following her death in 1911.

For many years, Caroline's nephew, Bishop Anson Phelps Stokes Jr., ran the charity with the assistance of an education officer. The endowment underwrote investigative trips, leading to reports on the British colonial system of education. Later, in the 1930s, the board of directors took an interest in housing, including the provision of homes for unwed mothers.[11]

After Bishop Stokes's retirement, Channing Tobias became the first Black president of the Phelps Stokes. He, too, had a religious background. Ordained a minister in the Colored Methodist Episcopal Church, Tobias spent most of his career working at the Young Men's Christian Association (YMCA), where he tried, unsuccessfully, to desegregate that organization. In 1957, Frederick Patterson, a prominent educator who had been president of Tuskegee University, a historically Black college in Alabama, had founded the United Negro College Fund in 1944, and the Phelps Stokes Fund refocused its mission and programmatic efforts to promote the agenda of Black universities. That put Phelps Stokes at odds with many Black leaders, who opposed even voluntary segregation, and when Williams agreed to succeed Patterson, he put himself in a controversial position.

Williams had attended a historically Black university, Lincoln, and often regretted that he did not send his two sons to predominantly Black colleges. Both of his boys had enrolled in excellent New England colleges, Amherst and Williams, but both left without degrees. Franklin was convinced their educational experience would have been better if they, like their dad, attended

Fiftieth reunion of the Lincoln University class of 1941. Franklin, as usual, is front and center. (Enid Gort collection)

a school like Lincoln, Howard, or Fisk. He had grown and matured immensely at Lincoln, where he began to understand and grasp his roots, and he thought his sons would have benefited as well.

Franklin Jr. disagrees with his father, denied ever feeling like an outsider at Amherst, and insists he left simply because he "never liked school." After serving in the military during the Vietnam War, Frank had a successful career in the travel industry. However, Frank agrees that his brother, Paul, may have had a different life had he enrolled in a historically Black college. Paul attended Williams College in the late 1960s, a time when Black consciousness was escalating. According to his older brother, Paul was a standout on the track team but dropped out after enduring blatantly racial mistreatment—and after the coach ordered him to cut his Afro. Paul drifted into the drug culture, which the family believed exacerbated a lifelong mental illness that would estrange him from his parents and brother for the remainder of his life. Paul's corpse was found in November 2018 in the Connecticut home where he had lived in seclusion for years. He died alone and had been dead for days or even weeks before his body was found.[12]

Would Paul's life have been different, better if he had attended Lincoln rather than Williams College? Perhaps. But Paul had always been a "troubled" boy. Franklin and Shirley were deeply saddened that, despite their best efforts to intervene, they could not save their son. Frank Jr. recalls his father crying only once, when he was overcome with emotion and frustration at his inability to help Paul.[13]

At Phelps Stokes, Williams quickly pointed out that historically Black colleges did *not* bar whites who wished to attend and was taken aback at the criticism he endured from longtime friends when he agreed to take over the foundation. One very close friend, Kenneth Clark, the renowned Black psychologist who along with his wife, Mamie Clark, created and conducted a series of experiments known as "the doll tests" to study the psychological effects of segregation on Black children, never understood or accepted Williams's point of view. "I think the historically Black colleges are symptoms of racism, and I think the Blacks who support them are not aware of the fact that they are supporting racism," Clark said in an interview in 1990.[14] Another friend, Robert Weaver, a former member of the NAACP national board, criticized Williams for taking a job with "that Uncle Tom organization."[15] Frank Mankiewicz, a longtime friend from California and the Peace Corps, told Williams that taking the Phelps Stokes position was the death knell of his public life, lamenting that Franklin "could have and should have been a leader of men."[16]

But Williams, like Thurgood Marshall, also a graduate of historically Black Lincoln University, believed there was value and merit in preserving the heritage and traditions of Black Americans. He distinguished between state-sponsored or government-mandated segregation in the Jim Crow tradition and private entities such as historically Black colleges and universities (HBCUs) that attracted and catered to Black scholars but did not exclude the small number of whites who wished to attend such schools. In any case, the HBCU issue underscored tension that long existed within the NAACP: How could the organization support scholarship programs exclusively for Blacks while opposing scholarships exclusively for whites?

Williams was able to put the criticism aside and focus on his new job, and promptly persuaded the board to divest itself of holdings in corporations that did business with South Africa, which was then governed by a white minority which openly engaged in the racially segregated policies of apartheid, a move that inspired other foundations and institutions to do the same. He was fortunate to have a board that included prominent African Americans such as Frank Horne, a well-known housing advocate (and uncle of his longtime friend, the singer, dancer, actress, and civil rights advocate Lena Horne) and

J. Wayne Fredericks, who had served as US Deputy Secretary of State for African Affairs.

His first act was to eliminate a provision requiring the presence of an Episcopal bishop on the board at all times; the first board member he chose was Ellen Sulzberger Strauss, a Jewish businesswoman and columnist whose family ran the *New York Times*. He recruited other exceptional individuals to the board, including Rachel Robinson, Jackie Robinson's widow, and Bishop Desmond Tutu, the South African theologian who would later win the Nobel Peace Prize.

Williams promptly increased the staff, opened a Washington office, and expanded the funding base beyond anything anyone had previously imagined. He wanted to increase direct communications between Africans and African Americans, and on his watch, the Roundtable was established. For a nominal fee, members were invited to a monthly lunch and engaging discussion with distinguished speakers. Among them were Ambassador Edward Perkins, the first Black American ambassador to South Africa; Thabo Mbeki, who followed Nelson Mandela as president of South Africa; John Daniel, a South African political scientist who was forced to flee his country because of anti-apartheid activities; and Albie Sachs, the revered South African anti-apartheid activist and judge who lost his arm in a car bombing due to his opposition to apartheid. The Roundtable developed into not only a profitable enterprise, but a recruitment tool.

By the mid-1980s, apartheid had become an international concern and Williams became a forceful opponent of government-sponsored racial segregation in South Africa. He called for closing down consulates, denying visas to South Africans, enforcing a boycott of South African goods, forbidding South African airlines to land in the United States, and pressuring our allies to do the same. On June 15, 1985, Williams was a guest on *The Open Mind*, a popular public affairs program hosted by Richard Heffner. The topic was "Apartheid: What to Do?" Williams calmly and firmly dissected apartheid, explaining the economic and political objective of state-sponsored segregation:

> Apartheid is a long-range strategy of the South African government . . . to control that Black population. . . . The economy can't function without Black support and Black participation, so that those who are necessary to it are available when needed at the price that [the white minority] care to pay, and those that are not needed are someplace else and not responsibile. Apartheid is a grand design, in short, of the South African government, to denationalize, to deny citizenship

rights and privileges to 90 to 95 percent of the Black population. . . .
The strategy is working and South Africa is moving toward its ultimate goal.[17]

When Heffner asked Williams if there was a danger that the divestiture and
boycotts that he was calling for could make things "worse" for South African
Blacks, Williams responded: "If you are a Black South African you have no
freedom to choose where to work, you have no freedom to choose where you
can live, you have no freedom to move where you want to, you can't move about
without carrying a pass. How can it be any worse than that?" He gave little credit
to the Reagan administration's half-hearted opposition to apartheid: "I don't
believe, quite candidly, that this administration cares a great deal about Black
South Africans. I think what they want to have happen in South Africa is to
avoid some kind of a bloodbath, avoid some kind of an outbreak that would
involve other countries in Africa and other countries in the world to avoid as
much interruption in the economic situation as they possibly can."[18]

Meanwhile, Williams was eager to build bridges between Phelps Stokes and
African Blacks. He also established the Distinguished American Visitors to
Africa Program and each year brought two guests, typically prominent Blacks,
on a trip to Africa. The purpose was twofold: Williams wanted to keep himself
and Phelps Stokes informed about happenings on the continent, and he also
wanted Blacks to become acquainted with their roots and share those experiences when they returned. Among those he brought were Marian Logan,
secretary of the Southern Christian Leadership Conference; Carl Stokes, the
first Black elected mayor of a major American city, Cleveland; and Percy Sutton, a prominent Black trial attorney, civil rights activist, and politician. Similarly, a fellowship program steered small grants to African colleges so they
could send scholars to American universities for advanced degrees, bringing
those degrees and the knowledge underlying them back home.

In short order, Williams revitalized every part of the Fund—institutional-
izing a Native American initiative, supporting poor white colleges in Appala-
chia, sponsoring research and securing nearly $18 million from the US Agency
for International Development to administer two southern African scholarship
programs, and supporting the Bishop Desmond Tutu African Refugee Scholarship Fund. He brought in Marie Gadsden, a career administrator of educational and philanthropic foundations and the first Black woman to chair the
board of the relief group Oxfam America, to run the Washington office. Gadsden brought credibility, competence, and balance to the capital station and
believed—accurately—that Phelps Stokes was neglecting two of its major charter
constituencies: poor whites and American Indians. Williams embraced her

efforts to aid poor white schools in Kansas, Tennessee, and Louisiana and to develop an American Indian College Program.

Williams wanted the Fund to engage in cutting-edge, scholarly research, and one of the first projects of the newly formed Research and Publications Division of the Phelps Stokes Fund was a groundbreaking study of lynching, its history and patterns. The objective was to "fill a void in reference materials on this aspect of race relations" and make the point that the civil rights movement wasn't merely about equal accommodations, voting rights, or a place to live. Rather, it was about life-and-death survival. Williams, who had a special interest in the topic since he narrowly escaped a lynching in Groveland in the late 1940s, coauthored the report with two of his former NAACP colleagues, Robert Carter and Roy Wilkins. The report, titled "The Usual Crime: A Study of Lynching in the United States,"[19] paints an extraordinary and haunting picture of the pervasive culture of lynching that permeated southern culture for hundreds of years.

A file at the Schomburg Center for Research in Black Culture in Harlem includes a handwritten chronology of lynchings that occurred in the United States, dating to 1899, and the reasons for which the individual was lynched. Many were lynched for felonies such as murder, rape, assault, sheltering a murderer, barn burning, and dynamiting; in Covington County, Alabama, three unknown "negro" men were lynched for the crime of "race prejudice." The file also includes a 1902 article from the New Orleans Picayune defending lynching as a valuable public service. "If . . . there had been no lynchings, and the law had been allowed to take its course, there would have been only 118 executions by judicial sentence, and 6,819 murders would have remained unpunished."[20]

A draft report by Williams, Carter, and Wilkins debunked the myth that lynching was necessary to protect white women, and the white race, from genetic and cultural pollution:

Though protection of the white woman (i.e., preservation of the white race from "bastardization" by the "Black unspeakable brute") was seen as that basic motivation for lynching, in actual fact even as an alleged cause this was never the case. Nevertheless, this continued to be the reason most often cited by laymen and apologists as late as 1947. The slowness of courts, given as a second major reason, was almost never true. Southern courts were noted for their "speedy and public trials" and the prompt dispatchment of the convicted. The classic lynchings involved removing an offender from the custody of the law, sometimes before, sometimes afterwards, and sometimes during the trial.[21]

Williams was always looking for new projects, and always receptive to suggestions. One time, an employee mentioned offhand that, as a rule and contrary to conventional wisdom, people in developing countries did not take better care of their elderly than people in developed countries. Williams was intrigued and commissioned an internal inquiry, which led to a successful grant proposal that led to a groundbreaking conference and publication on "Africa and the Americas: Aging in Cross-Cultural Perspective." He was bothered by the declining number of Black teachers in America, and that concern led to yet another conference and report.

Williams spent much of his time as president of Phelps Stokes at speaking engagements across the nation. On May 14, 1972, for example, he delivered a riveting commencement address at South Carolina State University:

We must not let ourselves be stampeded like mindless, unresisting sheep into the dank and rotting abyss of tyranny. You, as the future hope of our country, must demand leaders who can and will bring us out and let us breathe the air of freedom. We must not stop now. We have come too far to turn back. A nation that has progressed because of the sweat and blood of thousands of Blacks; a nation that first tolerated slavery then outlawed it; that accepted separate but equal as a valid constitutional concept then rejected it; a nation that has slowly, painfully—tragically evolved to the point where a Black woman is now running for the presidency, a nation that has come so far must not now give up the struggle to rid itself of racism and reaction.[22]

Simultaneously, he was chairman of the board at his alma mater, Lincoln University, a coincidence that thrust him into a battle over control of a $6 billion art collection.

Albert C. Barnes, a rags-to-riches manufacturer raised in Philadelphia poverty, worked his way through medical school, branched into chemistry and started a fabulously successful patent medicine company. In the early 1900s, Barnes began accumulating what would become the greatest collection of contemporary art in the nation, with masterpieces by the likes of Cezanne, Picasso, van Gogh, and Renoir.[23] Later, he began adding African art to his collection, perhaps a natural segue for a man who had always felt a strong affinity with the Black community.

When he was a child, Barnes's mother, a devout Methodist, brought him to religious camp meetings, including African American gatherings. He became "an addict to Negro camp meetings, baptizings, revivals, and the company of individual Negroes."[24] As a young man and adult, Barnes felt rejected by Philadelphia society and its institutions. In a 1987 book, *The Devil and Mr.*

Barnes, author Howard Greenfield wrote: "Since his childhood, his concern for Black people, and the underdog with whom he conceivably identified, had developed into a passion."[25] He associated with Black intellectuals such as philosopher Alain Locke, mentor of the Harlem Movement, and befriended Paul Guillaume, the French art dealer who was among the first to organize African art exhibits.

Barnes built a gallery outside Philadelphia to preserve and showcase his collection and established a foundation to run it. In painstaking detail, Barnes drafted a charter that set up a board of trustees, provided for its succession, and dictated who could view the works and under what terms. His conditions for the foundation, which controlled an arboretum, a botanical garden, and a school, were clear and rigid: nothing could be added to the collection—ever; nothing from the collection could be lent; the art objects must remain where placed by Barnes; and at no time were his buildings to host "any society functions, commonly designated receptions, tea parties, dinners, banquets, dances, musicales, etc."[26] Barnes made abundantly clear that the artwork, and the facilities that displayed it, would be readily accessible to the "plain people, that is, men and women who gain their livelihood by daily toil in shops, factories, schools, stores and similar places" and forbade the foundation from charging an admission fee on the limited days that the gallery and arboretum are open to the public. "The purpose of this gift is democratic and educational in the true meaning of those words, and special privileges are forbidden."[27] Barnes found enormous educational and psychological benefit to art and considered the gallery "an experiment to determine how much practical good to the public of all classes and stations of life may be accomplished by means of the plans and principles learned by the donor from a lifelong study of the science of psychology as applied to education and aesthetics."[28]

Barnes gave specific instructions for control of his foundation following his death and that of his wife. Initially, he intended that his alma mater, the University of Pennsylvania, and the Pennsylvania Academy of the Fine Arts would share control of the foundation.[29] But Barnes had a falling out with the university and academy and changed the terms of indenture on October 20, 1950, granting eventual control to Lincoln University. As the original trustees, including Albert and Laura Barnes, died or left the board, four of the five seats would be filled in perpetuity by nominees of Lincoln. By 1989, the Lincoln nominees had control and the chairman of the school's board of trustees, Franklin Hall Williams, became chairman of the Barnes Foundation.

Williams was intrigued and fascinated with Barnes: "The whole basis of his philosophy of teaching is that anyone can learn art appreciation. You don't have to be a highly trained elite art collector. As a matter of fact, he took the position that a lot of people who pretended to be experts in art didn't know what they were talking about."[30] His initial goal was to ascertain to "what degree the provision about 'plain' people was being realized, and how it might be more effective."[31] His long-term goal was to ensure that Barnes's wishes were respected, that the gallery was on firm financial footing, that it was run professionally, and that Lincoln University would use its newly acquired influence to establish a top-notch art department.[32] He had been concerned for a number of years that Lincoln and other universities were neglecting the humanities, as evidenced by a speech he delivered in 1965:

> The human mind is the most sophisticated Sputnik of them all.
> After all, a man is not a machine. And he is not simply an extension
> of the machine. He cannot function by combustible fuel, nor can
> the wheels by which he reasons be lubricated by some petroleum
> product. His mind can only be nourished and nurtured by ideas,
> self-engendered, self-examined, and self-powered. He must be taught
> to think, helped to think, encouraged to think. And this is where we
> need the Humanities.[33]

At the time, Lincoln was struggling. Its enrollment was down, its endowment meager and its financial situation precarious. Williams thought that a solid connection with the Barnes would help Lincoln restore its lost glory. But it was not to be.

Only eight months after becoming president of the foundation, Franklin died, and his dreams for both Lincoln and the Barnes were dashed by decades of questionable management, endless litigation, political interference, and outright corruption. The board was enlarged, seemingly against the express wishes of Barnes, so that Lincoln lost its controlling interest. John Anderson, an author who wrote the seminal book on Barnes, *Art Held Hostage*, predicted that the story would have played out much differently—and much better for Barnes and Lincoln—had Williams lived. "If there is one hero, it's Franklin Williams, a guy who really tried to find a reasonable middle course that would honor the Barnes indenture of trust while helping Lincoln University," Anderson said in a 2003 interview with the *Philadelphia Inquirer*. "I think if Williams had lived, there wouldn't be art held hostage. But then fate and Richard Glanton [a high-flying attorney who succeeded Williams as Barnes's president] intervened."[34]

In 1987, Williams received a cold call from a man he did not know, but certainly knew of: Sol Wachtler, New York State's chief judge. Wachtler, the son of a traveling auctioneer, spent much of his childhood in the Jim Crow South and was appalled by the "outrageous bigotry, and I mean harsh, cruel bigotry"[35] directed toward Blacks (and often Jews such as himself). Wachtler served in the US Army in the 1950s, and even though the military was officially desegregated by then, he was troubled by the status of Blacks in the armed forces. When Wachtler became a trial judge, he found that there were virtually no Black employees, let alone judges, in the New York State court system.[36] He eventually won election to the New York Court of Appeals, the highest court in the state, where no Black had ever served as a judge and where no Black worked as an employee: "It was wrong for the State of New York to give this image of being a liberal, progressive state, and yet have no African Americans as part of the judicial or legal system . . . where the perception has to be that justice is available to all, and that all people of every race and background can participate in the process."[37]

Not long after Governor Mario Cuomo appointed Wachtler in 1985 as chief judge, the highest judicial position in the state, the jurist was approached by the Coalition of Black Judges, which expressed their despair at the way Blacks were treated in the courts and their concerns with the underrepresentation of Blacks within the judiciary.[38] But what to do about it? Wachtler knew that even as chief judge he wouldn't be able to make progress and obtain institutional buy-in without presenting both factual and anecdotal evidence. He decided to create what would be the first court-based judicial commission on minorities in the United States. But he hadn't a clue as to who should chair the commission. Wachtler recalled:

> I didn't want to do one of these things where you form a committee, and the committee looks into something, and gives you a report, and you say, "Very nice," and then you move on after a press release or a photo op. I wanted to have a real job done, first of all, to find out where and why there was this lack of diversity, and then find out how to remedy this ill. I spoke to [civil rights attorney] Vernon Jordan about it. He thought it was a wonderful idea. He gave me three or four names, and one of those names was Franklin Williams.
>
> Then, by pure happenstance, shortly thereafter I was at a small dinner party with Thurgood Marshall. . . . I started talking to him about the commission and asked him for a recommendation, and he didn't hesitate for a minute. He said: "Frank Williams."[39]

Wachtler called Williams, unannounced, and explained at length what he had in mind. Williams listened intently and warned the chief judge, "You know, when you start digging into this problem, you're going to create wounds, and wounds that can't be covered over or cured with a Band-Aid."[40] Wachtler assured Williams that was exactly what he wanted, to expose racial injustice in the courts and essentially force the court system's hand. They agreed to meet in Williams's office at Phelps Stokes. According to Wachtler:

> We had a wonderful discussion, and there was an instant bonding between us. He said, "There are a couple of conditions that I would impose. Number one," he said, "it's going to cost a million dollars to do this thing right." I said, "Don't go to number two because we can't give you a million dollars." He said, "I don't want your million dollars." He said, "I will get the money provided that you come with me when I get it." I said, "I can't solicit funds." He said, "I don't want you to do anything. Just sit in the room and let me introduce you to indicate that the Chief Judge is behind the project."
>
> Number 2, he said, "I want to appoint my own staff. I don't want to have my office or the office of the commission any way related to the court system. I want to be completely apart," and he said, "I'm not going to talk to you about the progress of the commission, or what we're doing, or what we're not doing, except to ask you for your consent and access to the courthouses around the state because I'm going to want to have hearings around the state." They were all very easy things to consent to, and he accepted the job.[41]

Within a matter of weeks, Williams and Wachtler visited the Rockefeller Foundation, the Ford Foundation, and the Mellon Foundation, which combined to fund the New York State Judicial Commission on Minorities. In time, dozens of other organizations, including major law firms, banks, and foundations, contributed, ensuring that the Commission could complete its work independent of the courts. "He who pays the piper calls the tune," Williams repeatedly told Wachtler.

Wachtler began recruiting others for the Commission and reached out to Judge Samuel Green, a jurist from Buffalo who was assigned to the Appellate Division, the second highest court in the state. Green, a legendary Black judge who had against all odds become a City Court judge in 1973, hesitated and "told him I wasn't really interested in one of these 'feel-good' type committees or commissions."[42] Wachtler assured Green he was serious and emphasized that he had persuaded Franklin Williams to serve as chair. Green was unimpressed; he had never heard of Williams but agreed to meet with him in New York City. Williams won over Green instantly. "He was the most impressive Black man I had ever met or had ever had any dealings with, and I met quite a few. There was just something about the guy. He had class, style, was very, very, very bright, intelligent and down to earth at the same time. He seemed to just have had it all."[43]

Green agreed to be part of the Commission—which would include prominent judges, attorneys, academics, and others—only after both Wachtler and Williams guaranteed him that it would be independent of the court system. "I give Judge Wachtler a lot of credit for what he did," Green said in a 2016 interview. "He was dedicated, and he backed us up a hundred percent."[44]

On January 21, 1988, Wachtler held a press conference at the New York City Bar Association to announce the formation of the Commission and Williams's chairmanship. Wachtler and his chief administrative judge, Albert M. Rosenblatt, told the press conference that they were additionally troubled by a *New York Times*/WCBS-TV poll showing that 47 percent of Blacks in New York City believed judges and the courts favored whites. "What is terribly unsettling," Wachtler said, "is that there might be people out there who should be seeking redress in the courts who are not because they distrust the courts. What do you do when you don't trust the courts? You then take the law into your own hands."[45]

When Williams first met with the Commission, it was something of an audition. Few of the members knew him, and most didn't even know of him. He had almost no experience with the New York courts. Yet, he quickly made a strong impression. Juanita Bing Newton, a judge and original member of the Commission, recalled:

> The first time I ever even heard of Ambassador Williams, quite
> frankly, I questioned, "Who is this guy, and why is he being brought in
> to address these issues?" He was sort of an outsider to the court system.
> He didn't know a lot about the state courts. . . . We didn't know a lot
> about him, but that first meeting was very telling of what we were to
> expect in the ensuing months. He was a visionary. He was a charming,
> elegant man and the kind of person that gets you to say "yes" after a
> few minutes, even though you started off saying, "Absolutely not. What
> is this insanity?" Very polished, very diplomatic, as you would expect
> from a former ambassador, very discerning, as you would expect from
> someone who had his mettle tested in the courts in the civil rights era,
> tackling very challenging and different kinds of cases. I found him to
> be very strategic. He could hone-in and discern the issues. He could
> look at the pros and the cons. He asked a lot of questions. He was al-
> ways looking for the solution to the problem. I think the more he got
> involved in looking at the place of minorities in our court system the
> more shocked he was and surprised that the status of minorities in our
> court system was so troubling. We were not in a good place.[46]

The Commission would have a tripartite mandate: determine how the public and those in the courts perceive the treatment of minorities in the judicial system; review the representation of minorities in nonjudicial positions; and review the elective and appointive systems for electing judges and determine which resulted in greater minority representation.[47] Williams went about compiling a staff and reached out to a woman he did not know, Edna Wells Handy, a straight-talking former federal prosecutor. It is unclear who had suggested her to Williams. Wells Handy recalled:

> He was very concerned about a number of things, one, that I had a young child, and he asked me during the interview, "Who's going to take care of your child? There's going to be a lot of traveling." I said to him, "Let me give you some advice. Free. Never ask that question of a woman in an interview." I'd been Assistant U.S. Attorney, Assistant District Attorney, a Karpatkin Fellow. He said "You've done all this. How come I've never heard of you?" I said, "You're an Ambassador, and I never heard of you either." . . . I wasn't sure I was going to get called back, but I did.[48]

Williams hired Wells Handy, and they went about the task of compiling hard data. Over the coming months, the new commission visited all sixty-two counties in New York State, holding public meetings in every one of them. It held formal hearings around the state—two in New York City and one each in Albany and Buffalo. A special meeting was held in Green Haven Prison, and electronic town hall meetings were held in Westchester and Dutchess counties.[49]

Williams, Wells Handy, and a Manhattan attorney, James Goodale, chairman of the Commission, met with nearly every judge in the state at a series of conferences, and Wells Handy followed those up with meetings with court administrators. Commissioners met with the leaders of traditional and affinity bars throughout the state, and even set up a complaint hotline in Williams's office.[50] Monica Holmes was hired as research director. The research included a survey of litigators who appeared regularly in the courts, a survey of judges, and a major research study of the minority experience in the fifteen law schools in New York State. Judicial screening committees were queried.[51]

No matter where the Commission went, it heard the same story about minorities in the court system. It repeatedly heard about the lack of opportunity, the nepotism. It heard about separate lockers for Blacks, a noose left in a Black man's locker.[52] A witness in Albany testified that the "court personnel's attitude is [that an] inner city person is a nobody, and we feel helpless rage as we see them snickering and whispering snide remarks."[53] A *New York Law Journal* poll found that 71 percent of Blacks believed that a white would get a lighter sentence than a Black for the identical crime—a perception shared by 31 percent of the *white* respondents.[54] A witness in Buffalo told the panel that "95 percent of the clerks, court officials, city marshals, law assistants and attorneys are members of the majority community." In New York City, a former court employee insisted that "[minorities] . . . work at lower grades and lower pay ranges than all other employees."

The data and the anecdotal evidence persuaded Williams and the Commission that race relations within the courts were not only as bad as they thought but even worse than they feared. Although the Commission's work was not quite done, Williams decided to issue an interim report, concluding that the court system was doing little more than paying lip service to the notion of affirmative action. Wachtler and his chief administrator, Matthew T. Crosson, initially reacted defensively, claiming that the Commission's findings were overstated. Later, however, Wachtler backpedaled, admitting his criticism was a "knee-jerk reaction" to defend the court system and acknowledging that the situation was every bit as damning as the Commission documented.[55] Jonathan Lippman, then Crosson's deputy and one of Wachtler's successors as chief judge, said the report shocked the court system and resulted in permanent reforms: "I think Judge Wachtler opened more of a Pandora's box than he thought, originally. . . . There was more there than Sol or Matt or anyone really thought. I think Ambassador Williams . . . looked for it, found it and we're all the better for it."[56]

Wachtler agreed to join Williams at a press conference in Court of Appeals Hall in Albany, with the Emancipation Proclamation as a backdrop, where he took full responsibility for the court system's failings and promised enduring reform. In April 1991, nearly a year after Williams's death, the Commission, renamed in his honor by Wachtler, released a five-volume study (dedicated to its late chairman) that to this day is a blueprint for racial fairness in the New York courts. The Franklin H. Williams Judicial Commission is the ambassador's lasting legacy, and some thirty years after its formation, it remains a positive and persistent force.

Epilogue

With a history of coronary heart disease and a penchant for combative tennis matches with his pals at the Chip and Racquet Club, an interracial group of poker and tennis playing friends that he organized, Franklin Williams convinced himself that he'd collapse and die on the court. In fact, he rather relished dying in that fashion—quickly, dramatically and in the company of friends, doing something that gave him great pleasure.

But it was a cancer diagnosis that blindsided him.

In the summer of 1989, when Franklin was a vibrant seventy-one, he initially gave little thought to the lingering cough, dismissing it as a persistent August cold or perhaps an allergy. But as the cough got worse rather than better, Franklin visited his internist, who sent him to an allergist, who referred him to a pulmonary specialist, who ordered a biopsy that yielded a devastating verdict: stage 4 adenocarcinoma of the lung. Franklin was stunned. Like most men of his generation, he had smoked for a number of years but had quit decades earlier and never feared lung cancer. He took the news stoically and philosophically, deciding that he had lived a good and fulfilling life, spent with people he loved, and that he wasn't interested in treatment that would only delay the inevitable, prolong the suffering, and make his remaining time miserable.

However, family and friends prevailed on him to at least begin treatment, and once he was on board, he characteristically took charge, thoroughly researching his options and interviewing different specialists before selecting as his cancer "quarterback" Mark W. Pasmantier, a renowned oncologist associated with Weill Cornell Medical Center in New York City.

Over the following nine months, Franklin underwent a series of radiation treatments, coming to his office at Phelps Stokes most days, even if he needed to rest a bit in the afternoon. He knew his time was limited, was concerned with preserving his legacy, and talked openly with Enid Gort, who interviewed him for the oral history that underlies this book. He organized a special night out with Shirley and close friends for a formal dinner in the Rainbow Room on the sixty-fifth floor of Rockefeller Plaza, seemingly aware that he would never dine there again. Each day he made and received dozens of calls from friends and colleagues, including Sargent Shriver; the singer Harry Belafonte; Frank Mankiewicz, the famous journalist, political advisor, and president of National Public Radio; and, far less famous, a Colorado bean farmer whom he had befriended in the army.

Franklin wanted to say hello, and goodbye, to the white soldier he had met a half-century earlier and had not seen since and made a cold call. "Hello, George, you'll never guess who this is." The farmer responded: "Of course I know who this is. It's Franklin Williams. Frank, I could never forget your voice! It's great to hear from you!" For the next hour, two men who had not spoken in some fifty years—one a Black, urban lawyer, the other a white midwestern farmer—talked with easy affection and mutual understanding. The call ended with the farmer profusely thanking Franklin for opening his eyes to racial oppression so many years earlier.[1]

From across the country and around the world, friends and individuals he had influenced called or wrote to express their sentiments. On January 15, 1990, Walter C. Carrington, the former ambassador to Senegal, wrote Franklin a moving letter recounting his "remembrances of you that flood through me as I try to absorb the melancholy news of your impending death (I suppose I could have used a euphemism for the dreaded 'd' word, but what I always admired about you was that you believed in calling a spade a spade)."[2]

As a student at Harvard who founded the university's NAACP chapter, Carrington said he was inspired by Williams, viewing him as a "hero" and "role model to a whole generation of us in the 1950s."[3] He aligned with Williams and Jackie Robinson in their effort to promote the former within the NAACP as successor to Walter White. Carrington served in the Peace Corps with Williams and eventually become director of the Africa division. In 1980, President Jimmy Carter appointed him ambassador to Senegal, and in 1993, President Bill Clinton named him ambassador to Nigeria. Carrington credited Williams with helping him blaze that path:

> I've often wondered what the history of the Civil Rights Movement
> might have been had you become the Executive Secretary of the
> NAACP. With your drive, intelligence and feistiness, the Association
> would have been in the vanguard of the revolution which might have
> started a decade earlier than it did . . .

Working with you in the Peace Corps only reinforced my earlier beliefs in your unique qualities of leadership. Visiting you at the Embassy in Ghana imbued in me a model of diplomatic effectiveness that I would later try to emulate in Senegal. When we formed the Association of Black American Ambassadors, you were the natural, indeed the inevitable, choice to lead it. To all of us who were privileged to hold the rank of Ambassador in the sixties, seventies and eighties, you were our dean, our paradigm. . . . I've lived through a time of extraordinary Black leaders. As one not given to hyperbole, I can say honestly, Frank, that none were more abler [sic] than you.[4]

As Williams grew sicker and weaker, his hospital stays grew longer and more frequent. But the constant stream of visitors and well-wishers, and the endless telephone calls, kept him distracted from his suffering and boosted his spirits as his health deteriorated. He insisted on completing his oral history, taking breaks now and then to plan his funeral.

On the afternoon of May 19, 1990, doctors removed the last of the remaining tubes and sent him home in an ambulance. The end was at hand, and Franklin must have known it, but he showed no signs of distress or despondency. He missed Shirley and he missed being home, and it was clear there was nothing more that could be done for him in the hospital. The next morning, May 20, Franklin Hall Williams died peacefully, surrounded by family and friends and leaving behind both sons and a grieving widow (Shirley would live another eighteen years, until May 6, 2008), as well as instructions for his memorial service.

Williams made it crystal clear that he wanted a service free of religious overtones or even undertones; both he and Shirley rejected the theologies of organized religion, and the fact that he would soon "meet his maker" did not change that sentiment in the least. His service would be held at the Ethical Culture Society in Manhattan. Although Franklin never got around to joining the organization, both he and Shirley embraced its guiding credo: "Every person has inherent worth; each person is unique; it is our responsibility to improve the quality of life for ourselves and others; ethics are derived from human experiences and life is sacred, interrelated and interdependent."[5] It was a fitting epitaph.

All of the eulogists, including the South African Anglican cleric and theologian Bishop Desmond Tutu, a Nobel Peace Prize recipient known worldwide for his anti-apartheid activism, scrupulously respected Franklin's wishes. There were no references to a deity or an afterlife.

Bishop Tutu, whom Franklin had recruited to join the board of the Phelps Stokes Fund, spoke to the more than eight hundred mourners of Franklin's

Franklin and Shirley during the early years of their marriage, probably in the late 1940s or early 1950s. (Enid Gort collection)

"commitment to people and justice, his integrity, his opposition to apartheid and his concern for children."[6] The bishop recalled the wisdom of his own father, who counseled his son to improve the quality of his argument rather than increase the volume of his voice when debating an adversary, and said that Franklin was an object lesson in that sage advice. It was an accurate sentiment; Franklin almost never raised his voice. His words and logic were so persuasive, so irrefutable, that there was no need to shout.

Franklin and Shirley Williams in their later years, the mid-1980s. (Enid Gort collection)

Admiral Elmo Russell "Bud" Zumwalt Jr., now retired from the service, revealed that he first encountered Williams in the early 1970s, which was news to many who were aware only of the admiral's more recent service as chairman of the Phelps Stokes Fund. In the 1970s, Zumwalt, the head of the Navy, was struggling to "overcome the U.S. Navy's tokenism and institutional racism" two decades after President Truman ordered an end to military desegregation. The military was not listening to their commander-in-chief, let alone a four-star admiral who happened to be the youngest person ever to serve as Chief of Naval Operations, and he reached out to Williams for advice:

> The resistance began with many of the admirals and was reinforced by the support they got from many white conservative members of Congress. I was told the most effective person in dealing at the intellectual level with racist mindsets was Ambassador Franklin H. Williams. I called upon him to help.
>
> Later, I listened and watched the effect he was having as he spoke to hundreds of senior naval officers, as this brilliant and passionate man told of his own experiences with racism as a private first-class in the Army, and as he eloquently described his later battles against racism in the Civil Rights Movement as he struggled in his own mind to overcome his own prejudice against whites. I saw the dawn of true insight breaking through on the faces of his senior audience. . . . Very literally, while I struggled to comply with Truman's disregarded directive, Franklin converted [the group] into the spirit of dedicated compliance.[7]

With Franklin's guidance, Admiral Zumwalt had both the inspiration and guidance to, at long last, reduce racism in the Navy. In December 1970, the admiral issued a communique directing "every Navy facility to appoint a minority group officer or senior petty officer as a minority affairs assistant to the commanding officer."[8] That order was followed.

The burial was private, and as Franklin directed, his cremated remains were quietly deposited in Flushing Cemetery, near the weathered tombstones of his great-grandmother Lizzie Davis; his grandparents, Thadd and Cab Lowry; and his mother, Alinda Lowry Williams. There would be no statuesque monument to mark the spot, just a somewhat inconspicuous marker. Franklin thought his life's work should speak for itself.

With the benefit of hindsight, the life and contributions of Franklin Williams reveal a man who had a profound impact on the (still unfinished) struggle for equal rights for *all*, not just those in his own community, and who played a pivotal role at a pivotal time for the NAACP. He was a forceful yet rational advocate in an era where emotion too often overshadowed the debate. His posture as a civil rights activist who happened to be Black rather than a Black civil rights activist made him acceptable to whites who were turned off by the threatening, divisive, and sometimes segregationist rhetoric of the more militant fringe. He was a bridge between the Black and white communities, and a bridge within the Black community, fulfilling a role similar to that of James Farmer and skillfully navigating the "volatile and explosive" world of the new

Black Jacobins and the more genteel world of the "white and Black liberal establishment."[9]

Those bridge figures helped blaze the trail for all that followed, from *Brown v. Board of Education* to the Civil Rights Act of 1964 and all the way to the election and reelection of Barack Obama as president of the United States. Yet, while they were bridge builders rather than rock throwers, these pioneers were not appeasers. They could be confrontational. They would, through the power of their intellect and persuasive oratory, challenge the status quo and prejudice of both whites and Blacks.

Recent events such as the reemergence of the white supremacy movement have sadly demonstrated that racism remains an ugly undercurrent of American life, underscoring the need for a new generation of bridge builders to promote justice and racial harmony, to help us move forward rather than backward. The life story of Franklin Hall Williams is an object lesson for those with the courage and fortitude to build on what he, and many others, fostered, and to help this nation heal and advance through unity rather than tribalism.

Acknowledgments

The authors begin this section jointly by acknowledging each other in the full realization that this book never would have seen the light of day without the respective skills each brought to the project. Enid Gort contributed her scholarship, her skills as a researcher and interviewer, her unparalleled knowledge of Franklin Williams and his times, and her exclusive access to the Williams family and so many others, as well as the master's thesis that was the foundation for this project. John Caher brought his experience as a published author, a seasoned journalist and editor, a professional writer, and investigative reporter. But even then, there was help all along the way.

Enid Gort's dear friend Deborah Lesser examined the manuscript thoughtfully, and with the eagle eye of a serious scholar. She improved this book immeasurably and caught dozens of typos, errors, and poorly constructed phrases. Her suggestions are incorporated throughout. In addition, our editors at Fordham University Press, particularly Fredric Nachbaur, Eric Newman, and Gregory McNamee, were a writer's delight—smart, insightful, supportive. Our agent, Janet Rosen of Sheree Bykofsky Associates, provided a fresh eye on our original and rather rough first draft and worked diligently to find the right publisher.

Several friends and relatives graciously offered keen insight in one or more areas of this project, including James P. Caher, Louis Grumet, and Jodi Ackerman Frank. The contributions of each are reflected in the final product and deeply appreciated. The authors are indebted to the assistance and cooperation of the Franklin H. Williams Judicial Commission, especially its current and former executive directors, Mary Lynn Nicolas-Brewster, and Joyce Y. Hartsfield, respectively, Associate Counsel Karlene A. Dennis, and the four extraordinary jurists who chaired the Commission while this book was in progress: Hon. Richard B. Lowe III; Hon. Shirley Troutman; Hon. Troy K. Webber; and Hon. Richard Rivera.

Long before John Caher became involved in this project, Enid Gort was assisted by a great many people who augmented her research, offered access to individuals and information, and provided context to various events and history. Chief among them is the Williams family, in particular the late Shirley Williams and Franklin Williams Jr., and Michael Butler, who was a Tobias family descendant eager to share his extensive ancestral and anthropological knowledge of the State Street household.

Franklin Williams wanted his personal papers, which are voluminous, archived at the Schomburg Center for Research in Black Culture in Harlem, and today the Schomburg is a gold mine for anyone researching his life and times. Enid Gort largely catalogued the collection, in partnership with archivist Kathy Hadjo. That collection was crucial to this book, as were the endless research assistance, unlimited patience, and boundless kindness of Diana Lachatanere and her staff: Mary Yearwood, Berlina Robinson, and Andre Elizee. It is regrettable that Andre and Berlina did not live to see this book in print.

The influence of Hylan Garnet Lewis, who passed in 2000, and Arnold Rampersad, codirectors of the Scholar in Residence Program in the early 1990s when Enid Gort was a scholar at the Schomburg, is evident throughout this book. Lewis provided deep insight into the insidious impact of discrimination—an insight that only a Black person can truly have—while Rampersad, a noted biographer, mentor, and confidant, shared his expertise on the writing of a biography.

Special thanks to Adrienne Cannon, the Afro-American History and Culture specialist for the Library of Congress Manuscript Division, and the research staff in the Western Americana Collection at the Bancroft Library, University of California, Berkeley.

Notes

Note from the Authors

1. See Randall Kennedy and Eugene Volokh, "The New Taboo: Quoting Epithets in the Classroom and Beyond," *Capital University Law Review* 49, no. 1 (2021), https://www2.law.ucla.edu/volokh/epithets.pdf.

Introduction

1. Richard Severo, "James Farmer, Civil Rights Giant In the 50's and 60's, Is Dead at 79," *New York Times*, July 10, 1999.

2. Franklin Williams, "Race and Minority Groups," paper dated September 14, 1971, Schomburg Center for Research in Black Culture Archives (hereafter Schomburg Archives), Box 55.

3. Schomburg Archives, Box 1.

4. *Batson v. Kentucky* (476 U.S. 79, 1986).

1. Roots

1. Franklin Williams interview, May 5, 1988.

2. Chapter 1 is largely based on interviews conducted with Franklin H. Williams on May 5, 1988; September 25, 1989; and September 26, 1989.

3. See "Indians Plan Lawsuit over Queens, Long Island Land," *Newsday*, February 14, 1993.

4. Adrian Cook, *The Armies of the Streets: The New York City Draft Riots of 1863* (Lexington: University Press of Kentucky, 1974); Lawrence Lader, "New York's Bloodiest Week," *American Heritage*, June 1959, 44–59.

5. Lists of dead and injured victims of the Draft Riots are published in Cook, *The Armies of the Streets*, 2. It bears mention that the name of Elizabeth Tobias is not on the list of dead and injured, and therefore the family story cannot be confirmed. However, it is entirely possible that the mishap occurred exactly as recorded in family oral history but was never reported to authorities.

6. See "Matinecocks: Flushing Meadows Is Ours," *Little Neck Ledger*, February 8, 1983, and "Indians: Return LI Land," *Newsday*, February 14, 1993.

7. Gilbert Osofsky, *Harlem: The Making of a Ghetto* (New York: Harper & Row, 1966), and Elizabeth Blackmar, *Manhattan for Rent: 1785–1850* (Ithaca, NY: Cornell University Press, 1989), 57.

8. Mary (Mamie) Rodriguez interview, January 10, 1992.

9. Six Spencers, four Craigs, and three Davises resided at 164 East Eight-Fifth Street, according to the New York City Police Census of 1890. Volume 748–765, 22nd Election District, Book 758.

10. "Flushing Freedom Mile Historical Tour," a publication of the Queens Historical Society; "Surprising Flushing," published by the Downtown Flushing Development Corporation.

11. *History of Queens County, New York: With Illustrations. Portraits and Sketches of Prominent Families and Individuals* (New York: W. W. Munsell & Company, 1883), 91.

12. Joel Friedman interview, February 14, 1992.

13. Queens-County Clerk, real-property files, Deed to State St. property, Reel 1379, pages 16–20, May 16, 1905.

14. Franklin Williams interview, September 25, 1989.

15. "Flushing Notes," *New York Age*, September 28, 1905.

16. Osofsky, *Harlem*, 12–16. See also James Weldon Johnson, *Black Manhattan* (New York: Atheneum, 1930).

17. "The Negro of Farmville, Virginia: A Social Study," U.S. Department of Labor, Bulletin 3, Number, 14, 1898. See also David Levering Lewis, *W. E. B. Du Bois: Biography of a Race* (New York: Henry Holt, 1995).

18. Lewis, *W. E. B. Du Bois*.

19. Samuel J. Hough interview, January 6, 1995, Gorham Archives, John Hay Library, Brown University, Providence, RI.

20. Franklin Williams interview, September 26, 1989.

21. In *Middle-Class Blacks in a White Society: Prince Hall Freemasonry in America* (Berkeley: University of California Press, 1975), William A. Muraskin points out the difficulties inherent in identifying and defining the Black middle class.

22. Ibid.

23. Dennis C. Dickerson, *The African Methodist Episcopal Church: A History* (New York: Cambridge University Press, 2020).

24. Gail Buckley, *The Hornes: An American Family* (New York: Knopf, 1986), 60–62.

25. May Chinn papers, Schomburg Center for Research in Black Culture. See also Black Women's Oral History Project, Radcliffe College.

26. The genesis of Franklin's rather patrician name is unclear. "Hall" was reputedly the last name of two white sisters, childhood friends of Alinda who resided in Flushing. Where "Franklin" and "Donald" came from is anybody's guess.

27. For a greater understanding of the evolution of jazz and the musicians who created it see Eileen Southern, *The Music of Black Americans: A History* (New York: Norton, 1971); Samuel B. Charters and Leonard Kunstadt, *Jazz: A History of the New York Scene* (Garden City, NY: Doubleday, 1961); Frank Driggs, *Jazz Odyssey*, vol. III (Columbia Records, 1964).

28. Death certificate, Department of Health of the City of New York, number 736, Filed January 31, 1919.

29. Paul Weston interview, March 16, 1992.

30. See Robert S. Albert, "Cognitive Development and Parental Loss Among the Gifted, the Exceptionally Gifted and the Creative," *Psychological Reports* 29 (1971): 19–26; J. Marvin Eisenstadt, "Parental Loss and Genius," *American Psychologist*, March 1978, 211–222; Harris Finkelstein, "The Long-Term Effects of Early Parent Death," *Journal of Clinical Psychology* 44, nos. 1–2 (1988): 3–9.

2. Coming of Age

1. Speech, November 8, 1964, at the University of California Symposium on the Negro Family. See Schomburg Archives, Box 54.

2. Chapter 2 is based on interviews conducted with Franklin Williams on May 5, 1988, September 26, 1989, and October 2, 1989.

3. Ella Spencer was a serious artist whose work received critical attention after her death. See James A. Porter, *Modern Negro Art* (New York: Arno Press & New York Times, 1969), 77.

4. Roberta Braddicks Williams interview, November 2, 1990.

5. Franklin Williams interview, September 26, 1989.

6. John Holley Clark III interview, undated.

7. Ibid.

8. Lewis H. Latimer, a native of Flushing, invented carbon filaments for light bulbs, wrote the first book in the United States on electric lighting and was the first Black executive in the Thomas Edison company. See Lillie Patterson and Winifred Norman, *Louis Latimer: Scientist* (New York: Chelsea House, 1993).

9. Winifred Norman telephone interview, January 24, 1995.

10. Mary (Mamie) Butler Rodriguez interview, January 10, 1992.

11. Williams interview.

12. Ibid.

13. Indenture dated September 25, 1925. Office of the City Registrar, Queens County, Reel 2797, 415.

14. Mary (Mamie) Butler Rodriguez interview, January 10, 1992.

15. Samuel J. Hough interview, January 6, 1995.

16. Flushing High School archives.

17. "Gas Blast Destroys Boat Off Beechhurst, Hurls All Overboard," undated clipping, early 1930s, *North Shore Daily Journal*, Schomburg Archives, Box 1, folder 3.

18. Ibid.

19. Winifred Norman interview, February 21, 1995.

20. Philip Robinson, Scout executive for Queens, interview, February 22, 1995.

21. Franklin Williams's extracurricular activities are listed in the *Flushing High School Folio*, the school yearbook, for 1935. Flushing High School archives.

22. E. C. Schuerhoff, November 1934, Schomburg Archives, Box 1.

23. Joseph Mahoud interview, May 17, 1992.

24. Williams interview.

25. Rose Samms Wheeler interview, November 6, 1990.

26. See W. E. B. Du Bois, *Autobiography* (New York: International Publishers, 1968), 236.

27. Evelyn Cunningham interview, January 12, 1990.

28. Wheeler interview.

29. For a comprehensive discussion of club life in Harlem, see Myrtle Pollard, "Harlem As Is: Sociological Notes on Harlem Social Life," BA thesis, The City College of New York, 1936, 1:83–158. Schomburg Center for Research in Black Culture.

30. Gerri Miller, *Black Society* (Chicago: Johnson Publishing, 1976).

31. Schomburg Archives, Box 20, scrapbook A.

32. Incident witnessed by Enid Gort.

33. Flushing High School archives. See also, Schomburg Archives, Box 20, scrapbook A.

34. Williams interview.

35. Ibid.

36. Death Certificate, Register Number 8831, State of N.Y., Bureau of Records.

37. Franklin Williams did not list his Harlem addresses in his application for admission to the Bar, a form that seeks to elicit information about every residence an applicant has ever had. During the period between February 1935 and June 1941, the only address given is 3305 Murray Street, in Flushing. In fact, Williams bounced between Lowry's home in Flushing, Arthur Williams's apartment, and a rented room in Harlem.

38. Williams interview.

39. James Jones interview, February 26, 1995.

3. An "Ole Lady" at Lincoln

1. Schomburg Archives, Box A30, scrapbook, loose pages.

2. This chapter is largely based on interviews conducted with Franklin H. Williams on October 13 and 19, 1989.

3. Ashmun Institute, named for Jehudi Ashmun (1794–1828), a Congregational minister and supporter of the American Colonization Society, was the first institution in America to adopt Abraham Lincoln's name after his assassination on April 14, 1865. The charter of Ashmun Institute was amended by the state legislature on May 4 of that year and its name changed to Lincoln University. See *the Philadelphia Tribune,* Lincoln Centennial Supplement, February 13, 1954.

4. William A. Chapman Jr. interview, July 5, 1995.

5. Oswald Hoffler interview, September 6, 1995.

6. Robert Freeman interview, September 29, 1990.

7. Interviews with H. Clay Jacke, July 5, 1995; Rev. Edward K. Nichols Jr., August 26, 1985; Joseph Murray, July 6, 1995.

8. Freeman interview.

9. Ibid.

10. Bruce Wright interview, February 18, 1991. Juniors had the responsibility of protecting freshmen, but they could be harassed as well if they attempted to intercede.

11. "Kaleidoscope," *Lincolnian* II, no. 7 (November 19, 1935).

12. Ibid.

13. Lincoln Lion Yearbook, Class of 1941, unnumbered pages.

14. See Charles H. Wesley, *The History of Alpha Phi Alpha: A Development in College Life* (Washington, DC: The Foundation Publishers, 1969), 191.

15. The story of refugees from Nazi Germany who taught at historically Black campuses is told by Gabrielle Edgcomb in *From Swastika to Jim Crow: Refugee Scholars at Black Colleges* (Malabar, FL: Krieger, 1993).

16. Schomburg Archives, Box 21, scrapbook.

17. Schomburg Archives, Box 21, scrapbook A. Franklin Williams worked in Lincoln's library and student refectory. He received a $50 Robinson Shorter Scholarship in 1937, a State of Pennsylvania scholarship in 1940, and a $100 Alpha Phi Alpha scholarship for the academic year 1940–41.

18. John Edward Lowry began his college career at the University of Pennsylvania in 1916. He was drafted during World War I; where he completed his undergraduate studies is unknown. In 1919, he entered medical school at the University of Pennsylvania but was forced to drop out the following year because white patients would not allow him to examine them. John Edward Lowry Jr. interview, February 6, 1996.

19. "Meet the Hinksons of Philadelphia, Pennsylvania," *Ladies Home Journal,* August 1942, 75–79.

20. Georgine Upshur Willis interview, January 22, 1996.

21. Schomburg Archives, Box 1, scrapbook A. Evans Kephart, Senate of Pennsylvania, October 15, 1940.

22. Freeman interview.

23. Wright interview.

24. *Lincolnian,* December 19, 1937.

25. Williams's college yearbook is located in the Schomburg Archives, Box 1, Personal Papers.

26. Letter to Franklin Williams from Lewis M. Stevens, June 4, 1941, Schomburg Archives, Box A30, scrapbook.

27. Schomburg Archives, Box 55.

4. The Real World

1. Chapter 4 is largely based on interviews conducted with Franklin H. Williams on October 19 and 23, 1989.

2. Ted Spiegel, *Saratoga, The Place and Its People* (New York: Abrams, 1988), 28–55.

3. Robert Freeman interview, September 29, 1990.

4. Robert J. Kaczrowski, "Fordham University School of Law: A Case Study of Legal Education in Twentieth-Century America," *Fordham Law Review* 87 (2018), 861.

5. Ibid.

6. Joyce Phillips Austin interview, June 18, 1996.

7. See Jack D. Foner, *Blacks and the Military in American History: A New Perspective* (New York: Praeger, 1974), 72–108. See also Robert W. Mullen, *Blacks in America's Wars: The Shift in Attitudes from the Revolution War to Vietnam* (New York: Monad Press, 1973).

8. "One Tenth of a Nation," *The Lincolnian* XII, no. 3 (November 2, 1940), 2.

9. Franklin Williams's enlistment certificate shows that he was inducted into the US Army on May 8, 1942, at Fort Jay, a recruitment center on Governor's Island in the New York City harbor. He was immediately transferred to Fort Dix, New Jersey, for processing. Recorded photostat division, New York County Clerk's Office. January 10, 1945.

10. *New York Post*, September 10, 1946.

11. Along with Foner's *Blacks and the Military*, sources on Black participation in military units in the Southwest include William H. Lecke, *The Buffalo Soldiers: A Narrative of the Negro Cavalry in the West* (Norman: University of Oklahoma Press, 1967), and James P. Farley, "The Buffalo Soldiers at Fort Huachuca," *Huachuca Illustrated*, 1993.

12. In 1866, Congress established six regiments of Black troops. Two, the Ninth and Tenth, were cavalry, and four were infantry. Almost immediately, the four infantry units were reduced to two, the Twenty-Fourth and Twenty-Fifth. The famed Buffalo Soldiers, the legendary members of the Tenth Cavalry who had defeated the forces of Geronimo and destroyed what was left of Apache resistance, arrived at Fort Huachuca in 1913. They played a major role in the punitive expedition led by Brigadier General John J. "Black Jack" Pershing that pursued Pancho Villa, the Mexican revolutionary, deep into the Mexican heartland.

13. Foner, *Blacks and the Military*, 107.

14. Richard M. Dalfiume, *Desegregation of the U.S. Armed Forces: Fighting on Two Fronts 1938–1953* (Columbia: University of Missouri Press, 1969), 44.

15. Foner, *Blacks and the Military*, 130.

16. In 1942, a memo from the Adjutant General's office indicated that with the exception of Fort Huachuca, which housed one infantry division, "no Negro unit larger than a brigade be stationed at any post within the continental limits of the United States." See Ulysses Lee, *United States Army in World War II: The Employment of Negro Troops* (Washington, DC: Office of the Chief of Military History, United States Army, 1966), 103.

17. Schomburg Archives, Box 1, Series 1C, personal placement questionnaire.

18. The qualifications of Black inductees were uniformly disregarded no matter where they were assigned. Foner describes the experience of a Black biochemist who after successfully completing a number of technical training programs was assigned to a labor detail. *Blacks and the Military*, 147.

19. See https://data.bls.gov/cgi-bin/cpicalc.pl for an inflation calculator.

20. See Lee, *United States Army in World War II*, 281–286, for a detailed report about conditions at the Hook.

21. See recollections of First Lieutenant George Looney in Mary Penick Motley, *The Invisible Soldier: The Experience of the Black Soldier, World War II* (Detroit: Wayne State University Press, 1975), 83, and letters in Fort Huachuca Chronological Files. See also Corporal Everette Hodge's letter of November 5, 1942, protesting the assignment of Black soldiers as pickers in Arizona's cotton fields. Library of Congress, NAACP/Legal File, Box 150, Folder: Soldiers' Complaints.

22. Fort Huachuca Museum Chronological Files.

23. Lee, *United States Army in World War II*, 284.

24. Williams's experience was far from unusual. See ibid., 315–324, for a discussion of the difficulties Black soldiers faced when traveling during the war.

25. Joseph J. Rhoads was a scholar, educational administrator, and civil rights advocate who was the first African American president of Bishop College. Winfield Curry telephone interview, April 5, 1996.

26. Freeman interview.

27. Otto Rizzotto interview, April 5, 1996.

28. Schomburg Archives, Box 20, FBI File.

29. Ibid.

30. Ibid.

31. Franklin Williams interview, October 23, 1989.

32. Adrian Edwards interview, April 3, 1996.

33. See Lee, *United States Army in World War II*, 293.

34. Timothy J. Quinn, LTC, U.S. Army, Office of the Director of the Army Staff, November 8, 1995.

35. Roberta Braddicks Williams interview, November 2, 1990.

36. Ibid.

37. Shirley Broyard Williams interview, October 18, 1992.

38. Franklin Williams interview, May 5, 1988.

39. Anatole Broyard, *Kafka Was the Rage: A Greenwich Village Memoir* (New York: Carol Southern Books, 1993), 30.

40. Broyard Williams interview.

41. Franklin Williams graduated from Fordham University School of Law on October 10, 1945, with an 87.5 average. He passed the New York State Bar Exam in June 1945. Transcript, Fordham University School of Law.

42. Williams's application to the Federal Bureau of Investigation is among the archives at the Schomburg Center for Research in Black Culture Center. See Box 1, Personal Papers.

43. Ibid.

44. Thomas B. Dyett was a distinguished African America lawyer in New York City. He was the first Black to head the Civil Service Commission of the City of New York and the first to serve on the Character and Fitness Committee of the Appellate Division of the state Supreme Court. He also served as deputy commissioner of the New York City Department of Corrections. Dyett was also founder and general counsel to the Carver Federal Savings and Loan Association, the first African American institution of its kind in New York. Harold Stevens was the first African American to serve on the New York State Court of Appeals and was also presiding justice of the Appellate Division, First Department. Fritz W. Alexander II interview, April 23, 1996.

45. See Harry G. Bragg's letter of October 20, 1945, recommending Franklin Williams to Thurgood Marshall, Library of Congress, NAACP Legal Files, Box 218, Folder: Franklin H. Williams, 1945–1948.

5. The American Veterans Committee

1. Franklin Williams interviews, November 13 and 15, 1989, in which he recounted his AVC activities.

2. Schomburg Archives, Box 22, scrapbook A. Undated news clip.

3. http://biographies-memoirs.wikidot.com/harrison-gilbert-a.

4. Charles Bolte, The New Veteran (New York: Reynal and Hitchcock, 1945), 46.

5. Gilbert Harrison interview, November 1, 1996.

6. Bolte, The New Veteran, 54–73.

7. Ibid., 36, 37.

8. Schomburg Archives, Box 22, scrapbook, program from Des Moines Convention, June 14, 1946.

9. AVC Bulletin, February 1, 1946; February 15, 1946; May 1, 1946.

10. Christopher Matthews, Kennedy & Nixon: The Rivalry That Shaped Postwar America (New York: Simon & Schuster, 1996), 100.

11. New York Times, May 12, 1946.

12. Julian Feldman telephone interview, November 5, 1996.

13. See the New York Times of March 23, 1946, August 6 and 10, 1946.

14. See the following New York Times articles for information about the Metropolitan Area Council activities in 1946: March 23, 1946; August 6, 1946; August 10, 1946.

15. See Robert Cohen, *When the Old Left Was Young: Student Radicals and America's First Mass Student Movement, 1929–1941* (New York: Oxford University Press, 1993), for an account of the growth and demise of the student movement.

16. Justin Feldman interview, November 27, 1990.

17. *New York Times*, May 12, 1945.

18. Ibid.

19. Franklin Williams interview, November 13, 1989.

20. Ibid.

21. Feldman interview, November 27, 1990.

22. Schomburg Archives, Box 22, scrapbook A.

23. Franklin Williams interview, November 15, 1989.

24. Ibid.

25. Feldman interview, November 27, 1990.

26. Williams interview, November 15, 1989.

27. "National Planning the Militant Progressive Way," *New York Post*, September 10, 1946.

28. Feldman interview, November 27, 1990.

29. Gilbert Harrison interview, November 1, 1996.

30. "National Planning the Militant Progressive Way."

31. *Mademoiselle*, October 1946. See clipping in Schomburg Archives, Box 22, scrapbook A.

32. Michael Straight interview, December 4, 1996.

33. Feldman interview, November 27, 1990.

34. "Boos, Cheers, Mark Veterans' Session," *New York Times*, October 27, 1946.

35. See Neil A. Lewis, "Files Say Justice Marshall Aided F.B.I, in 50's," *New York Times*, December 4, 1996, and Denton L. Watson, "Thurgood Marshall's Red Menace," *New York Times*, December 10, 1996.

36. Williams interview, November 13, 1989.

37. Schomburg Archives, Box 22, scrapbook A, Memorabilia. Build AVC flyer.

38. Franklin H. Williams, "Democracy in Practice," *AVC Bulletin*, March 15, 1947.

39. "Veterans Warned on 'Drift to War,'" *New York Times*, June 20, 1947.

40. "AVC Session Nears Platform Dispute," *New York Times*, June 22, 1947.

41. NAACP Legal File Folder, FHW 1945–48, Memo to Walter White from Franklin Williams, June 30, 1947.

42. *AVC Bulletin*, 1946.

6. Civil Rights Lawyer

1. For a History Channel documentary on the NAACP, see https://www.history .com/topics/civil-rights-movement/naacp.

2. Williams's 1962 address to the Virginia State Conference of NAACP Branches is in the Schomburg Archives, Box 54.

3. Franklin Williams interview, October 31, 1989.

4. The Clerk of Court, U.S. Army Judiciary, General Court Martial, Arthur Essex CM242609.

5. The court-martial records of Lawrence J. Everett, AGPK-Cr201 and "Petition for Clemency and Brief in Support Thereof" were obtained from the Clerk of Court, U.S. Army Judiciary, Falls Church, Virginia.

6. Memorandum, December 16, 1945, Library of Congress, NAACP Legal Files, Box 218, Folder: Franklin W. Williams 1945–1948.

7. Ibid.

8. Ibid.

9. Gloster Current interview, April 30, 1991.

10. Jack Greenberg, *Crusaders in the Courts: How a Dedicated Band of Lawyers Fought for the Civil Rights Revolution* (New York: Basic Books, 1994), 32.

11. Current interview.

12. Greenberg, *Crusaders*, 33.

13. Memorandum to Thurgood Marshall from Franklin H. Williams, October 25, 1946, NAACP Legal Files, Box 218, Folder: FHW, 1945–1948.

14. Current interview.

15. Reminiscences of Julius Waties Waring, 1957, Columbia Center for Oral History, 1:50.

16. Memorandum for Orson Welles' Program, Lighthouse and Informer, John H. McCray, Publisher, September 19, 1946; LOC, NAACP Legal File, Box 219, Folder: Woodard, Isaac, Correspondence, 1946, September–November, 180.

17. P. M., September 27, 1946, *The New York Times*, November 6, 1946. Clipping from LOC, NAACP Legal Files, Box 219, Folder: Woodard, Isaac clippings, 1946–47.

18. Ibid.

19. Orson Welles, commentaries on ABC, July 28 broadcast.

20. Barbara Learning, *Orson Welles: A Biography* (New York: Viking Press, 1985), 331.

21. *Augusta Chronicle*, August 12, 1946.

22. Williams interview.

23. Memorandum to Thurgood Marshall from Franklin H. Williams, Re: Acquittal of Lynwood L. Shull in the case of Isaac Woodard, Jr. November 12, 1946. Library of Congress, NAACP Legal files, Box 219, Folder: Woodard, Isaac, Correspondence, 1946, September–November. Franklin Williams interview, October 31, 1989.

24. Williams interview.

25. There is contradictory evidence in the record about whether or not witnesses subpoenaed on Woodard's behalf ever took the stand. In Williams's memorandum to Thurgood Marshall, November 12, 1946, he reports that two witnesses gave testimony on rebuttal. However, Judge J. Waties Waring, in his oral history, states that federal prosecutors never produced witnesses to corroborate Woodard's testimony. See Reminiscences of Julius Waties Waring, 2:220.

26. See Glen Altschuler, "Unexampled Courage: How an Act of Racist Barbarism Sparked Racial Progress," *Pittsburgh Post-Gazette*, February 17, 2019.

27. Memorandum to Thurgood Marshall from Franklin H. Williams, Re: Acquittal of Lynwood L. Shull in the case of Isaac Woodard, Jr. November 12, 1946. Library of Congress, NAACP Legal files. Box 219, Folder: Woodard, Isaac, Correspondence, 1946.

28. Ibid.

29. "Frees Dixie Cop Who Blinded Vet," *Amsterdam News*, November 9, 1946; "Freedom for Woodard Attacker Protested," *Chicago Defender*, November 16, 1946; "Hit Verdict in Case of Blinded Vet," *Pittsburgh Courier*, November 16, 1946. See also the November 6, 1946, issues of the *Atlanta Constitution, Philadelphia Inquirer*, New Orleans *Times-Picayune, Baltimore Sun, New York Times*, and *Washington Post*.

30. "Woodard Unavenged," *Pittsburgh Courier*, November 16, 1946.

31. Reminiscences of Julius Waties Waring, 1:223.

32. Tinsley E. Yarbrough, *A Passion for Justice: J. Waties Waring and Civil Rights* (New York: Oxford University Press, 1987).

33. Reminiscences of Julius Waties Waring, 1:237–245.

34. Richard Kluger, *Simple Justice: The History of Brown v. Board of Education and Black America's Struggle for Equality* (New York: Vintage Books, 1975), 297.

35. See Audra D. S. Burch, "Why a Town Is Finally Honoring a Black Veteran Attacked by Its White Police Chief," *New York Times*, February 8, 2019.

36. *Rice v. Elmore*, 165 F.2d 387 (4th Cir. 1947).

37. *Briggs v. Elliott*, 342 U.S. 350 (1952).

38. Kluger, *Simple Justice*, 366.

39. Williams interview.

40. Ibid.

41. Gloster Current interview, May 30, 1991.

42. Gloster Current interview, February 26, 1997. See also Library of Congress Folder: Franklin H. Williams, Williams' Mileage Report, 1946.

7. In the Courts

1. See U.S. Census, "Income of Families and Persons in the United States: 1947," https://www.census.gov/library/publications/1949/demo/p60-005.html.

2. Home Office memo, November 1944, "Riverton Is Planned by the Company as Its Second Postwar Housing Project," Metropolitan Life Collection: Subject Files, Location 170604, V. F. Riverton #2.

3. After the war, the Metropolitan Life Insurance Company became the first company to join with municipal government in rebuilding blighted urban communities. In New York City, the company built and managed Parkchester, Riverton, Peter Cooper Village, and Stuyvesant Town. Elsewhere, the company owned units in Alexandria, Virginia, and Los Angeles and San Francisco, California. See "Company Highlights: 1868–1996," Metropolitan Life Collection: Subject Files, Location 170604, V. F. Riverton #1 & 2.

4. Quote by Metropolitan Life Insurance Company Chairman Frederick H. Ecker in Carlyle Douglas, "Ex Tenants Fondly Recall a Haven in Harlem," *New York Times,* March 15, 1995.

5. James Baldwin, *Nobody Knows My Name: More Notes of a Native Son* (New York: Dial Press, 1961), 64.

6. Ibid.

7. Robert Carter, telephone interview, February 13, 1998.

8. Roberta Braddicks Williams interview, November 2, 1990.

9. *Patton v. Mississippi*, 332 U.S. 463 (1947).

10. Hiroshi Fukurai, Edgar W. Butler, and Richard Krooth, *Race and the Jury: Racial Disenfranchisement and the Search for Justice* (New York: Plenum Press, 1993), 83–84.

11. Ibid.

12. See Civil Rights Act of 1875, Ch. 114, 18 Stat. 335.

13. *Strauder v. West Virginia*, 100 U.S. 303 (1880).

14. *Swain v. Alabama*, 380 U.S. 202 (1965).

15. Ibid., 223–224.

16. *Patton v. Mississippi*, 332 U.S. 463 (1947).

17. Ibid.

18. The Court held in *Norris v. Alabama* (1935) that it was the state's responsibility to prove that it did not exclude Blacks from juries, and that the defense could present testimony and census information to refute the state's claims. In *Smith v. Texas* (1940), the Court ruled that one Black juror was not sufficient to prove that discrimination did not take place.

19. *Patton v. State of Mississippi*, brief for petitioner, 12.

20. Ibid., 15.

21. *Patton v. Mississippi*.

22. Franklin Williams interview, October 31, 1989. Williams overheard Marshall praising him in a telephone call.

23. *Indianapolis Star*, November 14, 1946.

24. Ibid., November 21, 1947.

25. Ibid.

26. Warren M. Brown to Franklin H. Williams, Folder 54, File 1, LC, December 20, 1948.

27. It bears noting that in many of the cases where modern DNA evidence proved beyond doubt that an individual was wrongly convicted, police had obtained a false confession. See the Innocence Project, https://innocenceproject.org/dna-exonerations -in-the-united-states/.

28. Franklin Williams interview, October 31, 1989. All the quotations in this episode come from this interview.

29. *Haley v. Ohio*, 332 U.S. 596 (1948); No. 344, Misc. Robert Austin Watts, Petitioner v. State of Indiana, Respondent, Brief for Petitioner, Watts Folder 1, LC. See *Haley v. Ohio*, 92 L. Ed., Adv. Op. 239.

30. Robert Carter interview, July 24, 1999.

31. Ibid.

32. Franklin Williams interview, October 31, 1989.

33. Schomburg Archives.

34. See *Watts v. Indiana*, 338 U.S. 49, 69 S.C. 1347.

35. *Indianapolis News*, January 16, 1951.

36. See *Taylor v. Dennis*, 336 U.S. 929, 69 S.C. 93.

37. 338 U.S. 844, 70 S.C. 93.

38. 337 U.S. 949. See also *Long Island Daily Press*, April 15, 1949.

39. 337 U.S. 949.

40. *Briggs v. Elliott*, 342 U.S. 350 (1952).

41. See https://www.hmdb.org/marker.asp?marker=40503.

42. "Negro's Suit to Open Parks and Amphitheatre Put Off," *Courier-Journal*, July 30, 1947.

43. "Negro Balked in Show Suit: Court Rules Park Body out of Case," *Courier-Journal*, July 29, 1947.

44. *Sweeney v. City of Louisville*, 309 Ky. 465 (Ky. Ct. App. 1949).

45. Richard Kluger, *Simple Justice: The History of Brown v. Board of Education and Black America's Struggle for Equality* (New York: Vintage Books, 1975), 367–395.

46. Franklin H. Williams and Earl L. Fultz, "The Merriam School Fight," *The Crisis*, May 1949, 141.

47. "Student Papers in Local History," Johnson County Center for Local History, 1986, Kansas State Historical Society, Property Number 1600.

48. *Sipuel v. Board of Regents of University of Oklahoma et al.*, 332 U.S. 631; *McLaurin v. Oklahoma State Board of Regents*, 339 U.S. 637; *Sweatt v. Painter*, 339 U.S. 629.

49. Kluger, *Simple Justice*, 385; John Anderson Jr. interview, June 12, 1999.

50. *Kansas City Call*, April 8, 1949.

51. *Webb et al. v. School Dist. No. 90, Johnson County, et al.* 167 Kan. 395, 206, 2:1066.

52. Mary J. Webb interview, June 29, 1999.

53. Schomburg Archives, scrapbook 1E.

54. Peggy Cooper Davis interview by John Caher and Linda Dunlap-Miller, May 10, 2016. The interview was conducted by and for the Franklin H. Williams Judicial Commission.

8. Legal Lynching

1. James W. Ivey, "Florida's Little Scottsboro: Groveland," *Crisis* 266 (1949).

2. Franklin Williams oral history, February 11, 1985, David Colburn and Steve Lawson, Samuel Proctor Oral History Program, University of Florida.

3. Much has been written about the Groveland case. The authors have relied on accounts of the case provided by two NAACP attorneys intimately involved with it:

Franklin H. Williams and Jack Greenberg, who inherited the case after the NAACP transferred Williams to California in 1950. Franklin H. Williams discussed the case at length in an interview of November 15, 1989, conducted by Enid Gort. See also Williams's extensive news clipping files, Boxes 2 and 3, Folders 1–53 at the Schomburg Center for Research in Black Culture. See also Jack Greenberg, *Crusaders in the Courts: How a Dedicated Band of Lawyers Fought for the Civil Rights Revolution* (New York: Basic Books, 1994). The authors are especially grateful to Gilbert King, whose excellent work *Devil in the Grove: Thurgood Marshall, the Groveland Boys, and the Dawn of a New America* (New York: HarperCollins, 2012) provided valuable information about the forces at work behind the scenes in Groveland.

4. Florida State Archives, 20, 903, Transcript of Testimony, 629.

5. King, *Devil in the Grove*, 59.

6. Gary Corsair, *Legal Lynching: The Sad Saga of the Groveland Four* (Seattle: Create Space, 2012), 10.

7. Ibid.

8. Greenberg, *Crusaders in the Courts*, 94.

9. Corsair, *Legal Lynching*, 20.

10. Steven F. Lawson, David R. Colburn, and Darryl Paulson, "Groveland: Florida's Little Scottsboro," *Florida Historical Quarterly* 65 (1986): 8.

11. Ibid.

12. Pete Daniel, *In the Shadow of Slavery: Peonage in the South, 1901–1969* (Champaign: University of Illinois Press, 1972), 22.

13. *Christian Science Monitor*, August 26, 1949.

14. Ivey, "Florida's Little Scottsboro," 266.

15. Greenberg, *Crusaders in the Courts*, 95.

16. Lawson, Colburn, and Paulson, "Groveland," 3.

17. Ibid.

18. Ibid.

19. Corsair, *Legal Lynching*, 30.

20. Lawson, Colburn, and Paulson, "Groveland," 3.

21. Corsair, *Legal Lynching*, 30.

22. Greenberg, *Crusaders in the Courts*, 95.

23. Ted Poston, "Florida's Legal Lynching," *The Nation*, 296, undated. See Schomburg Archives, Box 2, folder 2.

24. Schomburg Center, FHW Box 2, Folder 12, unidentified news clipping "Jealousy is Source of Florida Terror."

25. Corsair, *Legal Lynching*, 3.

26. King, *Devil in the Grove*, 63.

27. https://www.bbc.com/news/world-us-canada-46847001.

28. *The Courier*, 1949, in Schomburg Archives, Box 2, clipping file 2.

29. Library of Congress, NAACP II, Box 99, Folder: Marshall, Thurgood, General 1947. Memorandum to Committee on Administration from Thurgood

Marshall, October 27, 1947. In Marshall's memo, he notes the following complaint from Williams: "The question which is ever present before the entire legal staff is the question of being required to do the most careful research in the preparation of the trial and appeal of cases in quarters that are so cramped as to make it impossible to do either."

30. Harry T. Moore and his wife, Harriette Vyda Simms Moore, were for three decades thorns in the side of racist law enforcement officials and other haters of Black people. Florida natives, they established the first branch of the NAACP in Brevard County in 1934 and thereafter were active in every aspect of the organization's activities including voters' rights and education. Their ceaseless investigations into lynching and police brutality ultimately led to their deaths in a Christmas Eve bombing in 1951. See "Legacy of Harry T. Moore," *Florida Frontiers*, PBS, aired October 1, 2017, and Ben Green, *Before His Time: The Untold Story of Harry T. Moore, America's First Civil Rights Martyr* (New York: Free Press, 1999).

31. Schomburg Archives, Box 2, folder 2, undated news clipping "Orlando Organizes to Help; Refugees of Florida Terror."

32. *Orlando Sentinel Star*, July 19, 1949.

33. Ibid.

34. Corsair, *Legal Lynching*, 81–82.

35. Ibid.

36. Franklin Williams interview, November 11, 1989.

37. Corsair, *Legal Lynching*, 83.

38. Greenberg, *Crusaders in the Courts*, 102.

39. Florida State Archives, Transcript of Testimony on Motion of Defendants to Withdraw Pleas of Not Guilty and to Set Aside Arraignment, Testimony of Franklin H. Williams, August 25, 1949, 5–7.

40. Interviews with Franklin Williams, November 15 and 17, 1989, and Poston, "Florida's Legal Lynching." There are minor inconsistencies in the two accounts, but the stories they tell are essentially the same.

41. Ibid.

42. Ibid.

43. Franklin Williams interview, November 17, 1989.

44. Spessard Holland Jr. became an outspoken antiwar activist and a participant, in 1963, in the March on Washington organized by Martin Luther King Jr. Forced to resign from his father's law firm, Holland and Knight, because of his liberal views, he practiced law on his own until his death in 1989. Nancy Dobson interview, March 24, 1997.

45. Florida State Archives, Transcript of Testimony, 5–7.

46. Greenberg, *Crusaders in the Courts*, 26.

47. Alex Akerman Jr. interview, April 1, 1991.

48. Ibid.

49. Williams interview, November 17, 1989.

50. Ibid.

51. Corsair, *Legal Lynching*, 50.

52. Lawson, Colburn, and Paulson, "Groveland," 11.

53. See *Moore v. Dempsey*, 261 U.S. 86 (1923) and *Powell v. Alabama*, 287 U.S. 45 (1932).

54. *Moore v. Dempsey*, 90–91.

55. Williams, in addition to presenting pretrial motions, carefully assembled the "four corners of the record" including motions, briefs, copies of the prejudicial newspapers, photographs, and other essential documents needed, as Thurgood Marshall reminded his staff, "[to] keep the record straight for the appeal." King, *Devil in the Grove*, 55.

56. Akerman interview.

57. *Clermont News Topic*, August 25, 1949.

58. Florida State Archives, 20,903, Special Rules for Circuit Court in and for Lake County, Florida.

59. Williams interview, November 17, 1989.

60. Poston, "Florida's Legal Lynching." See also Florida State Archives, 20,903, Transcript of Testimony, Volume I.

61. Undated *New York Post* news clipping, Schomburg Archives, Box 2, Folder 2.

62. Florida State Archives, Testimony, 4:465.

63. Ramona Lowe, "Force Defendants' Kin to Testify at Hearing," *Chicago Defender*, September 10, 1949; Schomburg Archives, Box 2, folder 2.

64. Florida State Archives, Testimony, 501, 503, 524.

65. Ibid., 482, 519.

66. Ibid., 483, 521.

67. William R. Ezzell, "The Law of the Groves: Whittling Away at the Legal Mysteries in the Prosecution of the Groveland Boys," *University of Massachusetts Law Review* 11, no. 2 (2016).

68. King, *Devil in the Grove*, 152.

69. Ibid.

70. Ibid.

71. See "Attorney Williams Expresses His Views on 'Faults of the South,'" *Mount Dora Topic*, September 8, 1949. See also Florida State Archives, 20, 903, Exhibit, XXI, "Special Rules for Circuit Court in and for Lake County Florida."

72. FHW papers. Box 2, folder 7. Unidentified news clipping.

73. *Mount Dora Topic*, November 29, 1952.

74. https://en.wikipedia.org/wiki/Ted_Poston.

75. King, *Devil in the Grove*, 175.

76. Greenberg, *Crusaders in the Courts*, 101–102.

77. Schomburg Archives, Box 3, Ted Poston interview.

78. Lowe, "Force Defendants' Kin to Testify at Hearing"; Schomburg Archives, Box 2, folder 2.

79. Schomburg Archives, Poston interview.

80. Corsair, *Legal Lynching*, 66.

81. Ibid., 157.

82. Williams interview, November 17, 1989.

83. Corsair, *Legal Lynching*, 184

84. In Ted Poston's *New York Post* article "Lynch Mob's Breath of Death Scorches Reporter Fleeing Florida," October 7, 1949, he described his flight from the courtroom and his harrowing departure from Tavares with Williams, Hill, and Lowe.

85. Ted Poston, "Horror for Sunny South," *New York Post*, September 8, 1949.

86. Ibid.

9. Passion and Power Plays

1. *McLaurin v. Oklahoma State Board of Regents*, 339 U.S. 637 (1950) concerned Oklahoma's required segregation in graduate or professional education. The lower court said the University of Oklahoma was correct in acting in accordance with that law. The Supreme Court disagreed. In *Sweatt v. Painter*, 339 U.S. 629 (1950), a Black man was refused admission to the University of Texas School of Law on the grounds that the Texas State Constitution prohibited integrated education.

2. Gilbert King, *Devil in the Grove: Thurgood Marshall, the Groveland Boys, and the Dawn of a New America* (New York: HarperCollins, 2012), 181.

3. *Shepherd v. State*, 46 So. 880 (1950).

4. Mabel Norris-Reese, "Justice Triumphs," *Mount Dora Topic*, May 18, 1950.

5. See Petition for Writ of Certiorari, *Shepherd v. Florida*, 341 U.S. 50, 53 (1951).

6. Jack Greenberg interview with the Columbia Oral History Project, in Juan Williams, *Thurgood Marshall: American Revolutionary* (New York: Random House, 1989), 154.

7. Franklin Williams interview, November 17, 1989.

8. Patricia Sullivan, *Lift Every Voice: The NAACP and the Making of the Civil Rights Movement* (New York: The New Press, 2009), 372.

9. King, *Devil in the Grove*, 201.

10. Williams interview.

11. King, *Devil in the Grove*, 203.

12. Gloster Current interview, April 30, 1991.

13. Nat Colley interview, undated.

14. Williams interview. Other details in this paragraph come from this source.

15. Memorandum from Walter White to Franklin Williams, Manuscript Division, Library of Congress, Box C235, File WCRO, Correspondence, 1950, August–October.

16. "The NAACP and the Communists," *The Crisis* 56 (March 1949): 72, in Albert S. Broussard, *Black San Francisco: The Struggle for Racial Equality in the West, 1900–1954* (Lawrence: University Press of Kansas, 1993), 79.

17. Williams, October 14, 1962, speech to the Virginia State Conference of NAACP Branches, Schomburg Archives, Box 54.

18. William H. Chafe, *The Unfinished Journey: America Since World War II*, 3rd ed. (New York: Oxford University Press, 1995), 79.

19. Williams interview.

20. "Itinerary, August 19–September 2nd, 1950," Manuscript Division, Library of Congress, West Coast Region, Box C235, WCRO, Correspondence, 1950.

21. See "Noah Webster Griffin Sr. (1896–1974)," in *Black Past*, https://www .Blackpast.org/african-american-history/griffin-noah-webster-1896-1974/.

22. Mrs. Noah Griffin interview, June 21, 1976. Broussard, *Black San Francisco*, 311.

23. Manuscript Division, Library of Congress, Box C235, File: WCRO, Correspondence, 1950, Aug.–Oct.

24. Letter to Roy Wilkins, September 18, 1950, Manuscript Division, Library of Congress, Box C235, File: WCRO, Correspondence, 1950.

25. Quintard Taylor, *In Search of the Racial Frontier: African Americans in the American West, 1528–1990* (New York: Norton, 1998), 251.

26. Quintard Taylor, "They Went West," *American Legacy: The Magazine of African-American History & Culture* 7, no. 3 (Fall 2001), 54.

27. Ibid.

28. Jeffrey D. Gonda, *Unjust Deeds: The Restrictive Covenant Cases and the Making of the Civil Rights Movement* (Chapel Hill: University of North Carolina Press, 2015), 26.

29. King, *Devil in the Grove*, 216–217.

30. Ibid.

31. Gary Corsair, *Legal Lynching: The Sad Saga of the Groveland Four* (Seattle: Create Space, 2012), 221.

32. Ibid.

33. *The Crisis*, April 1951.

34. Ibid.

35. *Cassell v. Texas*, 339 U.S. 282 (1950).

36. *Shepherd v. Florida*, 341 US 50 (1951).

37. Ibid.

38. https://www.crmvet.org/docs/51_naacp_ldef.pdf.

39. Ibid.

40. "Judge Closes Case in Slaying of Negro," *New York Times*, November 13, 1951.

41. Mabel Norris-Reese, "Irvin Sticks to Bizarre Story as He Awaits February 11," *Mount Dora Topic*, January 31, 1952.

42. "Florida AG Implicates 4 in 1951 Racial Slayings," Associated Press, August 17, 2006, http://www.nbcnews.com/id/14380016/ns/us_news-life/t/florida-ag-implicates -racial-slayings/#.XOhU_nmWzxM.

43. James C. Clark, "Civil Rights Leader Harry T. Moore and the Ku Klux Klan in Florida," *Florida Historical Quarterly* 73 (October 1999): 166.

44. Stephen Hudak, "Groveland Four: Who Were They?" *Orlando Sentinel*, January 11, 2019.

45. Sarah Wilson, "Florida Clemency Board Pardons Groveland Four 70 Years Later," WFTV (ABC) News, January 11, 2019.

10. California Deliverance

1. Kenneth Robert Janken, *White: The Biography of Walter White, Mr. NAACP* (New York: The New Press, 2003), 322.

2. Albert S. Broussard, *Black San Francisco: The Struggle for Racial Equality in the West, 1900–1954* (Lawrence: University Press of Kansas, 1993), 229.

3. Ibid, 228.

4. Ibid.

5. Second Quarterly Report—1951 to Gloster B. Current, Director of Branches, NAACP, from Franklin H. Williams, Regional Director, June 8, 1951, Schomburg Archives, Box 4, Regional NAACP Press Releases 1950–1956.

6. Broussard, *Black San Francisco*, 229.

7. Regional NAACP Press Releases 1954–60, Schomburg Archives, Box 4.

8. Ibid.

9. Letter from Franklin Williams to Board Members Warning About Leftists, Oct. 7, 1955, Bancroft Archives, Box 42, Folder No. 1, File: "Political Action Till, Emmett—protest meetings."

10. Schomburg Archives.

11. Franklin Williams interview, November 28, 1989.

12. Frank and Marion Barnes interview, undated.

13. NAACP Annual Report, 43rd Year, 1951, 15.

14. Amina Hassan, *Loren Miller: Civil Rights Attorney and Journalist* (Norman: University of Oklahoma Press, 2015), 3.

15. Williams interview, November 28, 1989.

16. NAACP Annual Report, Forty-fourth Year, 1952, 27. See https://www.sfgate .com/bayarea/article/Rev-Hamilton-T-Boswell-led-S-F-Blacks-2561042.php.

17. Letter to Gloster Current from Franklin H. Williams, August 10, 1951, reproduced from the Collections of the Manuscript Division, Library of Congress, Box C 235, File: WCRO, Correspondence: Jan.–June 1951.

18. Walter Carrington interview, December 12, 1992.

19. *The Stanford Daily*, April 13, 1957.

20. See "Pittman, Tarea Hall (1903–1991)," BlackPast.org.

21. Williams interview, November 28, 1989.

22. Ibid.

23. Ibid.

24. See James Baldwin, "Faulkner and Desegregation" (1956), in *James Baldwin: Collected Essays* (New York: Library of America, 1998), 9.

25. Schomburg Archives, scrapbooks, 1953.

26. Schomburg Archives, scrapbooks, 1956.

27. Schomburg Archives, West Coast clips.

28. Broussard, *Blacks in San Francisco*, 238.

29. Excerpts of speeches from the era, Schomburg Archives.

30. *Banks v. Housing Authority of San Francisco*, 120 Cal. App. 2d 1, 260 P.2d 668 (1953), cert denied, 347 U.S. 974 (1954).

31. Stephen Grant Meyer, *As Long as They Don't Move Next Door: Segregation and Racial Conflict in American Neighborhoods* (Lanham, MD: Rowman & Littlefield, 1999), 142.

32. See http://legalhistoryblog.blogspot.com/2015/05/banks-v-housing-authority -and-multi_13.html.

33. Charles J. Patterson interview, June 19, 1992.

34. Broussard, *Blacks in San Francisco*, 230.

35. See https://nul.org/mission-and-history.

36. Letter to Dr. May Edward Chinn from Franklin H. Williams, Bancroft Library, Call Number 78/180C/Box/Carton No. 5, Folder. OA Correspondence—Regional, Regional Secretary—Counsel, Franklin H. Williams (personal), Sept. 6, 1955.

37. Yvonne Ryan, *Roy Wilkins: The Quiet Revolutionary and the NAACP* (Lexington: University Press of Kentucky, 2014), 2.

38. Years later, James Booker a journalist for the *Amsterdam News*, reported that there were still some board members who wanted to dismiss Wilkins and replace him with Franklin Williams. However, by that time, Williams was long gone from the NAACP, and his career was on a different trajectory. See ibid., 138.

39. Ronald Gerald Coleman, *A History of Blacks in Utah, 1825–1910* (Salt Lake City: University of Utah Press, 1980).

40. Annual report of the NAACP, 1957.

41. Stuart John McElderry, *The Problem of the Color Line: Civil Rights and Racial Ideology in Portland, Oregon, 1944–1965* (Eugene: University of Oregon Press, 1998), 17.

42. Ibid., 66.

43. Kevin Allen Leonard, "Civil Rights Movement in the Pacific Northwest," in *Black Americans and the Civil Rights Movement in the West*, ed. Bruce A Glasrud and Cary D. Wintz (Norman: University of Oklahoma Press, 2019), 23–37.

44. See "Coast Nominee Barred; Brownell Refuses to Name Him Over N.A.A.C.P. Protest," *New York Times*, November 1, 1953.

45. Bradford Luckingham, *Minorities in Phoenix: A Profile of Mexican American, Chinese American, and African American Communities: 1960–1992* (Tucson: University of Arizona Press, 1994), 146.

46. Clipping from the *Courier*, Schomburg Archives, Box 22, scrapbook A memorabilia.

47. Mary W. Melcher, "Blacks and Whites Together: Interracial Leadership in the Phoenix Arizona Civil Rights Movement," in Glasrud and Wintz, *Black Americans and the Civil Rights Movement in the West*, 140.

48. See https://superiorcourt.maricopa.gov/llrc/phillips-vs-puhs/.

49. See https://superiorcourt.maricopa.gov/llrc/heard-vs-davis/. *Heard v. Davis* is posted at https://www.superiorcourt.maricopa.gov/LawLibrary/docs/PDF/Heard /MemorandumOpinion.pdf.

50. Schomburg Archives, Box 4, Regional NAACP Press Releases 1950–56: "NAACP Throws Brickbats and Bouquets at Racial Practices Ask Yuma (Arizona) to Remove Anti-Negro Signs in Business Places."

51. Elmer R. Rusco, "Civil Rights Movement in Nevada" in Glasrud and Wintz, *Black Americans and the Civil Rights Movement in the West*, 73.

52. Michael Coray, "African-Americans in Nevada," *Nevada Historical Society Quarterly* 35, no. 4 (Winter 1992): 240.

53. Nathanial Colley interview, undated.

54. Ibid.

55. Franklin Williams interview, November 30, 1989.

56. Ibid.

57. Franklin Williams Jr. interview by John Caher and Joyce Y. Hartsfield, November 9, 2016. The interview was conducted by and for the Franklin H. Williams Judicial Commission.

58. Williams interview, November 30, 1989.

59. Williams Jr. interview.

60. Williams interview, November 30, 1989.

61. Broussard, *Blacks in San Francisco*, 240.

62. Arnold Rampersad, *Jackie Robinson: A Biography* (New York: Knopf, 1997), 262.

63. Rachel Robinson interview, November 11, 1999.

64. Julia Bates interview, undated.

65. Memorandum from Franklin Williams to Roy Wilkins regarding Jackie Robinson, Feb. 15, 1957, Box #4, OA-Correspondence, Regional Secretary Counsel.

66. Rachel Robinson interview, November 11, 1999.

67. Williams interview, November 28, 1989.

68. Schomburg Archives, scrapbooks.

69. Ibid.

70. Broussard, *Blacks in San Francisco*, 231.

71. Western Region Annual Report, 1956.

72. Ibid.

73. Records indicated that Williams did not resign from the NAACP but rather took a leave of absence, suggesting perhaps that he wanted to preserve the safety net as long as possible.

74. Williams interview, November 28, 1989.

75. Ibid.

76. Ibid.

77. "PGA Opens Its Doors to Negroes, World Golfers," Associated Press, November 10, 1961.

78. William C. Rhoden, "A Pioneer's Tribute Is Both a Reward and a Reminder: Charlie Sifford Is Given the Presidential Medal of Freedom," *New York Times*, November 25, 2014.

79. Jason Zengerle, "The Man Who Was Everywhere," *The New Republic*, November 20, 2014.

80. Williams interview, November 30, 1989.

81. Ibid.

82. See Michael Beschloss, "Jackie Robinson and Nixon: Life and Death of Political Friendship," *New York Times*, June 6, 2014.

83. Franklin Williams interview, December 9, 1989.

84. See Black Past, https://www.Blackpast.org/african-american-history/martin-louis-e-1912-1997/.

85. Williams interview, December 9, 1989.

86. Ibid.

11. The Washington Years

1. See https://www.peacecorps.gov/about/history/founding-moment/.

2. Harris Wofford, Oral History, JFK Library, Boston.

3. https://www.jfklibrary.org/learn/about-jfk/jfk-in-history/peace-corps.

4. Elizabeth A. Cobbs, "Decolonization, the Cold War, and the Foreign Policy of the Peace Corps," *Diplomatic History* 20, no. 1 (1996): 79–105.

5. https://www.jfklibrary.org/learn/about-jfk/jfk-in-history/peace-corps.

6. Cobbs, "Decolonization," 81.

7. See Franklin Williams memorandum to Peace Corps Staff, March 6, 1963, Bush Papers, Box 1, John F. Kennedy Memorial Library.

8. Cobbs, "Decolonization," 82.

9. National Archives, April 1961.

10. See https://en.unesco.org/about-us/introducing-unesco.

11. John H. Morrow to the Department of State, Aug. 2, 1961, National Archives 59.

12. Cobbs, "Decolonization," 83.

13. Sargent Shriver interview, October 17, 1991.

14. Ibid.

15. Stanley Meisler, *When the World Calls: The Inside Story of the Peace Corps and its First Fifty Years* (Boston: Beacon Press, 2011), 23.

16. Ibid.

17. Meisler, *When the World Calls*, 24.

18. Franklin Williams interview, December 9, 1989.

19. Ibid.

20. Ibid.

21. Ibid.

22. Warren W. Wiggins interview, April 19, 1991. Wiggins, who served as deputy director of the Peace Corps, was Williams's boss during his brief stint as regional

director for Africa. Wiggins believed that Williams's willingness to accept a demotion to serve in the position demonstrated his growing interest in Africana.

23. Undated speech at Sacramento State College, likely early 1964, Schomburg Archives.

24. Ibid.

25. Franklin Williams interview, January 6, 1990.

26. In the January 6, 1990, interview, Williams recalled a conversation with Arthur Goldberg, a former US Supreme Court justice who left the Court in 1965 to succeed Adlai Stevenson as ambassador to the United Nations. According to Williams, Goldberg once said to him: "Frank, Adlai was always known as a cheapskate. He had never picked up a tab in his life."

27. Ibid.

28. *Congressional Record*, July 6, 1964.

29. Box 10 of the Schomburg Archives contains several typewritten pages that are unidentified but appear to be Williams's reflections on a number of issues and occasions during his time with the Economic and Social Council.

30. Ibid.

31. Ibid.

32. See "This Day in History," April 28, 1965, "U.S. Troops Land in the Dominican Republic in Attempt to Forestall a 'Communist Dictatorship,'" https://www.history.com/this-day-in-history/u-s-troops-land-in-the-dominican-republic.

33. The article from the June 26, 1965, number of the *San Francisco Chronicle* with Williams's comment is contained in the Schomburg Archives, Box 54.

34. Ibid.

35. Schomburg Archives, Box 54.

36. David L. Stebenne, *Arthur J. Goldberg, New Deal Liberal* (New York: Oxford University Press, 1996), 348–351.

37. Williams's diary notation.

38. Williams interview, January 6, 1990.

39. Schomburg Archives, Box 11, contains both articles.

40. Ibid.

41. The recording of the conversation between Thurgood Marshall and President Johnson can be heard at http://www.lbjf.org/aud/tel-wh/18790 3-aud-tel-wh-09403.mp3.

42. Franklin Williams interview, January 17, 1990.

43. Ibid.

44. Ibid.

45. Franklin Williams interview, January 22, 1990.

46. Ibid.

47. See "GhanaWeb," https://www.ghanaweb.com/GhanaHomePage/features/24th-February-A-Dark-Day-In-Our-National-History-99921.

48. Williams interview, January 22, 1990.

49. John W. "Jack" Foley interview, November 19, 1990.

50. Ibid.

51. See Seymour M. Hersh, "C.I.A. Said to Have Aided Plotters Who Overthrew Nkrumah in Ghana," *New York Times*, May 9, 1978.

52. Williams interview, January 22, 1990.

53. Ibid.

54. See A. B. Assensoh, *Kwame Nkrumah: Six Years in Exile, 1966–1972* (London: Arthur Stockwell, 1978), 1–68.

55. Enid Gort witnessed this event.

56. Williams made this comment during a June 14, 1964, commencement address at Verde Valley School in Sedona, Arizona. Schomburg Archives, Box 54.

57. The memories were included in a paper on "race and ambassador groups" that Williams authored. The paper is in the Schomburg Archives, Box 55.

58. Franklin H. Williams paper on Race and Minority Groups, September 14, 1971. Schomburg Archives, Box 55.

59. Speech at Windham College in Putney, Vermont, October 9, 1965, Schomburg Archives, Box 55.

12. After Washington

1. January 1969 speech at Columbia University on Black Power, Schomburg Archives, Box 55.

2. Williams makes his position clear in a written document dated August 2, 1968, and included in the Schomburg Archives, Box 11.

3. Lloyd Johnson interview, October 30, 1990. Johnson, whom Williams hired as his assistant at the Urban Center, later replaced him as director.

4. Franklin Williams interview, January 24, 1990.

5. Ibid.

6. Charles Hamilton remained at Columbia University until his retirement in 1998. He was W. S. Sayer professor emeritus of government and political science.

7. Franklin Williams interview, April 1, 1990.

8. Ibid.

9. Ibid.

10. Ibid.

11. Franklin Williams interview, March 24, 1990.

12. Franklin Williams Jr. interview, April 7, 2020.

13. Ibid.

14. Kenneth Clark interview, March 14, 1990.

15. Williams interview, March 24, 1990.

16. Frank Mankiewicz interview, April 16, 1991.

17. Video and a transcript of Williams's interview with Richard Heffner is available at https://www.thirteen.org/openmind-archive/civil-rights/apartheid-what-to-do/.

18. Ibid.

19. The report and reference materials are in the Schomburg Archives, Box 52 and Box 53.

20. Schomburg Archives, Box 52.

21. Ibid.

22. Schomburg Archives, Box 53.

23. John Anderson, *Art Held Hostage* (New York: Norton, 2013), 5.

24. Ibid., 12.

25. See Grace Glueck, "Small University Gains Control of the Barnes Foundation," *New York Times*, October 19, 1989.

26. In an October 5, 1989, interview with the *New York Times*, Williams read directly from the Barnes trust document. Enid Gort witnessed and recorded that interview.

27. Ibid.

28. Ibid.

29. Anderson, *Art Held Hostage*, 42.

30. *New York Times* interview.

31. Glueck, "Small University Gains Control."

32. Anderson, *Art Held Hostage*, 71–72.

33. Address at the presidential inaugural of Eugene C. Winslow at Windham College in Putney, Vermont, October 9, 1965, Schomburg Archives, Box 55.

34. Edward J. Sozanski, "Story Is Told on Barnes' Great Fight," *Philadelphia Inquirer*, June 1, 2003.

35. Sol Wachtler interview by John Caher and Joyce Y. Hartsfield, April 28, 2016. The interview and subsequent interviews by Caher and Hartsfield cited herein were conducted by and for the Franklin H. Williams Judicial Commission.

36. Ibid.

37. Ibid.

38. Report of the New York State Judicial Commission on Minorities, 19 *Fordham Urb. L.J.* 181 (1992). Available at https://ir.lawnet.fordham.edu/ulj/vol19/iss2/3.

39. Wachtler interview.

40. Ibid.

41. Ibid.

42. Justice Samuel Green interview by John Caher and Joyce Y. Hartsfield, June 7, 2016.

43. Ibid.

44. Ibid.

45. E. R. Shipp, "Panel to Study Racial Fairness of New York Courts," *New York Times*, January 22, 1988.

46. Juanita Bing Newton interview by John Caher and Joyce Y. Hartsfield, April 27, 2016.

47. Report of the New York State Judicial Commission on Minorities.

48. Edna Wells Handy interview by John Caher and Joyce Y. Hartsfield, April 28, 2016.

49. Ibid.

50. Ibid.

51. Ibid.

52. Ibid.

53. Interim report of the New York State Judicial Commission on Minorities, available at http://ww2.nycourts.gov/sites/default/files/document/files/2018-11/1989 %20Interim%20Report.pdf.

54. *New York Law Journal*, Public Opinion Poll, May 24, 1988.

55. John Caher, "Wachtler Hopes Study Heads Off Criticism Alleging Bias," *Albany Times Union*, August 20, 1989.

56. Chief Judge Jonathan Lippman (Ret.) interview by John Caher and Joyce Y. Hartsfield on June 2, 2016.

Epilogue

1. The conversation, on a speaker phone, was witnessed by Enid Gort.

2. Letter of January 15, 1990, from John Carrington to Franklin Williams, held in the Enid Gort collection.

3. Ibid.

4. Ibid.

5. "A Brief History of the Ethical Culture Movement," www.ethicalsociety westchester.org.

6. Notes of Enid Gort, who attended the memorial service.

7. Ibid.

8. "Naval History and Heritage Command. Z-grams—A List of Policy Directives Issued by Admiral Zumwalt while in Office as Chief of Naval Operations, 1 July 1970–1 July 1974."

9. Richard Severo, "James Farmer, Civil Rights Giant In the 50's and 60's, Is Dead at 79," *New York Times*, July 10, 1999.

Index

114th Field Artillery, 95

abortion, mother's death from, 3, 15
Addams, Jane, 64
Advocate, The, 133
Africa: FHW serves as regional director for the Peace Corps, 5; students at Lincoln University from, 37
"Africa and the Americas: Aging in Cross-Cultural Perspective," 175
African Methodist Episcopal Church, 12
African Student Aid Fund, 168
Agency for International Development, US, 173
Akerman, Alex, Jr., 99–102, 109, 120
Akerman, Amos T., 100
Akosombo Dam, 158
Alaska, 5, 126
All Souls Unitarian Church, 67
Alpha Phi Alpha, 35
Ambassador Franklin H. Williams Minority Scholarship Program, 168
American Civil Liberties Union, 61
American Indian College Program, 174
American Legion Post, 52, 56, 96
Americans for Democratic Action, 62
American Stock Exchange, 6, 167
American Student Union (ASU), 55
American Veterans Committee (AVC): founding and philosophy of, 53–54; liberal/progressives vs. communists, 55–62; Metropolitan Area Council and, 54, 56–57, 60
Amherst College, 169–70
Anderson, John, 177
apartheid, 2, 171–73, 186

Apple Green estate, 60
Arizona, 5, 134
Army, US: Blacks returning to Groveland from, 93; FHW and final call to white soldier, 184; FHW's army service, 41–48, 43; FHW's work on legal matters of Black soldiers, 65–72; racism in, 3–4, 7, 41–44; Wachtler on status of Blacks in, 178
Arnold, Thurmond, 142
Art Held Hostage (Anderson), 177
Ashmum Institute. *See* Lincoln University
Aspinwall House, 10
Association of Black American Ambassadors, 185
atomic weapons, 62
Austria, 55, 147
AVC Bulletin, 61
Azikiwe, Nnamdi, 32

Bailey, Lester, 124, 128
Baker, Carson DeWitt, 51
Baker, Ella, 67
Baker, Josephine, 128
Baldwin, James, 75
Ball, George, 152
Ballou, Terressa E., 116
Bane, Howard, 159–60
Bankhead, Tallulah, 45
Banks v. Housing Authority of San Francisco (1953), 131
Baptist Church, 10
Barnes, Albert C., 175
Barnes, Frank, 140–41
Barnes, Laura, 176

Barnes Foundation, 6, 168, 175–77
Batson v. Kentucky (1986), 4, 72, 77, 78, 81
"Battle Continues, The" (FHW speech for
    NAACP), 67
Bay Area Independent, 155
Bayley, Ed, 147–48
Belafonte, Harry, 135, 184
Bellevue Hospital Medical College, 12
Bernstein, Charles, 135
Bethesda Naval Hospital, 156
Bingham, Jonathan, 151
Bishop, Beth, 27
Bishop, Eloise, 27
Bishop, Rev. Shelton Hale, 27
Bishop College, 45
Bishop Desmond Tutu African Refugee
    Scholarship Fund, 168, 173
Black, Hugo, 65, 81
Black Dispatch, 89
Black Exclusion Law, 132–33
blackface, 132
Black Jacobins, 188–89
Black Niagara Movement, 64
Black Panthers, 166
"Blinding of Isaac Woodard, The" (song), 4
blood donations, 55
Bolden, Theodore, 32
Bolling, Richard Walker, 62
Bolte, Charles, 53, 58
Borden Inc., 6, 167
Boswell, Hamilton, 127
Boulware, Harold, 86
Bowen, Reeves, 117–18
Bowne House, 10
boycotts, 132
Boys' Choir of Harlem, 6
Boys Club of Harlem, 168
Boys Club of Lincoln University, 38
Boy Scouts, 24, 26
Braddicks, Robert (Bobby), 27
Bradley, Mamie Till, 124–25
Bragg, Harry G., 51
bridge figures, 1
Briggs v. Elliot (1952), 73, 86
"Broadcast and Print Journalism for Minori-
    ties" initiative, 166
Broadnax, Daniel, 24
Broadway, L. J., 79
Brooklyn College, 50
Brooklyn Dodgers, 130
Brownell, Herbert, Jr., 134
Brown v. Board of Education (1954), 110, 131,
    135, 139, 140, 189
Broyard, Anatole, 49

Broyard, Anatole ("Buddy"), Jr., 50
Broyard, Edna, 49
Buck, Pearl, 48
Bucknell University, 36
"Burden, The" (section of *The Crisis* maga-
    zine), 64–65
Burney, Mary Lois, 82
Burtoft, Lawrence, 92
Burton, Harold, 117
bus strikes, 63
Butler, Charles, Jr. (Charlie), 18, 20, 21, 22
Butler, Edith (Daisy) Craig, 17
Butler, Mary (Mamie), 20, 22
Buttenger, Philip, ix

California: FHW reorganizes NAACP in, 5,
    126–41
California Department of Justice. Constitu-
    tional Rights Section, 5, 141–43
California Labor School, 123
Cannady, Beatrice Morrow, 133
Cannady, Edward, 133
Cannon, Poppy, 112–13
Carey, Jim, 56
Caribbean Cultural Center, 168
Carrington, Walter C., 184–85
Carter, Jimmy, 144, 184
Carter, Robert L., 83–84, 85, 87, 90, 110, 117,
    174
Cassell v. Texas (1950), 118
Castro, Fidel, 148
Cavalcade (club), 29
Céline Ferdinand, 50
Central Intelligence Agency, 148
certiorari, 83, 85
Cezanne, Paul, 175
change of venue: for Groveland case, 99, 101,
    117; for Irvin retrial, 120
Chapman, Roy, 111
Chemical Bank, 6, 167–68
Chicago Defender, 105
Chinn, May: attends FHW's graduation from
    Lincoln, 38; attends FHW's swearing in
    as ambassador to Ghana, 152; attends
    FHW's swearing into ECOSOC, 152;
    encourages FHW to attend Lincoln, 30;
    as part of "Smart Set," 12, 13
Chip and Racquet Club, 183
Christian Endeavor, 24
Christmas, Doris, 36
Christmas, Lawrence, 36
Christmas, Marie, 36
CIA, 159–60
"Citizens First, Veterans Second" (slogan), 53

City College of New York, 30
Civil Rights Act (1875), 77
Civil Rights Act (1964), 189
Civil Rights Congress, 106, 123
Civil Rights movement, 63
Clark, James C., 120
Clark, Kenneth, 171
Clark, Mamie, 171
Clark, Michele, 166
Clermont News-Topic, 101
Cleveland, Harlan, 146
Clinton, Bill, 184
Coalition of Black Judges, 178
Cocteau, Jean, 50
Cold War, 145
Coleman, William, 84
Colley, Nathaniel S., Sr., 113, 131, 135–36, 141
Colored Methodist Episcopal Church, 169
Columbia University, 5, 163–67
communists and communism: attempt to in-
    filtrate NAACP, 122–25; exploit racism for
    fundraising, 123–25; FHW's distrust of, 2,
    106, 114, 122–25; Groveland case and, 106;
    infiltration of unions, 129; influence on
    American Veterans Committee, 57–62,
    106; JFK proposes Peace Corps to com-
    bat, 145–46; LBJ sends Marines into Do-
    minican Republic, 153; Nkrumah and
    Chinese Communists, 158–59; Scotts-
    boro case and, 106
Community Chest, 131
Comus Club, 49
confessions obtained under duress: in Grove-
    land case, 91, 94, 97, 103, 118–19; Miller v.
    Wigging (1949), 85; in Patton case, 79–80;
    in Watts case, 82–84
Congo, 150
Congressional Record, 152
Congress of Racial Equality (C.O.R.E), 1, 166
Connie's Inn, 29
Consolidated Edison, 6, 167–68
Constitution: FHW on importance of, 2, 4, 51,
    63, 64, 106; Marshall and Legal Defense
    Fund, 76; rights of Community Party
    and, 114; Supreme Court's views of, 65
cotton fields, 134
Council on Civic Unity (CCU), 129
Cow Palace, 145
credit standard, 138
Crisis, The (magazine), 64, 114, 120
Crosson, Matthew T., 182
Crusaders in the Courts (Greenberg), 68
Cuba, 148
Cuomo, Mario, 178

Current, Gloster F., 68, 73, 113, 114, 123
Cyprus, 147
Czechoslovakia, 55

Daily People's World, 123
Dancer, Clifford, 53
Daniel, John, 172
Daniels, Hayzel B., 135
Dark Days in Ghana (Nkrumah), 159
Davis, Alinda, 10, 188
Davis, Annise Elizabeth Tobias (Lizzie,
    maternal great-grandmother), 8–9, 10, 17,
    22, 188
Davis, John, 9, 35
Davis, Mary, 10
Davis, Peggy Cooper, 90
Davis, Sammy, Jr., 135
D-Day invasion of Normandy, 54, 95
debate teams, 36
defense industry, 116, 133
DeFrance, Adelaide, 27
Delta Rho Forensic Society, 36
DeMasi-Smith Fund, 26
democracy, defined, 64
"Democracy in Action" (FHW article), 61
Denmark, 147
DeSantis, Ron, 120
Dessaure v. New York (1949), 85
Devil and Mr. Barnes, The (Greenfield), 176
Devil in the Grove (King), 4
Dewey, John, 64
Dickey, John Miller, 32
Dickey, Sarah Cresson, 32
discrimination: Executive Order 8802 bans,
    116; in housing, 74–75, 116–17; reverse in
    jury selection, 79; in unions, 116
Distinguished American Visitors to Africa
    Program, 173
District Court, US, 87
Dixiecrats, 125
"doll tests," 171
Dominican Republic, 153
"Don't Buy Where You Can't Earn" slogan,
    128
Douglas, William O., 65
Draft Riots, 8
Du Bois, W. E. B., 11, 27, 35, 165
Dullea, Keir, 157
Dunbar National Bank; 27
Dyett, Thomas B., 51

Earle, Willie, 86
East Lake Park Community Center, 134
Ebey, Charles, 62

Edison, Thomas, 20
education: aid to, 129; equal access to, 65;
    federal aid for, 131
Egypt, 147
Eichler, Joseph, 136–37
Eisenhower, Dwight D., 69, 140
El Alamein, Battle of (1942), 53
elderly, 175
Ellington, Duke, 35
Ellis, John P., 96
El Paso Times, 47
Emancipation Proclamation, 182
employment, discrimination in, 5, 54, 65, 129
Essex, Arthur C., 67
Essex House, 75
Ethical Culture Lower School, 113
Ethical Culture Society, 185
Ethiopia, 147
Evans, Rowland, 155
Evers, Medgar, 54
evidence: illegally obtained, 80
exclusionary rule, 80
Executive Order 8802, 116
Exxon, 168

Fair Employment Practices, 66
Fair Employment Practices Commission, 138
Fair Employment Practices Committee
    (FEPC), 116
Farmer, James, 1, 6, 188
fascism, 55
Faulkner, William, 130
FBI: analyzes evidence in Fruitland Park rape
    case, 103; FHW applies to, 51; investiga-
    tion of Irvin shooting, 119; investigation
    of Moore killing, 120; vetting of FHW for
    ambassadorship, 61, 62
Federal Housing Agency, 136
Feldman, Justin, 56, 59, 60
Fence Talk (Harlem publication), 27
"Fifth Avenue, Uptown, A Letter from Har-
    lem" (Baldwin), 75
Fight for Freedom Campaign, 139
"Fight for Freedom" rally, 124
Finland, 56
First Amendment, 123
Fisk University, 170
Fleming, John, 72
Flushing Cemetery, 188
Foley, John W., Jr., 159
Ford Foundation: Columbia University and,
    163, 166; and donations to New York State
    Judicial Commission on Minorities, 179
Fordham, William, 98

Fordham Law School, 3–4, 40–41, 48
Fort Huachuca, 42–44, 46, 48
Fourteenth Amendment, 77, 133, 158
Frances, Abner H., 132–33
Francois, Terry, 131, 138
Frank, Louis, 61
Frankfurter, Felix, 65, 84, 118
Franklin, John Hope, 35
Franklin and Marshall College, 36
Franklin H. Williams Judicial Commission
    (formerly New York State Judicial Com-
    mission on Minorities), 6, 182
fraternities, 35, 38
Fredericks, J. Wayne, 172
"Freedom Is Possible" (flyer), 119
freedom rides, 63
Freeman, Mary, 46
Freeman, Robert (Bobby): asks FHW to be
    best man at wedding, 45, 46; business in-
    terests in Ghana, 155; FHW's roommate
    at Lincoln, 32, 33, 34; works with FHW
    summer after college, 39–40
fundraising: communists exploit racism for,
    123–25; to desegregate armed forces, 127;
    effect of communist ideology upon, 122;
    FHW and, 4, 70, 111, 139, 168; Jonas for
    NAACP, x; Marshall on impact of de-
    fending obviously guilty on, 68; *Shepherd
    v. Florida* as tool for, 119. *See also* NAACP
    Legal Defense Fund
Furth, Josef Herbert, 35–36
Futch, Truman G., 100–101, 103, 104, 106, 111

Gabon, 147
Gadsden, Marie, 173
gambling: Blacks barred from Nevada casinos,
    135; Groveland case and, 93, 95; parlors in
    Tenderloin district, 10
Garrison, William Lloyd, 64
Gaylord, Harry, 99
Gaylords, 75, 83
George Washington Carver High School,
    134–35
Ghana: FHW as ambassador to, 5, 156–60, 157,
    163; FHW embraces racial identity in,
    148; JFK secures funding for dam in, 158
Ghanaian Times, 148
G.I. Bill, 51
Gill, William, 133
Glanton, Richard, 177
Gloster, Jesse, 32
Goldberg, Arthur, 154
golf: as FHW's hobby, 125; segregation in,
    86–87, 142–43

Goodale, James, 181
Goode, Eslanda "Essie," 12
Goodlett, Carlton, 129
Gorham Sterling Silver Company, 11, 23
Gort, Enid: FHW recruits to work at Phelps
    Stokes Fund, ix–xi; FHW works on oral
    history project with, 184
Gort, Sy, x, xi
Gould, Norma J., 59
Grand Central Terminal, 27
Grant, Ulysses S., 77, 100
Great Britain, 147
Greater Phoenix Council for Civic Unity
    (GPCU), 134, 135
Green, Samuel, 179–80
Greenberg, Jack: on conflict between FHW
    and Marshall, 68, 112; Irvin retrial and,
    120; joins NAACP LDF staff, 110; as leg-
    end in civil rights litigation, 90; works on
    Groveland appeal, 111–12, 117
Greenfield, Howard, 176
Green Haven Prison, 181
Greenlee, Charles: arrest and trial of, 93, 97,
    99, 104, 107, 109; not part of Groveland
    appeal, 111; parole and death of, 120
Griffin, Noah, 113, 115–16
Groveland case: appeal to Supreme Court,
    111–12, 117–19; background of, 91–99;
    communist fundraising for, 123–24; trial,
    100–107
Groveland News-Topic, 101
Guatemala, 147
Guillaume, Paul, 176
Guthrie, Woody, 4

Haley v. Ohio (1948), 83
Hamilton, Charles, 166
Harlem: conflict with Columbia University,
    165–66; FHW on board of Boys' Choir
    of Harlem, 6; FHW's adolescent trips to,
    27; FHW speaks at Harlem Hospital, 67;
    musical revolution in, 14; resentment of
    Columbia University, 163; Riverton as
    segregated section of, 75; "Smart Set"
    in, 27
Harlem Hospital, 12, 67
Harlem Movement, 176
Harrison, Gilbert, 53, 58, 59
Harvard University, 184
Hastie, Williams, 81
Hawaii, 5
hazing ("rabbling"), 34–35
health insurance legislation, 54
Heard v. Davis (1954), 135

Heffner, Richard, 172–73
Height, Dorothy, 6
Heller, Harry, 54, 56, 57
Herald-Post, 47
Hill, Horace, 98, 100, 107–9
Hill, Joseph Newton, 35
Hinkson, Cordelia (Betty), 36
Hinkson, Major DeHaven, 36
Hinkson, Mary (Bunny), 36
Hispanics, 137
Hitler, Adolf, 38, 41, 98
Holbrook, Edward, 11–12
Holland, Spessard, Jr., 99
Hollins v. Oklahoma (1935), 80
Holmes, Monica, 181
Hoover, Herbert, 12
Horne, Frank, 171
Horne, Lena, 135, 171
housing: discrimination in, 116–17, 129; fair
    and affordable, 5, 53, 55, 65; for unwed
    mothers, 169
Houston, Charles Hamilton, 63, 81
Howard, Charles, 58
Howard University, 81, 170; Law School, 98;
    Medical School, 22
Howden, Edward, 129, 131
Howells, William Dean, 64
Hughes, Langston, 32
Humphrey, Hubert H., 35, 143
Hunter, Jess, 100, 102–4, 106
Hunter College, 50

Idaho, 5, 126
immigrants, 3, 12, 18
Independent Progressive Caucus, 57–62
Indian burial grounds, 9
Information Agency, US, 153
Innis, Roy, 166
Interfaith University Religious Conference
    (IURC), 53
International Labor Defense, 106
International Union of Electrical Workers
    (IUE), 56
Iowa Code, 58
Iran, 160
Irvin, Walter: appeal of, 112; arrest and trial of,
    92–95, 99, 104, 107, 109; conviction over-
    turned, 118; parole and death of, 120;
    wounding of, 119

Jackie Robinson Foundation, 168
Jackson, Jesse, 6
Jackson, Robert H., 117–18
Janus (neighborhood theater), 24

Japanese Americans, 116, 129, 137
Jews: Bernstein, as first Jewish jurist in Arizona, 135; FHW appoints Strauss to Phelps board, 172; as members in American Veterans Committee, 54, 55; prejudice towards, 41; treatment of, in Jim Crow South, 178
Jim Crow restrictions: FHW on the stance of the American Veterans Committee (AVC) on, 59; FHW on Black resistance to, 64; FHW's resentment of, 99; Groveland case and, 91; in labor unions, 133; NAACP's primary goal to end, 110; in public schools, 5, 87–89, 110, 134–35; in rail transportation, 45–46, 47; restrictions in Army, 41; at Rose Bowl Café, 58; Supreme Court's views on, 65; Waring becomes leader in upending, 72
Johnson, Anna, 13
Johnson, Arnold, 57
Johnson, Earl, 13–14
Johnson, Ellen Sirleaf, xi
Johnson, Lloyd, 166
Johnson, Lyndon Baines, 5; appoints FHW ambassador to the UN Economic and Social Council (ECOSOC), 5, 151; appoints FHW as ambassador to Ghana, 5, 155–56; assesses FHW with Marshall, 155–56; creates Office of Economic Opportunity, 155; difficulties with Nkrumah, 158–59; Goldberg tries to persuade to get out of Vietnam, 154; orders Marines into Dominican Republic, 153
Jonas, Gil, x
Jones, Adele, 70
Jones, Eugene, 20
Jones, Eugene Kinkle, 20
Jones, Mary, 45
Jones-Quartey, K. A. B., 155
Jordan, Vernon, 6, 178
judicial system: fair treatment from, 65
jury service: Cassell v. Texas, 118; exclusion of Blacks from, 4, 85; jury pools, 77; jury stacking, 101, 117; Nevada restricts Blacks on, 135; racial bias in, 80, 83; reverse discrimination in, 79; Waring on desegregating, 72
Justice, US Department of: brings charges in Woodard case, 71–73

Kafka, Franz, 50
Kaiser Shipyards, 128
Kansas Supreme Court, 88
Kefauver, Estes, 140

Kennedy, Jacqueline, 158
Kennedy, John F.: assassination of, 5, 151; FHW works on 1961 presidential campaign, 143; Peace Corps initiative, 145–46, 147; secures funding for Akosombo Dam in Ghana, 158; wary of American Veterans Committee, 54
Kennedy, Joseph P., 144
Kennedy, Randall, xiii
Kennedy, Robert, Jr., 144
Kennedy, Robert F., 144, 158, 165
Kentucky Court of Appeals, 87
King, Gilbert, 4
King, Martin Luther, Jr., 1, 6, 35, 63, 165; FHW on, 169
Kissena Park, 24, 25
Knobel, Lawrence, 54, 58
Kotoka, Emmanuel Kwasi, 160
Kramer Brothers Freight Line, 29
Kress's Five and Ten, 29
Kuchel, Thomas H., 152
Ku Klux Klan: Black as former Klansman, 81; FHW on, 2; in Georgia, 94, 100; Groveland case and, 95, 96; McCall as member of, 93; Moore bombing and, 120; in Oregon, 133; threatens NAACP during Woodard trial, 71
Kunstler, William, 85

La belle et la bête (film), 50
Ladd, Edward, 53
Ladies Home Journal, 36
Lash, Josh, 55
Latimer, Lewis H., 20
Lawrence, D. H., 50
Leesburg Commercial, 104
Lehigh University, 36
Les enfants du paradise (film), 50
Lewisohn Stadium, 70
Lightly, Wadsworth, 53
Lincoln, Abraham, 64
Lincolnian, The, 34
Lincoln University: Arthur Williams attends, 26; Barnes Foundation and, 175–77; Chinn encourages FHW to apply to, 30; famous alumni, 3, 5, 32, 37, 58, 148, 157, 170; as first degree-granting historically Black university in US, 3; FHW attends, 31–38; FHW on board of, 6; as HBCU, 169–70; originally called Ashmum Institute, 31
Lippman, Jonathan, 182
Locke, Alain, 176
Logan, Marian, 173

London Missionary Society, 169
Louis, Joe, 4, 70, 98
Lowe, Ramona, 105, 106, 108
Lowry, Caroline Davis (Cab, grandmother), 9, 10, 11, 22, 23, 28, 29, 188
Lowry, Ethel Skinker (Eddie's wife), 22–23, 26, 38, 51
Lowry, Frederick Lawson (Freddie, uncle), 12, 13, 17, 22, 26
Lowry, Gussie Hernandez (Freddie's wife), 22, 23
Lowry, John Edward (Eddie, uncle), 12, 13, 17, 22, 26, 29, 35, 36, 38, 51
Lowry, John Edward, Jr. ("Chunk"), 26
Lowry, Thaddeus (grandfather), 11, 188; bars children from contact with father, 15–16; conflict with Gussie, 23; conflict with Roberta, 28; on controlling children's friendships, 20; loses job and pension, 23; moves from Virginia to New York, 10–11; moves into Eddie Lowry's family, 29; personality of, 11–12; presides over "Smart Set," 12–13, 13; relationship with FHW, 22
Luce, Clare Boothe, 143
Lumet, Sidney, 157
lunch counter sit-ins, 63
lynching: Earle case, 86; FHW narrowly escapes, 2, 7, 91; Groveland case and, 99; as part of southern culture, 134; Phelps Stokes Fund and study of, 174

MacArthur, Douglas, 127
Macedonia African Methodist Episcopal (AME) Church, 10
Macy's department store, 54
Mademoiselle, 59
Madison Square Garden, 127
Major League Baseball color barrier, 138
Malcolm X, 1
Mandela, Nelson, 172
Mangum, Bob, 154
Mankiewicz, Frank, 171, 184
Marathon Parkway, 9
marches for civil rights, 63, 132
Marshall, Thurgood, 1; 1960 presidential campaign and, 143; as alumnus of Lincoln University, 3, 32; assesses FHW with LBJ, 155–56; on board of ACLU, 61; clashes with FHW, 4–5, 67–69, 82–83, 90, 112, 113; colleagues' assessment of, 90; FHW and Rivkin resolution, 61; FHW works as special counsel to, 4; as graduate of HBCU, 171; informs FBI about Communist efforts to infiltrate the NAACP, 61;

Irvin retrial, 120; on judicial precedent, 4; as legend of civil rights litigation, 1, 90; makes trip to Asia to investigate treatment of Black troops, 126–27; as member of Alpha Phi Alpha, 35; NAACP Legal Defense Fund and, 4, 68, 76, 80–84, 85, 86, 88; named special counsel to NAACP, 113; permits FHW to argue Groveland case before Supreme Court, 117; recommends FHW to Wachtler, 3, 178; Watts v. Indiana, 85
Marshall Plan, 61
Martin, Louis E., 144
Marxism. See communists and communism
Masons, 12
Matinecock tribe, 8–9
Mauldin, Bill, 54
Maxwell, Joseph, 95
Maxwell, Matthew, 95
Mays, Willie, 138
Mbeki, Thabo, 172
McCall, Willis Virgil, 103, 107, 118–20
McCarthy, Joseph, 122
McLaurin v. Oklahoma State Board of Regents for Higher Education (1950), 88, 110
Meharry Medical College, 32
Meier, Bill, 25
Mellon Foundation, 179
Methodist Church, 10
Metropolitan Area Council, 54, 56–57, 60
Metropolitan Life Insurance Company, 74–75
Michigan, University of, 145
Militant, 123
Miller, Dorie, 47
Miller, Loren, 6, 81, 83, 127, 131, 135–36, 141
Miller v. Wigging (1949), 85
Mimo's (club), 29
Ming, William Robert, Jr., 81, 83
minimum wage, 54
Mississippi, Supreme Court of, 79
Mitchell, Henry, 32
Molly (caretaker from orphanage), 17, 19
Moon, Henry Lee, 113
Moore, Harriette, 120, 123–24
Moore, Harry Tyson, 96, 120, 123–24
Moore v. Dempsey (1923), 101
Mormons, 132
Morningside Heights, 165
Mosk, Stanley, 140–43, 144
Moskowitz, Henry, 64
Motley, Constance Baker, 90, 96, 110
Moulin Rouge (club), 29
Mount Dora Topic, 101, 104, 120
Moyers, Bill, 151, 153

Muhammad Ali (Cassius Clay), 143
mulattos, 132
Murphy, Audie, 54
Murphy, Frank, 65
Murray, Philip, 56
Mussolini, Benito, 38
Myers, Lillian, 25

NAACP (National Association for the
  Advancement of Colored People): Carrington founds chapter at Harvard, 184;
  communists attempt to infiltrate, 106, 114,
  122–25; falsely told FHW a communist,
  62; Florida State Conference, 96; founding of, 64; FHW as executive director of,
  44; FHW as executive secretary of, 27;
  FHW as fundraiser for, 168; FHW attempts to oust Wilkins from NAACP
  board, 153; FHW on legal department,
  63; FHW reorganizes in West, 5, 126–41;
  FHW's speech to Virginia State Conference, 65; FHW works as civil right lawyer
  with, 63–73; FHW work with, 4, 5; hires
  Houston, 63; Jonas as fundraiser for, x;
  names Baker "Woman of the Year," 128;
  political infighting in, 112–13; primary
  goal to eliminate Jim Crow, 110; "Young
  Turks" in, 132, 153
NAACP Legal Defense Fund (LDF): crime
  scene tampering, 103; FHW and Mar-
  shall work for, 76–90; FHW's work with,
  65, 66, 66–73; FHW vs. Marshall on
  use for guilty individuals, 4, 68, 80, 82;
  Scottsboro case and, 106; sees Shepherd v.
  Florida as fundraising tool, 119. See also
  Groveland case
Nathan, Robert, 59
National Archives Records Administration, 48
National Campaign to Register One Million
  New Negro Voters, 143
National Conference of Christians and Jews
  (NCCJ), 138
National Distillers, 28, 29
National Guard, 95
National Liberation Council, 160
National Negro Congress, 114
National Negro Labor Council, 123, 124
National Public Radio, 184
National Socialist Party, 53
National Urban League, 133, 134
Nation of Islam: FHW on, 2–3; Malcolm X's
  break with, 1
Native Americans, 168, 173
Navy, US, 187–88

Nazis, 55
Nazi-Soviet Pact (1939), 55, 56
Netherlands, 147
Nevada, 5, 134, 135–36
New Deal, 53, 142
New Orleans Picayune, 174
New Republic, 59
newspapers, reporting on racism, 47–48. See
  also specific newspapers
Newton, Huey, 1
Newton, Juanita Bing, 180
New York City Bar Association, 180
New York Court of Appeals, 178
New York Herald Tribune, 155
New York Law Journal, 182
New York Post, 59, 105
New York Real Estate Board, 55
New York State Bar examination, 51
New York State Judicial Commission on Mi-
  norities, 6, 179–81
New York State Supreme Court, 40
New York Times, The, 50, 54. 172, 180
New York University Law School, 90
Nichols, Roy, 32
Nigeria, 147, 184
Nixon, Richard, 140; 1960 presidential cam-
  paign, 143
Nkrumah, Kwame: alumnus of Lincoln Uni-
  versity, 32, 37, 148, 157; FHW and Peace
  Corps, 148, 150; FHW as ambassador to
  Ghana and, 156–59, 157
Norman, Gerald, 20
Norman, Winifred, 20
Norris-Reese, Mable, 104–5, 106, 111, 112, 120
Norris v. Alabama (1935), 80
Novak, Robert, 155

Oakland Fire Department, 128
Obama, Barack, 189
Ocala National Forest, 119
Office of War Information, 53
Open Mind, The, 172
Oregon, 5, 132–33
Orlando Sentinel Star, 95, 96–97, 104
"Outline of Procedures for Legal Cases"
  (Marshall), 80
Ovington, Mary White, 64
Oxfam America, 173

Padgett, Norma Lee, 91, 93, 102–4
Padgett, Willie Haven, 91–92, 94, 102–4
Paine, Howie, 58
Palace Chow Mein Company, 29
Paladino, Helen, 41

Palangyo, Peter K., 160–61
Paris: Baker breaks color barrier at department store, 128; FHW visits to promote Peace Corps, 147
Paterson, Chat, 62
Patterson, Frederick D., 35, 169
Patton, Eddie "Buster," 77–81
Patton v. Mississippi (1947), 76–81, 83
Peace Corps: Carrington's service in, 184–85; JFK and, 145–46, 147; Nkrumah's views on, 148, 150; Shriver recruits FHW for, 5, 146–48, 147, 150–51; Soviet Union blocks UN support for, 150–51; UN and, 146–47
Pearl Harbor, 41, 47
Pegler, Westbrook, 47
Pennsylvania, University of, 36, 176
Pennsylvania Academy of the Fine Arts, 176
People's World, 124
peremptory challenges, 77–78
Perkins, Edward, 172
Perkins, Paul, 120
Perry, Marian Wynn, 110
Pettus, Ken, 62
Peyser, Annette, 96
Phelps Stokes Fund: FHW heads, 168–69; FHW recruits Gort to work at, ix–xi; FHW recruits Tutu to board of, 185–86; FHW's final days at, 183–84; Palangyo and, 161; purpose of, ix, 5–6; studying of lynching and, 174; support for poor whites, 169, 173–74; Zumwalt as chairman of, 187
Phi Beta Kappa, 50
Phi Kappa Epsilon fraternity, 38
Phi Kappa Sigma fraternity, 3
Philadelphia Inquirer, 177
Philips, Joyce, 40
Phillips vs. Phoenix Union High Schools and Junior College District (1953), 135
Picasso, Pablo, 175
Pinky Price's rooming house, 98, 109
Pittman, Tarea Hall, 128–29
plaster casts, 102–3
Plaza Hotel, 60
Plessy v. Ferguson (1896), 131
Plimpton, Francis T. P., 151
PM (newspaper), 52
pogroms, 55
Poland, 55
Political World, 123
poll tax, 47
Poole, Cecil, 129
Poston, Ted, 105, 106, 108
Powell, Adam Clayton, 44, 131

Prempeh II, Otumfuo Nan Sir Osei Tutu Agyeman, 150
price controls, 54
primaries, 73
Professional Golfers Association (PGA), 142–43
prostitutes: brothels in Tenderloin district, 10–11; false rape charges against Black soldiers and, 67; at Fort Huachuca, 44; Scottsboro case and, 105
public housing projects, 129
public schools, 5, 87–89, 110, 134–35. See also Brown v. Board of Education (1954)

Quakers, 9–10
Queens College, 63
Queens County Medical Society, 13

"rabbling" (hazing), 34–35
"race prejudice," 174
race-stacking, 78, 82
racial quotas, 55
racism: FHW and, 3, 7, 17, 37, 163; intermarriage criminal offense in Nevada, 135; Jim Crow restrictions in transportation, 45–46, 47; in newspaper reporting, 47–48; students at Lincoln University from Africa and, 37; in US Army, 3–4, 7, 41–44; in US Navy, 188
Raiford prison, 97, 99, 119
railroads, 45–46, 47
Rainbow Room, 184
Randolph, A. Philip, 124, 143
rape: Blacks falsely accused of, 4, 67; Fruitland Park, FL case, 103; lynchings for, 174; Marshall on getting people off on "technicalities," 68; Scottsboro case and, 105, 106; Taylor v. Dennis (1949), 85. See also Groveland case
Rawls, Lawrence, 168
Reagan, Ronald, 54, 173
Red Rooster (club), 29
Red Scare era, 106, 114
Reeves, Frank, 81
Reeves, George, 54
religion: African American and influence upon Barnes, 175; differences in polarizing Flushing, 10; Episcopal Church sponsors integrated troop of Boy Scouts, 24; FHW's lack of interest in, 185; impact upon Martin Luther King Jr., 6; importance of, in Black community, 127; prejudice toward Catholics, 12, 41; quotas at religious institutions of higher

religion (continued)
    learning, 55; role in Underground Rail-
    road, 9–10. See also specific churches and
    denominations
Renoir, Pierre-Auguste, 175
Republican Party, 12, 57, 58, 100, 140, 141, 152
Reynolds, William Bradford, 129
Rhoads, J. J., 45
Rice v. Elmore (1947), 73
Rickey, Branch, 130
Rivera, Geraldo, 166
Riverton, New York, 74–75, 83
Rivkin, Arnold, 60–61
RKO Keith Theater, 163
Robertson, Carolyn, 25
Robeson, Paul, 12, 35
Robinson, Jackie, 4, 112, 130, 138–39, 143
Robinson, Rachel, 139–40, 172
Robinson, Spottswood William, III, 81
Rockefeller Foundation, 179
Rockefeller Plaza, 184
Rogers, Fred, 71
Rogers, Will, Jr., 54
Roman Catholics, 12, 41
Roosevelt, Eleanor, 48, 53, 112
Roosevelt, Franklin, Jr., 56, 58, 59
Roosevelt, Franklin D.: Blacks in military and,
    43–44; FHW advises on returning veter-
    ans, 69; FHW on FDR and Blacks, 142;
    issues Executive Order banning discrimi-
    nation, 116; Martin liaison between FDR
    and Blacks, 144; New Deal and, 53, 142;
    Supreme Court appointees and, 65
Roosevelt, James, 155
Roosevelt, Kermit, 160
Roosevelt, Theodore, 58
Root, Elihu, 58
Root, Oren, 58, 59
Rose Bowl Café, 58
Rosenblatt, Albert M., 180
Rothenberg, Don, 62
Roundtable, 172
Rowan, Carl, 153
Rubiero, Miguel Augustus, 152
Rusk, Dean, 159

Sachs, Albie, 172
Salvation Army, 96
San Francisco Chronicle, 153
San Francisco Fire Department, 127
San Francisco Housing Authority (SFHA),
    129, 131
Sapp, Claude, 71
Schmeling, Max, 98

scholarships: DeMasi-Smith Fund and, 26;
    FHW and eligibility for, 37; NAACP and
    scholarships exclusively for Blacks, 171;
    Palangyo approaches FHW for, 161; Phi
    Kappa Epsilon as scholarship fraternity,
    38; Shirley's parents force her to turn
    down, 50; from Stevens Institute, 168.
    See also specific scholarships
Schomburg Center for Research in Black
    Culture, 168, 174
Scott, Elisha, Sr., 88
Seale, Bobby, 1
segregation: in Chinatown housing project,
    129; "doll tests" to measure psychologi-
    cal effects of, 171; federal education aid
    and, 131; in golf, 86–87, 142–43; housing,
    in Riverton, New York, 74–75; links civil
    rights movement to godless commu-
    nism, 122; Nevada bars Blacks from
    militia, 135; in Oregon, 133; in public
    schools, 5, 87–89, 110, 134–35; in veter-
    ans' organizations, 52; voluntary,
    HBCU's as, 169–70
Senegal, 184
Shalala, Donna, xi
sharecropping, 93–94
Shelbourne, Roy M., 87
Shepherd, Henry, 92, 94, 95, 106–7, 108
Shepherd, Sammie: appeal of, 113; arrest and
    trial of, 92–95, 97, 99, 102, 104, 106–7,
    109; conviction overturned, 118; death
    of, 119
Shepherd v. Florida (1951), 117
Shriver, Eunice, 146
Shriver, Robert Sargent, Jr.: initial meeting
    with FHW, 144; last days of FHW and,
    184; leads "War on Poverty," 155; recruits
    FHW for Peace Corps, 5, 146–48, 147,
    150–51; works on Kennedy presidential
    campaign, 143
Shull, Lynwood, 70–73
Sifford, Charlie, 142–43
Sillah, Abu, x
Sipline, Moses, 95
Sipuel v. Board of Regents (1948), 88
sit-ins, 63, 132
Skinker, Buckley Merriman, 22
Smart Set, 12–14, 13, 30
Smith, Bessie, 37
Smith College, 50
Smith-Hoover campaign (1928), 12
Smith v. Texas (1940), 80
Smut, The (Harlem publication), 27
Society of Friends, 129

soil samples, 103
South Africa: apartheid in, 171–72; FHW compares to US, 2
South Carolina State University, 175
Southern Christian Leadership Conference, 173
Southern Pacific Railroad, 127
Soviet Union: blocks UN support for Peace Corps, 150–51; communists fear Nazi invasion of, 55; FHW criticizes Marshall for meeting with Russian officials, 61
Spadeville (Harlem publication), 27
Spanish Civil War, 55–56
Spaulding, Nelson, 97
Spencer, Ella, 17
Spencer, Samuel Jr., 53
Spingarn, Joel Elias, 64
Stalin, Joseph, 55–56
Stanford University, 128
State Department, US, 151, 156
Stevens, Harold, 51
Stevens, Wallace, 50
Stevens Institute, 168
Stevenson, Adlai, 140, 147, 151–53, 154
St. George's Episcopal Church, 24
Stokes, Bishop Anson Phelps, Jr., 169
Stokes, Carl, 173
Stokes, Caroline Phelps, 168
Stone, I. F., 52–53
Stout, Nancy, 82
St. Philip's Episcopal Church, 27
Straight, Michael, 59, 60, 61
Strauder v. West Virginia (1880), 77
Strauss, Ellen Sulzberger, 172
Strauss, R. Peter, 155
Struckmeyer, Fred C., 135
Stuckey's Still, 95
students: FHW thinks they are ignorant of history, 163–64; protesters at Columbia University, 166; as "Young Turks," 132, 153
Stuyvesant Town, 75
Supreme Court, US: FDR appointees, 65; FHW argues cases before, 4; Marshall vs. FHW re taking cases to, 4–5, 68; overturns Groveland case, 91; Scottsboro case and, 105–6; on stacking juries by race, 72. *See also specific cases*
Sutton, Percy, 173
Swain v. Alabama (1965), 78
Swarthmore College, 36
Sweatt v. Painter (1950), 88, 110
Sweden, 147
Sweeney, P. O., 86
Sweeney v. Louisville (1949), 87

talented tenth, 27
Tallahatchie River, 124
Tavares Court House, 100
tax rolls, 80
Taylor, Thelma, x
Taylor v. Dennis (1949), 85
Tenderloin District, 10–11
Terkel, Studs, 54
Texas Southern University, 32
Thomas, Ernest, 93, 95–96
Thomas, L. E., 98
Thompson, Lewis, 114
Thurmond, Strom, 143
Till, Emmett, 124
Tobias, Channing, 169
Tobias, Mary, 9
Tree, Marietta, 152
Trotter, William Monroe, 64
Truman, Harry, 69, 70, 71, 127, 187
Tuskegee University, 169
Tutu, Bishop Desmond, 172, 185
Tyson, Coy, 94

Underground Railroad, 9–10
unions: discrimination against Blacks and, 116; Jim Crow restrictions in, 133; musicians, 141–42; union members as "Young Turks," 132; waterfront, 129
United Airlines, 167
United Methodist Church, 32
United Nations: American Veterans Committee (AVC) support for, 61; Congress on the Prevention of Crime and Treatment of Offenders, 153; Economic and Social Council, 5; Shriver wants Peace Corps under, 146
United Nations Economic and Social Council (ECOSOC): FHW makes speech on women's rights, 154; LBJ nominates FHW for ambassador to, 5, 151; passes resolution to establish Peace Corps, 147
United Nations Educational, Scientific and Cultural Organization (UNESCO), 147
United Negro College Fund, 169
Unity Caucus, 57–62
universal military training, 61
University of Florida, 99–100
University of Ghana, 155
University of Utah, 132
unwed mothers, 169
Upshur, Georgine, 37
Upshur, William A. Jr., 37
Urban Center, 166
Urban League, 20, 131, 154

URS Corp., 167
"Usual Crime: A Study of Lynching in the United States, The," by FHW, Robert Carter, and Roy Wilkins, 174
Utah, 5, 126, 132
utility power and bills, 167

vagrancy, 105
van Gogh, Vincent, 175
Vaughn, Jack, 156
venereal disease, 44
veterans: bonuses for, 61; honorably discharged Communist, 61; paraplegics, 54; as "Young Turks," 132
Veterans of Foreign Wars (VFW), 52, 56
Vietnam War, 154, 158–59, 165, 170
Villard, Oswald Garrison, 64
visas, 172
Volokh, Eugene, xiii
voting: Blacks' names left off lists, 77; NAACP and rights, 65; Nevada bars Blacks from, 135; registration for Kennedy vs. Nixon campaign, 143

Wachman, Marvin, 159
Wachtler, Sol, 6, 177–82
Walling, William, 64
Waring, Julius Waties, 72–73
"War on Poverty," 155
War Production Board, 45
Washington, 5, 126
Washington, Booker T., 65, 165
WASPS, 55
waterfront unions, 129
Watson, Barbara, 27
Watson, James S., 27
Watts, Robert Austin, 82–84
Watts v. Indiana, 85
WCBS-TV, 180
Weaver, Robert, 171
Weill Cornell Medical Center, 183
Weinberger, Andrew, 81
welfare recipients, 167
Welles, Orson, 70
Wells Handy, Edna, 181
Whaley, Ruth Whitehead, 40, 41
White, Gladys Powell, 112
White, Jane, 27
White, Walter: divorce and interracial remarriage, 112–13; executive secretary of NAACP, 27, 44, 64, 112–13; fears communist infiltration of NAACP, 114, 122, 124, 132; mentors FHW, 69, 112, 113, 116, 127
whites, poor, 169, 173–74

Who's Who in American Colleges and Universities, 38
Wilkie, Wendell, 48
Wilkins, Roy: 1960 presidential campaign and, 143; co-authors report on lynching, 174; concerns on communism, 122, 124; conflict with FHW, 112–13, 122, 126–27, 132, 139, 141, 153; Groveland case and FHW, 96; introduces FHW to Jackie Robinson, 139; investigates conditions at Fort Huachuca, 44
Willet family, 9, 10
William Beaumont General Hospital, 45, 46
Williams, Alinda Lowry (mother), 8, 12, 13, 13–15
Williams, Arthur Lee (father), 8, 14, 15, 15–16
Williams, Arthur Robert (brother), 14, 15, 20, 21, 23, 25, 26, 28, 38, 40, 48
Williams, Franklin Hall, Jr. (son): attends Amherst, 156, 169–70; birth of, 74; early education and, 113; on father's confrontation with white neighbors, 137–38; on FHW's inability to help Paul, 171; move to California, 114, 115; on racial incident at Shriver home, 144; serves in Vietnam War, 170
Williams, Franklin Hall Donald Lowry
Beliefs and opinions: conciliatory attitude, xi, 137–38, 161; distrust of communism and communists, 2, 106, 114, 122–25; on Ku Klux Klan, 2; lack of interest in organized religion, 185; on Nation of Islam, 2–3; on women's rights, 154
Early life and education: ancestry of, 8; attends Lincoln University, 3, 31–38, 170; birth of, 14; Chinn encourages him to go to Lincoln University, 30; experiences racism, 3, 7–8, 17, 37; friendship with Charlie Butler, 18, 20, 21; hobbies and school activities, 17, 23–24, 26, 125; joins Boy Scouts, 24–26; loss of mother, impact upon, 16, 17, 22–23; marriage to Shirley Broyard, 49–51, 186, 187; military service, 3–4, 7, 41–48, 43; personality of, 27–28, 32; racial identity and, 18, 20, 148, 149; relationship with brothers, 19, 20; relationship with grandfather, 22; rooms with Robert Freeman at Lincoln, 32, 33, 34; social life in Harlem, 27; strife in and breakup of family, 23, 28–29; works odd jobs for college tuition, 29; works with R. Freeman summer after college, 39–40; YMCA denies membership to, 3, 24–25, 163

Legal career: applies to FBI, 51; argues
cases before Supreme Court., 4; argues
Watts v. Indiana before Supreme Court,
85; US Army service, 41–48, 43; attends
Fordham Law School, 3–4, 40–41, 48;
chairs New York State Judicial Commission on Minorities, 6, 177, 178–82; as civil
rights lawyer with NAACP, 63–73;
clashes with Marshall, 4–5, 67–69, 82–83,
90, 112, 113; clerks with Dyett and Stevens, 51; clerks with Ruth Whaley, 41;
conflict with Wilkins, 112–13, 122, 126–27,
132, 139, 141, 153; on Constitution, 2, 4, 51,
63, 64, 106; Groveland case, 4, 91, 96–109,
107, 111, 117; joins California DOJ Constitutional Rights Section, 5, 141–43; narrowly escapes lynching, 2, 7. 91; passes
New York State bar examination, 51; rep-
resents Isaac Woodard, 4, 7; as successful
fundraiser, 4, 70, 111, 139, 168; temporary
director of Freedom Fund, 139; transferred to West Coast office of NAACP, 5,
113–15, 115, 126–41; works as special counsel to Marshall, 4; work with American
Veterans Committee, 52–62; work with
NAACP Legal Defense Fund, 4–5, 63–
65, 66, 67–73, 69, 76–87, 85, 88–90
Washington years: as ambassador to
(ECOSOC), 5, 151–53; as ambassador to
Ghana, 5, 156–60, 157, 163; on coup that
ousted Nkrumah, 5, 159–61, 166; Shriver
recruits for Peace Corps, 5, 146–48, 147,
150–51; works on 1960 Kennedy campaign, 143
Post-government life and work: accepts
position at Columbia University, 163–67;
board member of various companies,
167–69; as chairman of Barnes Foundation, 175, 176–77; extramarital affairs bar
run for public office, 75–76, 168–69; final
days and death of, 6, 183–88; Gort and
oral history project, 184; heads Phelps
Stokes Fund, ix–xi, 5–6, 161, 168–69,
183–84; at home on West Eighty-Ninth
Street, 162; legacy of, 2, 6, 188–89
Williams, G. Mennen "Soapy," 144
Williams, Jimmie, 27
Williams, John Frederick (brother), 14, 19, 20,
21, 23, 29, 38
Williams, Oliver D., 40

Williams, Paul Anatole: attends Williams
College, 169–70; birth of, 114; death of,
170–71; questions father on racism, 163;
on racial incident at Shriver home, 144;
witnesses scene between father and
Innis, 166
Williams, R. I., 96
Williams, Roberta Braddicks (Arthur's wife),
28–29, 38, 40, 48, 75–76
Williams, Shirley Marie-Louise Broyard: parents insist she turn down scholarship, 50;
attends FHW's swearing in as ambassador to Ghana, 152; attends FHW's swearing in to ECOSOC, 152; friendship with
Rachel Robinson, 139–40; friendship with
Shrivers, 144; friendship with Warings,
73; FHW's death and, 185; Gorts' friend-
ship with, xi; on husband's infidelity, 75–
76; marriage to FHW, 49, 49–51, 186, 187;
move back East, 144; move to Ghana,
156–57; move to Riverton, 74; move to
West Coast, 114, 115, 116; return to Amer-
ica, 161; son's education and, 113; as wife
and mother, 161, 186, 187
Williams, Wesley, 27
Williams College, 169
"Williams Policy," 167
Wilson, James H., 27
WMCA radio station, 155
Wofford, Harris, 143–44, 145
women's rights, 154
Woodard, Isaac, Jr., 4, 7, 69–73, 98
Wormser, I. Maurice, 40
W. Pasmantier, Mark, 183
Wright, Bruce, 37
Wright, Walter Livingston, 35

Yankee Stadium, 98
Yates, James L., 92, 103, 119
YMCA: denies membership to FHW, 3, 24–25,
163; FHW asked to speak at YMCA in
Paterson, NJ, 67; sponsors Boys Club at
Lincoln University, 38; Tobias tries to
desegregate, 169
Young, Andrew, 6
Young, Whitney, 6, 154
"Young Turks," 132, 153
Youth Conference on Civil Rights, 128

Zumwalt, Elmo Russell "Bud, " Jr., 187–88

Enid Gort is an anthropologist and Africanist. Her articles have appeared in numerous academic journals, including the *Journal of African Studies* and *Social Science and Medicine*. She wrote the chapter "Swazi Traditional Healers, Role Transformation and Gender" in *African Feminism: The Politics of Survival in Sub-Saharan Africa*, edited by Gwendolyn Mikell. A consultant on the award-winning PBS documentary on Ambassador Franklin H. Williams, *A Bridge to Justice*, she holds a degree in education from Kean College and master's and doctoral degrees from Columbia University.

John M. Caher is the author or coauthor of eight books and the principal writer of a PBS documentary on Franklin H. Williams, *A Bridge to Justice*. Caher has degrees from Syracuse University (Utica College) and Rensselaer Polytechnic Institute. His reporting has garnered more than twenty awards, including prestigious honors from the American Bar Association, the New York State Bar Association, and the Erie County Bar Association.

CPSIA information can be obtained
at www.ICGtesting.com
Printed in the USA
LVHW101454160922
728180LV00006B/7/J